ANDROPOV

ANDROPOV

NEW CHALLENGE TO THE WEST

A Political Biography by
Arnold Beichman and Mikhail S. Bernstam
Introduction by Robert Conquest

STEIN AND DAY / Publishers / New York

First published in 1983
Copyright © 1983 by Arnold Beichman and Mikhail S. Bernstam
All rights reserved, Stein and Day, Incorporated
Designed by Louis A. Ditizio
Printed in the United States of America
STEIN AND DAY/*Publishers*
Scarborough House
Briarcliff Manor, N.Y. 10510

Library of Congress Cataloging in Publication Data

Beichman, Arnold
Andropov, new challenge to the West.

Includes index.
1. Andropov, IU. V. (I͡Urii Vladimirovich), 1914–
2. Heads of state—Soviet Union—Biography. I. Bernstam,
Mikhail S. II. Title.
DK275.A53B47   1983   947.085′4′0924 [B]   83-42830
ISBN 0-8128-2921-2

This book is dedicated
to the political and
religious prisoners
in the Soviet Union

Contents

Acknowledgments

The basic methodological problem of this book was to put into the context of the political and social history of the Soviet Union the dispersed bits and pieces of data about the political life of Yuri Vladimirovich Andropov. Although this method is essentially what all Sovietologists and Kremlinologists usually do, our book places its main emphasis on the socio-political aspects surrounding Andropov's past.

This approach, we felt, was appropriate because in the first period of Andropov's career, i.e., before the 1950s, he was much more involved with people in towns and villages than with leadership fights and intrigues in the Kremlin. His career, however, was predetermined by the outcome of the struggle for power in the upper echelons of the Soviet political machine.

Andropov's practical achievements, which led to his promotion to top positions in the Soviet hierarchy, were due to his operational skills in dealing with masses of people whose fate was, to a significant extent, dependent on Andropov's conduct. These same operational skills were visible once more in his career when he served as Soviet Ambassador to Hungary from 1954 to 1957 and, later, as chief of the KGB from 1967 to 1982.

Andropov's attitude toward people and his record in this regard is traced in this biography in as much detail as possible. In our judgment, this is the main variable to take into account in offering an assessment of the present Andropov and the future Andropov as he takes on the leadership of the Soviet Union.

There are many lacunae in Andropov's life for which no data seem to be available, but in as great a detail as possible, we have presented his political record, his concepts of power and ideology. From this record, it may be possible to make judgments about the policies and decisions that it will be Andropov's to make in the time that remains to him to serve as General Secretary of the Communist Party of the Soviet Union.

In the course of this undertaking a number of people helped make this book possible. The entire work was researched and written during a stay at the Hoover Institution on War, Revolution and Peace at Stanford University, California. We wish to express our special thanks to W. Glenn Campbell, director of the Hoover Institution. Others whose help and advice we would like to acknowledge include: Dennis L. Bark, John H. Moore, Richard T. Burress, Sidney Hook, Alain Besançon, Robert Conquest, Peter J. Duignan, Lewis H. Gann, Carroll Aikins Beichman, and David L. Arans. We are, however, solely responsible for the contents of the book.

Arnold Beichman
Mikhail Bernstam

Stanford, Calif.

Introduction

by Robert Conquest

Even if Andropov were to die or be overthrown tomorrow, his accession to power in the USSR would have many lessons for us. It is a question not only of what type of man, with what type of record, can today become leader of that huge country, but also of the way in which the facts of such a man's political personality can be misunderstood or misrepresented in the West.

When Andropov succeeded to power, there were articles—some of them by "experts"—to the effect that he was a "reformer," even a "liberal." Human-interest stories about his open-mindedness and Western tastes proliferated (most of them have been tracked down and shown to be imaginary in a careful investigation by Edward Jay Epstein published in *The New Republic* [February 7, 1983]).

This discovery of "liberal" Soviet rulers has been repeated every time a change takes place at the top. Those who present it argue, indeed, that the USSR is pretty liberal already, but that the newest man is more liberal yet. This sort of thing seems to fill some psychological need; at any rate it has no rational explanation or factual basis.

In this book, on the contrary, we have research into Andropov's true background by an academic scholar (and a man with immediate personal experience in these matters) presented by the skills of a journalist (himself a man of scholarly interests). The result is readable reality.

The natural bent of both authors is to seek and present the human factor in the background of the new General Secretary of the Central Committee of the Communist Party of the Soviet Union, and in particular his long association with the terror machine that has inflicted so much harm on the Soviet peoples. And this is indeed of the greatest interest to anyone concerned to know the real roots of the man, though also of the utmost significance in understanding the whole Soviet phenomenon.

But, to my mind, what is even more striking is the clear depiction of the circumstances of Andropov's first emergence into the central politics of the USSR. Above all, what is clearly demonstrated here is the way in which Stalin, in the last four or five years of his life, selected from the legions of young apparatchiks blooded in the Great Terror and hardened in the power struggles that followed, a chosen band of young super-Stalinists —Andropov among them—to replace his old senior followers and to serve as instruments to inaugurate a second terror to match the first.

As Khrushchev said in his Secret Speech in 1956, Stalin "aimed at removing the old Political Bureau members and bringing in less experienced persons, so that these would extol him in all sorts of ways,"—though naturally "extolling" was not to be their only task. Setting up fake trials of their predecessors, launching a new attack on the population, killing leading Jews and deporting the mass of them to the Arctic—such were the tasks for which the new men struck Stalin as suitable.

Of the fifteen or twenty we can identify, Andropov is not among the most senior. But on Stalin's death he shared the instant demotion inflicted on all of them by those who now ruled the USSR. And, also like the others, he only began to rise again when the power struggle among Stalin's successors grew so sharp that Khrushchev needed allies among skilled purge operators, regardless of their past. Andropov's talents in this field proved themselves, of course, in his later rise to power over the Secret Police and finally in the achievement of the leadership itself.

There are those in the West who would simply have us ignore the historical and psychological background of men like Andropov. They would pay no attention to the fact that he and those like him are the products of a history quite alien to our own and are the exemplars of a political psychology of a type hardly seen in the West outside small sects of millenarian psychopaths.

Indeed, though in the Soviet case the fact is disguised by Western-type suits and a Western-type vocabulary, the record and the motivations of a man like Andropov are as different from our own as those of any Ayatollah.

The book establishes beyond reasonable cavil what Andropov is like, but also what the USSR is like, and how it is likely to remain. The picture may not be a pleasant one. But truth is better than illusion, especially among us citizens of the West who in our conduct of foreign affairs are going to have to cope with the real Soviet leadership rather than the Soviet leadership as we would like it to be.

ANDROPOV

1

Image Making

ONE of the most popular songs in Soviet cities during the Brezhnev and, now, the Andropov era goes like this:

Vodka now costs us five rubles
Yet we ain't gonna stop drinking.
Give Brezhnev this message from us:
We will even pay ten rubles a bottle—
But if it goes up to twenty rubles—
Well, then we'll march on the Winter Palace
And seize it once more.

Of course, this isn't a song one chants at home, but it is heard on the streets of Moscow, Leningrad, and other cities at night, performed by carousing Soviet citizens. It is a song with a social significance surely not lost on the Soviet Politburo, the secret police, and other Soviet elites.

Vodka is one of the most cherished articles of consumption in the Soviet Union. Normally it is plentiful, except during changes of regime or significant deaths like that of Stalin or Brezhnev. At such moments, vodka disappears—there is always the risk that imbibers might be emboldened, under the influence of vodka, to say or even do silly things. On November 10, 1982, when Brezhnev died, vodka disappeared from the shelves of the liquor stores. As soon as the new Party General Secretary, Yuri Vladimirovich Andropov, came to power, the vodka reappeared on the shelves of the emptied liquor stores.

The popular song quoted above contains a warning, not too significant but still a matter of concern, to the men on top. For what it implies is that if the price of vodka gets out of hand (a ruble is about $1.20 in purchasing power) the Russian people, or at least that high percentage of the population who are vodka drinkers, will march and seize one of the symbols of the Russian Revolution. For the Winter Palace referred to in the song once belonged to the czars. With the abdication of Czar Nicholas II, the Winter Palace became the seat of power for the Provisional Government. On November 7, 1917, Lenin's Bolsheviks seized the Winter Palace, an act that became part of the legendry of the most fateful event of the twentieth century, the Communist Revolution. It is now the handsome Leningrad Art Museum. What the vodka revelers are saying is that if things get bad enough—say, vodka at $25 a bottle—it could be the straw that breaks the docile proletariat's back.

Hyperbole in alcoholic moments is natural. But one can be certain that the patriarchs of the Politburo are well aware that what may appear to be the boozy threats of a few Moscow drunks weaving their way home after a night on the town may also be a sign of the alienation of large masses of the Soviet peoples.

And so, perhaps, we have a contributing reason for the triumph of Andropov on November 15, 1982. On that day, he beat his opponents in the Politburo to become the new *Vozhd,* the Leader, the General Secretary of the Communist Party. In that strategic position, he could expect in time to eliminate the collective leadership, his potentially Disloyal Opposition, which usually encumbers the victor in the early days of a Soviet succession. This happened to Stalin, Khrushchev, and Brezhnev, and no doubt it encumbers Andropov now, unless, of course, the Disloyal Opposition gets him first.

The contributing reason is the fact that Andropov was for fifteen years in charge of internal repression in the Soviet Union. He was The Man Who Kept the Lid On, who is presumed to know everything about everybody, even right up to the pinnacle of power; the man with the dossiers, the dungeons, the labor camps; the man with the vast informer network located on each factory and farm. Andropov was, until May 1982, chief of the KGB (*Komitet Gosudarstvennoi Bezopasnosti* or the Committee on State Security), a police organization that goes back to the early days of the Russian Revolution. Then it was called the *Cheka,* an acronym from the Russian that means "Extraordinary Commission." It was founded December 20, 1917 and has had many names and initials and chiefs since—GPU, OGPU, NKVD, NKGB, MVD, MGB, and now KGB. It's still the same old all-powerful *Cheka.* In fact, KGB operatives are still referred to, affectionately within the club, as *chekisty.*

Andropov has accomplished the unprecedented. From the Lubyanka, the huge stone prison building on Dzerzhinsky Square that houses the headquarters of the KGB, he has traveled to the official seat of Soviet power a mile away, the Krem-

lin. None of his predecessors at the security managed that leap.
Indeed, no fewer than five of them were executed:

1. Genrikh G. Yagoda, NKVD chief from 1934 to 1936, shot by
   Stalin's order March 15, 1938.
2. Nikolai I. Yezhov, NKVD chief from 1936 to 1938, executed
   sometime in 1940.
3. Lavrentii P. Beria, NKVD chief from 1938 to 1946 and MVD
   Minister from March 1953 to June 1953, executed sometime
   between June and December 1953.
4. Vsevolod N. Merkulov, NKGB chief in 1941 and from 1943 to
   1946, executed in December 1953.
5. Viktor S. Abakumov, MGB Minister from 1946 to 1951,
   executed in 1954.

Truly Andropov is the Great Survivor, after such an ignomi-
nious record of corpses and un-persons among the heads of the
secret police. Andropov has broken what seemed to have become
an inevitable pattern of behavior in the highest echelons of the
Soviet power elite. His accession to the top post came after a long
struggle for power with many ups and downs, a struggle that
began a year before Brezhnev's death on November 10, 1982, and
during which there were reports of internecine party battles,
murders, suicides, and even corruption within Brezhnev's
family.

Added to this achievement is another one. Andropov came on
the world scene not as the former head of the sinister KGB, with
all that such a post implies, but as a closet liberal, a lover of
American jazz, a man with Western tastes, a man of intellectual
discrimination and tolerance. And he managed to accomplish
this extraordinary miracle with the full and even enthusiastic
cooperation of leading U.S. media, which offered no evidence for
Andropov's sanctification except the words of putative KGB

defectors.[1] Ignored by the media were other aspects of Androp-ov's past, such as incitement of international terrorism, the crushing of the dissident movement, and—as a member of the Politburo—chemical warfare in Afghanistan, the military dicta-torship over Poland, guerrilla warfare in southern Africa, the threat of nuclear warfare, and more.

In the January 24, 1983, issue of *The New Yorker* magazine (page 97) there appeared a cartoon that, rather artfully, reflects the buildup in the American media of Yuri Andropov, a buildup that began almost from the moment he took power.

The scene is the tastefully furnished living room of a well-to-do middle-class couple. He is in a sports jacket and flannels, a pipe in his mouth, reading a book while seated in his big, favorite easy chair. Opposite him and in front of a well-stocked bookcase and a bay window with flower pots sits his wife on a couch. She is looking up from the newspaper she is reading; she says: "What a nice name that is—Yuri Andropov."

The cartoonist, B. Tobey, has caught the flavor of the Ameri-can will-to-believe when aided by a congruent public relations campaign. What was so startling about this buildup is that the very newspaper writers and columnists who for years dug up skeletons in J. Edgar Hoover's closet and who harried the one-time CIA director, Richard Helms, exposing both men and their organizations as villainous conspirators against the welfare of the Republic, would jettison their concern about freedom from police surveillance and welcome the arrival of Yuri Andropov, enforcer of totalitarianism in half the world. Probably the great-est compliment of all was paid to Andropov by Vice-President George Bush. In an interview with the *Christian Science Moni-tor,* December 20, 1982 (p. 20), Bush said:

My view of Andropov is that some people make this KGB thing sound horrendous. Maybe I speak defensively as a former head of

7

the CIA. But leave out the operational side of KGB—the naughty things they allegedly do . . .

So extraordinary a whitewash by an American political leader and presidential hopeful—who implied an equation between the CIA and KGB; who was saying that the "naughty things" the KGB does cannot be proven (which is what "allegedly" means); who implied that some people are spreading bad, "horrendous" stories about the KGB for dubious purposes; and who is asking that the "operational side" of the KGB be overlooked—would surely indicate that Andropov's public relations campaign is getting more than a little help from his alleged adversaries. He was even being exonerated in advance from any complicity in the plot to assassinate Pope John Paul while the Italian judiciary was still investigating the plot in early 1983. According to the *Wall Street Journal*'s editorial page, February 2, 1983, a strange silence about the assassination investigation had even befallen the Vatican and the Catholic press.

In Yuri Andropov we have a man who may well become as redoubtable a Soviet dictator as Lenin and Stalin before him. He is a man who knows the weakness of Western public opinion. As former head of the Soviet secret police and master of a vast array of internal and external agent networks, he knows how to deal with his own country's public opinion as well. His agents and informers collect data daily on the mood of the population everywhere, in each factory, each bar, each apartment building, in food queues. His network knows who is saying what. It is a system of total surveillance brought to perfection by modern computer technology.

The Soviet peoples are different today; their mood is different and visibly so. They are not so fearful as they were under Stalin, and no longer have they the hope and expectations that they had during the Khrushchev era. A people that is no longer so fearful as it once was, nor so hopeful, is dangerous to a dictatorship.

These people could, indeed, given some unexpected catalysts, "march on the Winter Palace / And seize it once more."

In a totalitarian society, the man who has been for fifteen years head of its secret police—who has controlled the internal militia and the secret agents and political commissars, who is privy to the military and political secrets of Western countries—has the kind of knowledge that makes for unlimited power. One can be certain that Andropov's *apparatchiks* in the KGB are going to take their orders from him, not from some senescent Politburo member. Andropov will see to that, for he cannot forget that Nikita Sergeyevitch Khrushchev, the numero uno—so he thought—of the Soviet hierarchy, was removed from office in October 1964, obviously unaware of the success of his own dear colleagues' plotting against him. That is an eventuality Andropov has the experience to guard against.

The story of Andropov's life needs telling in as much detail as is possible, because he is no ordinary policeman. Not only does he run what is probably the most effective intelligence agency in the world, with no oversight or outside control, he also runs, in cooperation, the Soviet military, the most formidable military force in the world, nuclear and non-nuclear, on land, on and under the sea, and in the air. And, moreover, he has persuaded a good part of the non-totalitarian world that the Soviet Union is a peace-loving country threatened by American capitalism and imperialism.

Andropov will need all his power. The problems his country faces are enormous. The Soviet economy is in disarray. Even the forced labor of the Gulags cannot produce butter *and* guns, consumer goods in any quantity let alone quality. The Russian people are becoming and will become an ethnic minority in the Soviet Union in two decades or less.

As for the present, the ethnic Russians have just lost the majority of the 272,000,000 population. By the mid-1990s, the ethnic Russians, due to their increasing mortality and rapidly declining fertility, will begin negative population growth. Their numbers will decline at an accelerating rate, but their relative share in the total USSR population will decline even faster because the Turko-Muslim nationalities of the southern Asian border lands will still grow at about 3 percent annually. The bulk of the Soviet gross national product and the absolute majority of food production areas are concentrated in the Russian and other Slavic parts of the country. The Soviets are experiencing in 1983 their fifth consecutive disastrous harvest. Food has been rationed in many localities since 1981. The demographically declining Russian areas and rapidly growing southern border lands, the protracted food crisis and general decline of economic productivity, especially labor shortages, pose a major threat to the entire social and political structure of the USSR.

No Communist leader can ever forget how the Soviet peoples in the millions welcomed the invading Germans in World War II and even joined the German troops. And no Communist leader can forget that the only revolutions in the world by working people have occurred in East Germany, 1953, Poland, three times, and Hungary, 1956. Nor can he forget the minatory significance of Poland's Solidarity movement, crushed but not dead.

A man who could outflank as tough a crew as his Politburo associates knows how to wield power. His survival will depend on how well he wields influence and coercion over the West, particularly the United States, whose economy can help stabilize and whose leaders can help legitimize the Andropov era.

2

Biographical Fictions, Biographical Facts

L IKE any good Soviet dictator-to-be, Yuri Andropov came up the hard way. In the Soviet political tradition, that means not only to have survived Stalin's purges and executions but also to have participated in such events as an apparatchik and then to have survived. It also means having survived through the post-Stalin "thaws" when Stalin's successors organized their own Night of the Long Knives against those, like Andropov, who had been prepared to do Stalin's bidding.

It simply wouldn't do to make such a personal history public if the new Party Secretary hopes to play a successful role on the world stage. To be feared by the Soviet peoples is one thing and useful for the Party Secretary. But for the world without, his image must be refurbished, with all disfiguring warts removed.

When his rival for the supreme position in the Soviet hierarchy, Konstantin Chernenko, nominated Andropov on November 12, 1982, he said: "There is no need, I think, to recount his biography. Yuri Vladimirovich [Andropov] is well-known to the Party and the country . . ."[1]

Chernenko's statement is untrue. Andropov was not known, except as a name, to the Party and most certainly not to the country and the world at large. The non-communist world has been the target of a tremendous "disinformation" campaign to create an Andropov who never existed. Soviet media has tried to hide the man who was.

The official biography of Andropov was published in the USSR at the time of his ascendancy. It ran about 100 newspaper lines, some 500 words.[2] This so-called biographical sketch was published word for word in thousands of Soviet newspapers and sent abroad by Tass. The story was a masterpiece of *suppressio veri suggestio falsi,* a Latin phrase that means to suppress the truth is to suggest falsehood. Following is the *Pravda* version and the true events:

1. *Pravda*'s "truth": He is a college graduate. The truth: He is not. He holds a diploma from a technical school, which, in Russia, is lower than a junior college. He was a dropout from two colleges.[3]

2. *Pravda* says: After starting out as a manual worker, he became a sailor on small freighters on the Volga river. The truth: Between his job as an office clerk (not a manual worker) and his riverboat job, he tried to learn a real trade, as a movie projectionist. He failed at this. Until he became part of Stalin's purge *apparat,* he seemed to be a born loser.

3. *Pravda* says: After the riverboat job, he entered a technical school and became a Komsomol youth organization local representative. The truth: His career began as an ostensible Komsomol organizer, but actually in 1936 he was a Komsomol representative in the shipyard, which was managed by

the secret police, then called the NKVD. In his position as the local Komsomol functionary he was more connected with the local NKVD management than with the central Komsomol apparatus.

The official biography would have it appear that his secret police connections began only in 1967, when he was appointed KGB head. Actually, his work with the secret police began more than three decades earlier, in 1936. In other words, by May 1982 (when, ostensibly, he gave up his post as KGB head) he had been in secret police work for almost half a century, and the friends and allies he made back in his early NKVD days helped him in his career in the Komsomol organization.

4. *Pravda*'s "truth": His first important appointment in the Komsomol apparatus came in 1938 as the first secretary of the Yaroslavl provincial Komsomol committee. The truth: His first appointment in Yaroslavl was as a second secretary, in the notorious year of 1937—notorious because it was the peak year of Stalin's brutal terror against the Soviet people as well as the purge of party and military elites.

New people, like Andropov, who were brought in during the 1936–37 purges were vigorous participants in effectuating Stalin's design. They could not have survived otherwise. That part of his history Andropov wishes to consign to the memory hole. The fact that he became the first secretary of the Yaroslavl provincial Komsomol committee a year later means that his promotion was over the body of his purged predecessor and he was thus rewarded by Stalin's lieutenants. To have mentioned the year 1937 in the official Andropov biography might have reminded people of what Andropov must have done not only to survive the purge but to rise in the hierarchy during the purge.

5. *Pravda* says: In 1940, Andropov was promoted to a higher post—first secretary of the Komsomol in the Karelo-Finnish Republic, a territory newly established after the Soviet-

Finnish war. The truth: What seems to be a routine promotion was really an assignment to lead Stalin's purge in this new Soviet territory.

6. *Pravda*'s "truth": From the opening days of the Great Patriotic War—the Soviet phrase for the German attack on June 22, 1941—and until war's end in 1945, he was actively engaged in the partisan movement against Hitler's armies in the Karelo-Finnish republic. The truth: This would-be war hero was in charge of Stalin's forced labor battalions. He was far behind the front lines and not at all in the partisan movement. In other words, he saw no action. His real job during the war was to manage timber production in the notorious Soviet prison camp at Belomor in the Karelo-Finnish Republic.

7. *Pravda* says: In 1944 he was moved from the Komsomol to party work in Petrozavodsk, the Karelo-Finnish Republic capital. The truth: This was a demotion not, as the official biography would have it, a promotion. His new position implied that he was a failure during the war, a period where many people made, by Soviet standards, successful careers.

8. *Pravda* says: From 1947 to 1951, Andropov worked as a second secretary of the Karelo-Finnish Republic. The truth: What the official biography omits is that within the same four-year time span, his two superiors, the first secretaries, were arrested one after the other. They were both charged with treason. One was executed and the other tortured and imprisoned. Andropov was eventually brought to Moscow to work in the Central Committee of the Soviet Communist Party as a high official. His later promotion in 1951 was over the bodies of his two superiors.

9. *Pravda* says: From 1951 to 1953, Andropov was an inspector and chief of a sub-department of the Central Committee. The truth: The inspectorial post was an extraordinary one personally established by Stalin for his closest henchmen, who were to participate in the new purges that Stalin had scheduled

for 1953. But Stalin died in March 1953, and so the purge was averted. Andropov's early career ended with Stalin's death, and he was subsequently dropped from the Central Committee apparatus and even from the Supreme Soviet, the USSR's quasi-Parliament.

10. *Pravda* says: In 1953, the Party sent Andropov to the Foreign Office and, thereafter, to Hungary as the Soviet Ambassador. The truth: After his dismissal from the Central Committee and the Supreme Soviet, he was transferred to an obscure position as counsellor—not ambassador—in the Soviet Embassy in Hungary. It was a year after this appointment (and after the execution of secret police chiefs like Lavrentii Beria and Viktor Abakumov and their underlings) that Andropov was promoted to the rank of Ambassador.

11. *Pravda* says: After helping with the suppression of the October 1956 uprising in Hungary by the invading Red Army, Andropov returned to the USSR and began his comeback. He was able to reenter the Central Committee apparatus, first as a departmental chief, then as a Committee secretary, and, in 1967, chief of the KGB. In 1973, he became a full Politburo member, and in May 1982, he returned to the Secretariat, which put him in line as Brezhnev's successor.

The truth: What the biography overlooked is that the faction within the Soviet hierarchy to which Andropov belonged from at least 1957, when he rejoined the Central Committee apparatus, was led by Mikhail A. Suslov. It was Suslov who was responsible for Andropov's comeback and promotions. Andropov eventually replaced Suslov when the party ideologist died in January 1982. And it was only from his appointment as Suslov's replacement on the Party Secretariat that he was in a position to challenge his rivals for the succession.

Suslov, kingmaker from beyond the grave, and Suslov's faction represented the most narrow-minded, reactionary Marxist clique within the contemporary Soviet leadership. It was Suslov

15

and his factionalists, including Andropov, who opposed the jejune Khrushchev reforms and the so-called "thaw" in the late 1950s and the early 1960s. And it was this faction that engineered and eventually ousted Khrushchev by an inner Politburo coup in October 1964.

Despite Chernenko's announcement of Andropov's appointment as party chief, an announcement that described Andropov as "one of the closest comrades-in-arms of Leonid Ilyich [Brezhnev]," Andropov was, at least in the last year of Brezhnev's life, his rival for the leadership. Andropov's victory over Brezhnev's heir-apparent, Chernenko, was a posthumous triumph for Andropov's patron, Suslov.

It is necessary to note that in the official post-succession biography of Andropov, no predecessor in the party post or in the Politburo is mentioned—no Suslov, no Brezhnev, no Khrushchev, no Stalin. Only Lenin stands before Andropov. Thus the fiction of party unity and the apostolic succession is maintained.

3

The
Beginning:

1914-1930

THE Russia into which Yuri Vladimirovich Andropov (the Yuri is equivalent to "George") was born June 15, 1914 (June 2, 1914, old style calendar), was a land of agricultural abundance and rapid economic development. The infant, born in the railroad station of Nagutskaya, province of Stavropol, came into the world just six weeks before the outbreak of war.

There is some evidence of an ancient Greek heritage in the area where Andropov's family lived. The name Stavropol derives from the Greek word, *stavros,* which means old or ancient, and *polis,* which means city. The name of the railroad station, which was also home for the Andropov family, is Turkish in origin. It was a region in which lived peoples of different ethnic origins—Greeks, Turks, Kalmyks, Caucasians, Ukrainians, and Russians.

The family name of Andropov hints of Greek origin. *Anthropos* in Greek means man or human being, while the Russian suffix, "ov," is like the word "ben" in Hebrew or "ibn" in Arabic—son of. In other words, Andropov means "son of man," a rather impious thought.

The railroad station of Nagutskaya, on the main line that connected St. Petersburg and European Russia with the Caucasus, the industrial and oil center of Baku, capital city of Azerbaijan, is between the Black Sea and the Caspian Sea. To the south, some 200 miles away, was the border with Turkey and Iran. Much of this area is beautifully described by Aleksandr Solzhenitsyn in the opening chapters of his novel, *August 1914.*

The area was at the peak of rapid prosperous economic development brought about by land reforms enacted by the czarist government in 1906 and 1910. These countrywide reforms enabled about one-quarter of the peasant households in Stavropol province to acquire, as private owners, more than 1.6 million acres of prime agricultural land. The peasants were able to establish farms with an average size of 40-50 acres.[1]

The station of Nagutskaya was a few miles away from a rich farming village of the same name. Andropov's father worked for the railroad administration, undoubtedly as the stationmaster. This can easily be determined from earlier Soviet sources, which identify Andropov's father's status as an "employee" not as a "worker."[2] The use of the word "employee" in Soviet publications always means that the person was more than just a lowly clerk or ordinary worker. Therefore, Andropov is denied the aristocratic (by Soviet definition) status of pure proletarian origin.

What is striking about Andropov's family origins is that practically nothing is known about that family other than his own date and place of birth and that his father's first name was

Vladimir. Nothing has ever been published in known Soviet sources about his mother, about any siblings, living or dead, about relatives, including his wife, or about his years before he reached the age of 16 in 1930.[3] It is likely, now that Andropov has taken power, that court biographers will soon publish books about Andropov's life and confirm a *post hoc* heroic stature of him. Such was the case for Stalin, Khrushchev, and Brezhnev.

The Russia into which Andropov was born seemed to be in a state of relative quiet. Examination of Russian newspapers of the period describe how, the day that Andropov was born, Czar Nicholas II had gone to Bucharest to meet King Carol of Rumania; that the Russian Duma, the legislative chamber, had voted to accept the national budget for 1914–1915. There was a story from the Caucasus, where Andropov was born, that workers' strikes were expected, and local mayors were warning about violence. Another story described how of a flight of five Russian airplanes, one had crash-landed in East Prussia and the two-man crew had been arrested by local police. More serious was a story that Admiral von Tirpitz, worried about Russian naval reinforcements in the Black Sea had discussed with Kaiser Wilhelm the need for Austria-Hungary to beef up its own naval rearmament. Wilhelm was meeting with the Austrian heir-apparent, the Archduke Franz Ferdinand, to pass on von Tirpitz's concern and to discuss the future of the Dardenelles.[4] Two weeks after this meeting, Franz Ferdinand was assassinated in Sarajevo.

The arts were flourishing in St. Petersburg. The Russian ballet was performing. Anna Pavlova had just returned from a triumphant tour of America. Halévy's *La Juive* and Glinka's *Ruslan and Ludmilla* were being performed. And in Baku, there was the story about a man with the first name of Mahomet, described in the newspaper as the "Don Juan of Baku" who had been killed by five angry and jealous husbands. The newsstory said they had been first sentenced to 15 years each for the murder, but on appeal, one was released as not guilty while the other four had their sentences reduced to five years.

Another newspaper described the visit of Emil Vandervelde, secretary of the Second International, who had met with the editors of the Bolshevik newspaper, *Pravda,* in St. Petersburg and discussed with them the legal methods used by workers to organize. The paper, which was legal under the czar, then had as one of its editors Vyacheslav M. Molotov, later Stalin's Foreign Secretary and Premier.

The newspaper reported that heavy rains in the Caucasus had washed out the railroads, and all traffic had been halted between May 31 and June 2. Two days before Andropov was born, a tremendous rainstorm blanketed the entire Caucasus and trains stopped moving.

At Ekaterinodar, a few miles from Andropov's birthplace, the Black Hundreds, an anti-Semitic national socialist group, was protesting that the municipal assembly had refused it an appropriation to establish "people's libraries," and it planned to appeal to the provincial government.

A prostitution ring was broken up by St. Petersburg police when the madam, who had a list of call-girls, had tried to interest military officers. The police were informed and arrests followed. The St. Petersburg and Moscow press reported that a prisoner in a Kursk jail had hanged himself after being reprimanded by the turnkey. There was a prison riot in Vilnus, the capital of Lithuania. The stock market was flourishing in Russia, especially railway and metallurgical stocks, while oil and banking stocks were having a smaller rise.

The editorial pages were full of criticism and complaints about inflation, unstable prices, and government policies that created wide-swinging price fluctuations.[5]

All in all, judging by the independent Russian press, one could say that Yuri Andropov was born into a limited autocratic society with far more freedom and civil liberties than have ever existed in the Soviet Union. Certainly, the press was far freer then than it has been since the Bolshevik revolution.

His official biography says that as late as 1930 he was still living in the northern Caucasus in the town of Mozdok, about 100 miles southeast of his birthplace, Nagutskaya. There is no indication whether he was living alone, with his family, or with anybody else.[6]

The area in which he grew up was, for three years (from 1918 to 1920 inclusive), among the bloodiest battlefields of the civil war. There was widespread guerrilla warfare and large-scale movement of troops by all sides on the railroads. The Red Army in 1920 consisted of some 5 million soldiers.[7] However, Soviet records of the period show that as many as 25 million soldiers were transported by railroad, which meant an average of five trips for each soldier.[8] So much railroading meant that each railroad station was an important tactical point in the civil war. Histories and records of the Communist revolution make many references to the battles for the Nagutskaya railstation. From June to November 1918, as many as 100,000 soldiers of all sides, combined, including anti-Communist peasant guerrilla detachments, fought in the Nagutskaya area.

One of the battles in this area lasted as long as 28 days without interruption.[9] Some of these events are recounted in *The Russian Revolution,* the classic work by William Henry Chamberlain.

The significance of these military events is that the Stavropol area was everybody's target. In addition to military and guerrilla operations, the Communists conducted a campaign of terror against petty bourgeois individuals, particularly government officials.[10] A government stationmaster was especially on the spot because he had to provide equipment for troop movements under conditions of complete chaos. The 1918–1920 period could be thought of as the war of all against the stationmaster. An actuary studying the Russian revolution would say that the probability of survival of a stationmaster in Nagutskaya would be nearly zero.

Did his father die in the war between the Reds and the Whites? Did he die later? How well this blank fits the life of a man who has been involved with the secret police for almost half a century, and whose official biography makes Lenin his only "ancestor."

4

Great Leap
Forward:

1930-1937

IN 1930, Yuri Andropov was a youth of 16 with no visible
signs of interest in any particular profession or vocation. Yet
within ten years, at the age of 26, he was a leading member of a
team sent to terrorize the population of the newly established
Karelo-Finnish Republic. The reason for this terror campaign
was that the Karelo-Finnish Republic, a new administrative
unit created in 1940 at the end of the war between the two
neighboring countries, contained what Soviet rhetoric designated as "politically unreliable elements."

Perhaps even more remarkably, at the age of 23, Andropov
had already made his contribution to the expansion of the Soviet
prison camp system in the upper Volga valley. With this system,
Stalin was able to exterminate the peasantry—resistant or

passive—whom he had ordered deported as part of the brutal collectivization program that began in 1930.[1]

In 1930, Andropov joined the Komsomol, the organization of Communist youth. In and of itself, this affiliation was not particularly meaningful since the vast majority of young people in the USSR are compelled to join the Komsomol. In Andropov's case, what made his affiliation important was that after being part of the non-participating majority, he became part of an active minority within the Komsomol that helped fulfill Stalin's aims. One Soviet historian described the Komsomols as the youth who "took an active part in all economic-political campaigns and fought the kulaks relentlessly." (Kulaks were relatively better off farmers whom Stalin exterminated.) In a speech, the Komsomol first secretary quoted Stalin as saying that "the very first task of all Komsomol education work was the necessity to seek out and recognize the enemy, who was then to be removed forcibly, by methods of economic pressure, organizational-political isolation, and methods of physical destruction."[2]

How active was the young Andropov during Stalin's collectivization campaign in the northern Caucasus from 1930 to 1932? From his official biography, no definitive activity can be discerned. In 1930, young Andropov was living in Mozdok, about 100 miles from his place of birth. In Mozdok, an oil-refining town, he became a clerk in a telegraph office. After a few months, he tried unsuccessfully to become a movie projectionist. All this time he was also a member of the Komsomol. Obviously no significant assignment was given him; otherwise his official biography would have mentioned it, and if he had such an outside assignment as a *Komsomolets,* he would not have been assigned so menial a non-manual job as a junior telegraph clerk. Even had there been some minor Komsomol activity, the biography would have mentioned it.

In 1932, at age 18, he left for Rybinsk, about 1,000 miles north of Mozdok, in the province of Yaroslavl. His departure had nothing to do with any improvement in his condition, because in Rybinsk he found employment at a job even lowlier than the one he had held in Mozdok. In Rybinsk, he became a river boatman, a position at the very bottom of the Soviet social structure.[3]

Even though he was still on the lowest rung of the ladder in Rybinsk, at least he had forsaken a part of the Soviet Union that was now racked by famine and terror. As the forced collectivization neared completion in the northern Caucasus in 1931, and hundreds of thousands of peasant families were being deported to the frozen north, what peasantry remained began a desperate resistance. Stalin ordered drastic measures against the peasants of the Kuban and Stavropol provinces, the area where Andropov was born and where he was still living in 1932.

The collectivization system, forcibly introduced by Stalin, produced chaos, not grain. Therefore, Stalin ordered the seizure of all grain, even including what would have been the daily food ration for the peasantry.[4] The Northern Caucasus population lost, by the most conservative estimate, about 600,000 people, or about 10 percent of the population.[5] When the famine and forced deportations reached their final climax in 1932, Andropov was already in Rybinsk.

After a few months as a riverboat sailor, he enrolled in the Rybinsk technical school of water transport.[6] At this point, it should be remembered that Andropov had little formal education (he had only graduated from elementary school in the northern Caucasus) and no useful job training. Had Andropov held a high school diploma, instead of entering a technical school he would have been allowed to matriculate at a college.

In 1936, he received his technical school diploma in Rybinsk.[7] However, he never practiced his vocation as a river transport technician because something important happened in the mid-

1930s to Andropov. He became a professional and salaried Komsomol organizer at his technical school. He was relieved of his duties as a full-time student.[8]

The mid-1930s was a particularly providential time for a young man starting what he hoped would be a Party career. After the assassination of Leningrad party leader Serge M. Kirov in December 1934 (which Khrushchev later revealed had been engineered by Stalin) and the mass terror and party purges that the assassination unleashed, there were many openings and opportunities for career-minded young men.

The man who replaced the murdered Kirov as Leningrad party boss was Andrei A. Zhdanov, party boss in the lower and middle Volga provinces, who retained general control of the area even though he had been promoted to Leningrad. Zhdanov later became Stalin's heir-apparent and responsible for party ideology. (In later chapters we will discuss Zhdanov, when Andropov crosses his path again.)

While Zhdanov administered the terror in Leningrad, he continued to be in charge of the terror in the Volga area. In the summer of 1935, he made an inspection trip of the cities and Volga countryside, launching a new wave of repression. Many Party and Komsomol cadres were removed and purged.[9]

It was in this particular terroristic environment that Andropov began a career that 47 years later would bring him to the top of the Soviet hierarchy.

During 1935 a group of young water transport technicians from Rybinsk with an ambitious proposal got to Stalin (perhaps via Zhdanov), something unprecedented because Stalin was not usually accessible to young men from the provinces.

Their proposal was to expand the Moscow-Volga Canal, under construction since August 1933, to Rybinsk. A dam to contain the waters of the Volga and thus create a huge artificial lake was envisioned, as well as an electric power station.[10]

From every conceivable standpoint—economics, engineering,

national growth and development in terms of gross national product—this proposal should have been ignored as the silly pipe dream of a group of inexperienced youths just out of technical school. But the idea had one advantage for Stalin that made this project eminently desirable, and he personally supported it.[11]

Stalin supported the Rybinsk project because it was congruent with his ideas for the Soviet Union, namely, to "remake Nature," in the words of one of the revolutionary slogans, by huge Pharaonic projects—dams, artificial seas and lakes, canals, and power stations. All this would be the substitute for air, road, and rail transport.[12] For Stalin, these projects were part of the developing prison camp system. It was an opportunity to use the labor of hundreds of thousands of people, deemed politically unreliable, on projects that might be of some use to his utopia. It was also an opportunity to develop model slave labor camps for later and more effective use for gold mining and providing timber. In other words, these water projects, while of dubious economic benefit, were great for exterminating the "class enemy."[13]

Such were the ideas behind Stalin's approval of the project of the young Rybinsk technicians and the Komsomol brigadiers among whom Andropov held the leading position. Preliminary work began in 1936 and heavy construction in 1937.[14]

As the Rybinsk project went into full swing, Andropov, a mere graduate of a technical school, was given his first assignment: to supervise the Komsomol work at the Rybinsk shipyard.[15] The shipyard produced river barges and large cranes for mounting on these vessels. The cranes were then used in building the power station dam and moving earth for the artificial sea.[16]

In July 1937, NKVD construction of the Moscow-Volga Canal was completed. The 500,000 Belomor prisoners who had previously built the White Sea Canal were moved by the NKVD to the Rybinsk project, named by the Soviets *Volgostroi,* or the

27

Volga Construction Project. With the influx of armies of newly arrested political prisoners, the Volgostroi became the largest NKVD project in the Soviet Union at the time. The NKVD took over the administration of the Rybinsk project, thereby bringing the shipyard's Komsomol officials under its direct control. Heading the Volgostroi project was the notorious Yacub Rappoport; the chief engineer was Sergei Zhuk.[17] Both are referred to in some detail in *The Gulag Archipelago*, Volume II, by Aleksandr Solzhenitsyn.

For Andropov, to have worked with Rappoport and Zhuk at this time would be like having worked for Heinrich Himmler and Adolf Eichmann, in the later Nazi period.

By the end of 1937, the construction project had become so demanding, not only of manpower but also of important infrastructural stores and manufactures, that a host of subsidiary factories and lesser enterprises sprang up in the province.[18] It could be said that half the province of Yaroslavl was occupied by the NKVD, which turned the area into a huge concentration camp, with the civilian population doing the camp's subsidiary work.

And now a remarkable event occurred:

Here was young Andropov, a mere 23 years old, doing Komsomol work at the Rybinsk shipyard under NKVD auspices. And suddenly and for no apparent reason this young man was propelled upward to the post of Second Secretary of the Yaroslavl Komsomol.

We must assume that such a promotion was a reward for service over and above the call of Party or Komsomol duty, to have achieved the eminence of *nomenklatura* status at so tender an age. (*Nomenklatura* refers to the Soviet personnel management system whereby all senior appointments require approval by the Central Committee Secretariat. This system makes it possible for a tiny group of the Soviet elite to control the Party as an instrument of its effective rule of the USSR.) But during the bloody days of Stalin's purges, which crested in 1937, there were, as suggested earlier, many opportunities and job openings.

And a year later, Andropov became First Secretary—at age 24! Such a promotion meant that he was now one of an important triumvirate—Rappoport, who ran the prison camp and project, Nikolai S. Patolichev, First Secretary of the Yaroslavl party (and in 1983, Minister of Foreign Trade), and Andropov. As a member of the triumvirate, Andropov assisted in the administration of the province, half of which could be regarded as a Russian Auschwitz minus the gas chambers.

5

Patrons and Clients:

1937-1940

ON December 20, 1967, in the Kremlin Palace of Congresses, Andropov delivered a speech entitled "Fifty Years of Safeguarding the Security of the Soviet Motherland." His audience consisted of, for the most part, KGB officers and party officials.

It was an important occasion for Andropov since it was his first formal appearance as head of the KGB or Committee for State Security, speaking in his own right. Seven months earlier the party had appointed him to this strategic position.

Andropov's speech demonstrated what would seem to be a certain independence of thought—independent, that is, of the prevailing party line as it had once been enunciated by Nikita Khrushchev.

It will be recalled that in February 1956 and again in October 1961, Khrushchev had exposed the horrors of mass terror and the purges during the Stalin era. His speeches were a chilling recital of what life and death were like in Stalin's USSR. Khrushchev singled out the executed secret police chiefs, Beria and Yezhov, as Stalin's designated killers.

During the Khrushchev years, millions of people executed or jailed at Stalin's orders were rehabilitated. This act of rehabilitation meant that these millions, some of them still alive after years of tortured existence in the slave labor camps, were declared guiltless. Their rehabilitation was an admission by the party and the Soviet State that great wrongs had been committed against so many of its citizens and their families.

With Khrushchev's ouster in October 1964, the party line on Stalin shifted into reverse. Now it was said that while there had been certain abuses of "socialist norms" in the Stalinist past, it should not be exaggerated. Even Khrushchev had warned against over-interpretation. The post-Khrushchev line on Stalin went even further: forget it, don't mention it, accentuate the positive.

While there was now nothing wrong in praising Stalin on suitable occasions, no reference to the black years would be countenanced. There was general agreement in the party that the NKVD, the KGB's predecessor, was not to be singled out for attack as Stalin's instrument for the mass terror. The NKVD role was to be ignored; its past activities would neither be praised nor justified.

Now comes the remarkable Andropov speech of December 20, 1967. He said:

> In the pre-war period, the State Security organs had no more important task than to frustrate the designs of enemy intelligence agencies and other destructive activities on the part of Fascist

Germany and militarist Japan. If the enemy failed to disorganize our rear positions and failed to undermine the military prepared-ness of the Soviet State, this achievement, to no small extent, is due to the State security organs. [Applause][1]

Despite Khrushchev's past view of the tragic years of Stalin's rule, despite the revelations made by Soviet leaders themselves and their attempt to conceal what had actually happened, de-spite the rehabilitation of millions of innocent people, Yuri Andropov stood up in the Kremlin and broke the leadership consensus: silence about the past and the NKVD. Andropov in the passage quoted above was defending the NKVD. Never mind what his Politburo comrades (he was, in 1967, a candidate member of the powerful Politburo, but not a full voting member) had agreed upon. With breathtaking audacity he was rebuilding the damaged reputation of the security organs and what must have been the morale of their officers. And nobody, from Brezh-nev on down, said nay to Andropov's personal campaign to rehabilitate the NKVD.

Even further, Andropov was saying that the millions and millions of innocent people whom Stalin had doomed in the 1930s had really been Nazi or Japanese spies and deserved every-thing they got. This sort of terminology for Stalin, and now for Andropov thirty years later, had justified the Great Terror. Stalin's declaration of war against internal opposition, actual or fictitious, was on the basis of an accusation that was never proven. In charging that vast numbers of Soviet peoples were somehow Nazi or Japanese spies, witting or unwitting, Stalin was implying, and Andropov was accepting, that there was a vast reservoir of disloyal subjects in Stalin's Soviet Union eager to work with the enemies of the Soviet revolution.

At the peak of the terror, Stalin addressed a Plenum of the Central Committee on March 3, 1937, in which he launched a series of accusations against those arrested by the secret police, the sharpest of which was that they were really German and Japanese agents. Said Stalin:

> Bourgeois states must have infiltrated into the rear of the Soviet Union twice as many or three times as many saboteurs, spies, wreckers, and murderers, as these same states infiltrated into each other's countries. Isn't it clear that as long as capitalist encirclement exists, saboteurs, spies, wreckers and murderers will exist, having been infiltrated into the rear by the agents of foreign states? Our party comrades forgot about this. And having forgotten, they fell into disarray. This is why espionage and sabotage of Trotskyite agents, of Japanese and German political police were not fully anticipated by some of our comrades.[2]

And thirty years later Andropov was reiterating these charges against Stalin's victims, dead or alive, even using the same language and images just as if there had never been a so-called destalinization campaign by the Party leadership. It is understandable that Andropov, a graduate of what might be called the "Class of 1937," should have spoken as he did if only to demonstrate a loyalty to the memory of a dead leader who had made the careers of Andropov and other Soviet leaders possible by purging their predecessors.

The years 1937 to 1940, when Andropov was Komsomol leader of Yaroslavl province, saw the greatest turnover of Party personnel in Soviet history. The rule was: either you rose or you fell—there was no middle road. Either you were purged, jailed, disgraced, or executed, or you were promoted to a higher nomenklatura position. By the beginning of 1939, Stalin could tell the 18th Communist Party Congress that "within the last five years, the party was able to promote to leading positions in the State and Party apparatus more than 500,000 young Communists."[3] At least the same number of people who had held these offices had been purged. In many cases, the turnover had been two or three times in this same period.

During the 1937-1939 period, in the province of Yaroslavl we know of only two leading functionaries who retained their leadership positions in the same geographical area. They were Yacub Rappoport, head of the Volga Construction Project, and Yuri Andropov. In the same two years, at least two first secretaries of the Yaroslavl provincial party were removed. These two secretaries were Andropov's superiors since the Komsomol organization was subordinate to the party. At the same time, another Andropov superior, the Yaroslavl Komsomol first secretary, disappeared without trace, and Andropov replaced him in 1938. In the country at large, almost the entire Komsomol leadership was destroyed in November 1938.[4]

Andropov, leading a charmed life, not only survived these purges, he also profited from them. In view of Andropov's steady rise during these turbulent years, the conclusion is inevitable that he had become a beneficiary and a participant in the Soviet leadership's system of patronage.

Before Andropov was designated second secretary of the Yaroslavl Komsomol in 1937, he had over him three superiors—the first secretary of the Yaroslavl Communist provincial party, whose name has been lost to posterity despite a diligent search of the records; Aleksandr N. Yegorov, first secretary of the Rybinsk party, which it should be remembered was administered by the NKVD from Moscow because of the Volgostroi project; and Yacub Rappoport, head of the Volgostroi.

The provincial party secretary probably was not Andropov's patron since he disappeared in 1937 and Andropov did not. According to the usual pattern of Stalin's purges, if the patron was "guilty," all his clients were "guilty." Yegorov was an influential party figure, but he suffered a severe demotion in

1937, from this high party post down to an obscure position as head of the education section of the provincial Soviet, than which there could be nothing lower, short of being dead.[5]

With the elimination of the first two, Yegorov and the unknown secretary, we are left with Rappoport as Andropov's patron, unless one assumes that Andropov's promotion from Rybinsk to Yaroslavl was an accident.

Yacub Davidovich Rappoport is a strangely unknown figure in Soviet history, and yet he held important positions in the secret police apparatus throughout his life. He, too, lived a charmed life at a time when few secret police officials survived Stalin's purges. Rappoport's career in the security services began as early as 1917 with the establishment of the Cheka. In 1930, Stalin appointed him to a team charged with the establishment of his concentration camp universe.[6] A year later, Rappoport was appointed deputy head of the construction for the infamous White Sea-Baltic Canal where, it is estimated, a quarter million people perished within the 1932–1933 period.[7] From 1933 to 1937, he was deputy head of the Moscow-Volga Canal. For supervising these projects, Rappoport was twice awarded the Order of Lenin. In 1937, he was promoted to chief of the newly designated upper Volga, or Volgostroi, project.

Rappoport seems to have been Stalin's chosen instrument in the creation of a slave economy. For added to all his other accomplishments and appointments, Rappoport, from the early 1930s through the 1940s, was also deputy chief of the entire Gulag, the all-Union system of prison camps and forced labor.

Sometime after the end of the Soviet-Finnish war and after the establishment of the Karelo-Finnish Republic in spring 1940, Rappoport was transferred to this area with a new assignment: to expand what was left of the White Sea-Baltic prison camp into a vast system of forced labor in the timber industry. During the Soviet-German hostilities in World War II,

Rappoport received other important assignments while still in charge of the northern system of concentration camps. In October 1952, he received his last Order of Lenin for the construction of the Volga-Don Canal during 1949–1952, when he held the rank of Lieutenant-General in the MVD, forerunner of the KGB.[8] Andropov and Rappoport worked together not only from 1937 to 1940 in Yaroslavl province but also from 1940 on when they both moved to the Karelo-Finnish Republic.[9]

In 1938, a new party boss, Aleksei I. Shakhurin, was appointed head of the Yaroslavl provincial party to replace his vanished predecessor. It was Shakhurin's first appointment to a higher level, provincial chief, and judging by his career line, he was a client of Andrei Zhdanov, Politburo member and close to Stalin.[10]

By appointing Shakhurin, Zhdanov wanted to retain control of the important upper Volga area party apparatus. At this time, Zhdanov in alliance with Politburo Member Andrei A. Andreyev and Georgi M. Malenkov, a powerful apparatchik, fought against an opposing faction, led by Lazar M. Kaganovich, who fancied himself as Stalin's heir-apparent.[11] One of the rules of the Kremlin power struggle was: crush the clients of your opponent in the bureaucracy and substitute your own.

In such a confrontation between the big fish, not only a first secretary like Shakhurin but even a first secretary of a provincial Komsomol, a really small fish like the young Andropov, counts in the order of battle. Andropov's next important promotion to the position of first secretary of the Yaroslavl provincial Komsomol was undoubtedly due to the joint endorsement of his candidacy by Shakhurin, the party man, and Rappoport, the NKVD man.

From this date on, 1938, Andropov became part of the unceasing factional inner struggle that characterizes Soviet politics. Any new party figure who emerged on the scene in any place where Andropov was assigned would, in the course of fulfilling his own political ambitions, have to take into consideration Andropov's presence.

In August 1938, Nikolai S. Patolichev arrived in the province of Yaroslavl as a special representative of the Central Committee of the CPSU (Communist Party of the Soviet Union). He was charged with strengthening defense-related production of synthetic rubber at the largest industrial plant in the Soviet Union, located in the city of Yaroslavl.

Patolichev represented what was at the time the anti-Kaganovich faction of Zhdanov, Andreyev, and Malenkov.[12] In fact, his arrival on the scene led to the beginning of a significant relationship between him and Andropov, a 15-year relationship that determined Andropov's career from 1938 to 1953.

In January 1939, Stalin transferred Shakhurin from Yaroslavl to the same position in Zhdanov's fiefdom, the province of Gorki. This transfer made possible Patolichev's promotion to first secretary of the Yaroslavl's provincial party organization.[13] Within a few months, Patolichev raised Yegorov from the obscurity of his provincial education post, to which he had been demoted in 1937, and appointed him to an important party position in Yaroslavl. It was from this position that Yegorov was in a few years promoted to the core of the Central Committee party apparatus in Moscow.[14]

Judging from his memoirs published in 1977, Patolichev also highly approved Andropov's performance as Komsomol leader. He also expanded Andropov's sphere of influence to include ideology, culture, and education.[15]

One of the most important achievements of Patolichev's tenure was the construction of a 56-mile road between Rybinsk and Yaroslavl. Since Rappoport was unable to supply prison labor for the project because they were all busy building Rybinsk's artificial sea, Patolichev, aided by Andropov, Yegorov, and NKVD provincial chief Nosov, introduced an old form of tyranny, corvée, unpaid road labor under government orders. The population of the province was mobilized for the project. Patolichev was so proud of this road that in his memoirs he says that he and the other provincial leaders, as the project drew to a close, flew over the area in an airplane and that from the air the scene below looked like "a birthday cake" (*prazdnichnyi pirog*).[16] A macabre simile when one considers that on the ground below were the hundreds of thousands of people who had been forced to build this road.

6

Between Two Wars:

1940-1941

"EVERYTHING is closed in, stuffy, and repugnant; one wants to destroy everyone, or simply kill oneself."[1]

This letter by a Komsomol member was written at the height of the purges and the denunciations. It encapsules the atmosphere of tragedy in the years we have been describing. The Komsomol provincial organizations were decimated.[2] But those who led the purges, who followed Stalin's orders, were promoted in 1939 and 1940.

One of these functionaries was Yuri Andropov. From being a first secretary of one of dozens of provincial Komsomols, he rose to become the first secretary of the Komsomol of one of the then eleven Union Republics, namely the Karelo-Finnish Republic.

This promotion was largely due to Patolichev, then allied to

Zhdanov. And it was Zhdanov, in charge (among his other duties) of the newly established Karelo-Finnish Republic, who evidently supported Andropov's rise.[3]

The Karelo-Finnish Republic, the eleventh incorporated into the USSR, was organized after the Soviet-Finnish war, which ended in 1940 in a Pyrrhic victory for the USSR. Khrushchev himself called it "a moral defeat," but it was also a political defeat.[4]

Official Soviet sources suggest that the idea of a Soviet attack on Finland came from Zhdanov, who saw in such a war a way to expand his political influence.[5] Zhdanov was at the time First Secretary of the Leningrad Provincial Committee, a full Politburo member, a Central Committee Secretary, and a possible heir-apparent to Stalin. In pressing for an attack on Finland, Zhdanov was staking his career on its outcome.

The decision to conquer Finland, either by political or military means, was taken in June 1939, two months before the Hitler-Stalin Non-Aggression Pact.[6] The actual war started on the morning of November 30, 1939. During the war, the Soviets concentrated 1.4 million regular troops against 600,000 Finnish soldiers and volunteers. The Soviet artillery advantage on this front was 2.8 times that of the Finns. As far as tanks were concerned, the Soviets had them, the Finns had practically none.[7] But the Finns had their Mannerheim line of fortifications, which the Soviet troops were unable to overcome for three months.

During the 1939–1940 winter, hundreds of thousands of Soviet soldiers froze to death for lack of warm winter clothing. Far fewer were actually killed in battle. The Finns lost some 60,000 soldiers. The Soviets claimed they lost 48,745 troops.[8] Khrushchev in his memoirs, however, stated: "I'd say we lost as many as a million lives."[9]

The Soviet leadership was in disarray as a result of this shambles of a war. The memoirs of Khrushchev and Patolichev do not disguise the disorder at the top levels of the Soviet Party. In fact, Khrushchev describes an amazing scene toward the end of the Finnish war in which Stalin, "in a white hot rage," berated the Defense Commissar Voroshilov for the Soviet defeats. Voroshilov "was also boiling mad," and he "hurled Stalin's accusations back into his face." Khrushchev reports that Voroshilov shouted at Stalin: "You have yourself to blame for all this! You're the one who annihilated the Old Guard of the army: you had our best generals killed."

Says Khrushchev: "Stalin rebuffed him and at that, Voroshilov picked up a platter with a roast suckling pig on it and smashed it on the table . . . Voroshilov ended up being relieved of his duties as People's Commissar of Defense."[10]

The outcome of the war, however, was as much a defeat for Zhdanov as it was for Voroshilov. Zhdanov was deeply involved in the war; first, as political commissar on the Finnish front and, second, because the war was his idea. Just one month after the war's end, in mid-April 1940, Malenkov won Stalin's approval to get rid of Zhdanov's pattern of Party management of industry, introduced in 1939, and to establish Malenkov's own management system.[11] This decision also meant that Malenkov had overtaken Zhdanov and could now begin building up his own position as Stalin's heir-apparent.

The alliance between Malenkov, Zhdanov, and Andreyev was now broken. It was a critical moment for Patolichev, Andropov, and other clients of this now shattered coalition. Fortunately for Patolichev and his circle, however, the moment of the Soviet Union's political defeat in this war and the moment of Zhdanov's personal defeat within the Soviet leadership, coincided with the sprouting of a personal relationship between Patolichev and Stalin himself.

Toward the end of March 1940, an extraordinary Plenum of the Central Committee was convened to discuss the lessons of the Soviet-Finnish war, the prospects for Soviet foreign policy, and the Soviet structure of economic management.[12] Zhdanov played two roles at this plenum—he was both main speaker and also main target. Patolichev, as a candidate member of the Central Committee since 1939, and provincial chief of Zhdanov's fief, was one of the first speakers. As a reputed Zhdanov client, Patolichev was vulnerable to Malenkov's offensive against Zhdanov.

Upon the completion of Patolichev's speech, General Andrei V. Khrulev, chief of Red Army logistics, ran over to Patolichev as he took his seat. Khrulev, according to Patolichev's published memoirs, asked him excitedly if he were not the son of his revolutionary comrade in arms, Semyon Patolichev, who had been killed in the Soviet-Polish war of 1920. Yes he was. Khrulev then interrupted the meeting, shouting, "Let's go immediately to Stalin!" Patolichev says he was embarrassed by Khrulev's outburst, not realizing that Stalin had been a good friend of his father.

Patolichev found it bizarre that his father's relationship with Stalin should be the occasion for an interruption of a Central Committee Plenum meeting of such importance. However, Khrulev knew better. He had gone up to Stalin during the meeting and identified Patolichev. When the session adjourned, Stalin and other Party leaders surrounded Patolichev and talked with him about his heroic father and, eventually, about more current matters.[13] Much to his surprise, Patolichev quickly became a member of Stalin's inner circle. From this point on, Patolichev's career as well as those of his major clients, like Andropov, became independent of Zhdanov's fate.

Evidently among the matters discussed between Stalin and Patolichev was the work of the Komsomol. A few months later, Stalin proposed to Patolichev that he take over the leadership of the all-Union Komsomol.[14] Although Patolichev doesn't say this, one can sense a certain paternal flavor in Stalin's offer. Patolichev declined the offer, and Stalin didn't insist—otherwise it would have been an offer that Patolichev couldn't refuse. However, from this first meeting with Patolichev in March 1940 and thereafter, Stalin apparently regarded him as an expert in Komsomol matters.

During the 1940 Plenum meeting, a decision was adopted to establish the new Karelo-Finnish Republic and to appoint its leadership.[15] When the question of a first secretary of the Karelo-Finnish Republic Komsomol came up, Andropov's name surfaced and his nomination was approved. From the fact that Patolichev specifically mentions Andropov's transfer from Yaroslavl to the Karelo-Finnish Republic and from our knowledge that Patolichev and Stalin had discussed Komsomol matters, we can conclude that Andropov's promotion was the result of Patolichev's recommendation.[16] An appointment of this rank necessitated Stalin's personal approval and personal deliberation instead of the usual system for low-level appointments where a list of suitable candidates would be submitted to him for approval. In other words, the appointment meant that he was now Stalin's personal choice as a result of Patolichev's nomination.

Andropov's appointment was compatible with the balance of forces in the party apparatus as it related to patronage and clientage.

On the one hand, Zhdanov was of course interested in expanding his rule over his now enlarged empire, the Karelo-Finnish Republic, by placing in important posts individuals from his old trusted fief in Yaroslavl province. On the other hand, Malenkov saw further ahead than Zhdanov in this case. Malenkov should have welcomed such personnel transfers from Zhdanov's Yaroslavl stronghold because Malenkov was already taking over from the weakened Zhdanov the central party apparatus. Malenkov planned to fill vacancies with his own people everywhere, including Yaroslavl.

Andropov's appointment and promotion to the Karelo-Finnish Republic has another and different perspective, for he wasn't the only Party functionary sent in 1940 to run the new Republic. He was one of a team that consisted of a number of important Party officials collected from various provinces of the USSR to staff the new Republic. The complete list of the team cannot now be reconstructed from available records, but some of its constituent members are known. Among them was Fyodor Grekov, a party apparatchik from Yaroslavl.[17] Another team member was A. S. Varlamov, appointed secretary of the central committee of the Republic, charged with the cadre and party apparat. Varlamov evidently represented Malenkov's faction on this team, a faction in the Central Committee apparatus that opposed Zhdanov.[18]

A particularly important component of the team were two NKVD officers. One of them, V. A. Andreyev, was immediately appointed Minister of the NKVD for the Republic.[19] The other was Sergei Ya. Vershinin, a special representative of the main NKVD headquarters in Moscow, which means that he had been assigned personally by Lavrentii P. Beria, then head of the NKVD, to the Republic.[20]

From all these assignments, it is clear that the team in which Andropov was an important figure was not wholly Zhdanov's personal entourage. To some extent, the team was a counterforce to Zhdanov's establishment in Karelia, an establishment that had been in existence since 1938.

However, the first secretary of the Karelo-Finnish Republic, Gennadi N. Kupriyanov, was a Zhdanovite who was transferred in 1938 from the Yaroslavl provincial party apparat and was reappointed to the same post when the Republic was established. The second secretary of the Republic was also a Zhdanovite, N. N. Sorokin.[21]

To be a member of such a significant team meant that Andropov was now somebody whom the party bosses in the central apparat in Moscow were including in their personnel calculations. He was now in a situation where his role was to be more than just a tool in the hands of competing party leaders. Nor was he only a client of Patolichev while ending his relationship with the power-impaired Zhdanov. He was now an active participant in the struggle for dominance in the party apparat. He was amassing, as an important asset, personal experience in the art of party infighting, faction against faction, from purge to purge, the integral practices of Soviet political life and death.

It was now 1940; Andropov was in charge of the Karelo-Finnish Republic Komsomol organization whose membership totaled 23,000 young men and women in their late teens and twenties.[22] His position could be considered roughly equal to that of Otto W. Kuusinen, an old Comintern leader with the then honorific title of chairman of the Supreme Soviet of the new Republic. Kuusinen during the 1950s and 1960s would become Andropov's patron, but in 1940 Kuusinen, for someone of his earlier status, was in a position of relative obscurity. Stalin had announced at the outset of the Soviet-Finnish war that Kuusinen would head a Finnish puppet government to be formed at the successful conclusion of the war. The plan foundered on Finnish obstinacy and military resistance.

In 1940, Andropov had been a Communist Party member for just one year, although he had been a candidate-member for several years before. (His late entrance in the party in 1939 was due to an extension in waiting time for admission to the party.) And yet he was virtually on a par with Kuusinen who had been a Party member since 1905, had been for many years secretary of the Comintern, and at one time had even been its acting chairman.[23]

Another way to evaluate the rapidity with which Andropov, now 26, was moving up in the Party apparatus at this time is to compare him with the 34-year-old Leonid I. Brezhnev, who in 1940 had nine years of Party seniority and who then held a minor position, fourth secretary of the Dnepropetrovsk provincial party committee in the Ukraine—somewhat less important that Andropov's Republic Komsomol chairmanship.

Despite Andropov's achievement, his position was far from secure. As a protégé of Patolichev and as a man still considered to be part of the Zhdanov establishment, he was vulnerable to attack by Malenkov's and Beria's representatives on the team sent to the Karelo-Finnish Republic. And equally troubling for Andropov was that he was also vulnerable to attack by powerful local Zhdanovites led by Kupriyanov, because Patolichev had defected from Zhdanov. In his memoirs, published in 1975 in the USSR, Kupriyanov does little to conceal his hostility to Andropov.[24]

The first known Malenkov attack on Patolichev, as the route that would lead to the downfall of Zhdanov, began in August 1940. The attack failed because Stalin came to the defense of Patolichev and even offered him the job, as mentioned earlier, of first secretary of the all-Union Komsomol.[25]

In spring 1941, Malenkov launched another vicious attack on Patolichev and through him on Zhdanov, holding both men responsible for the failure of synthetic rubber production as part of Soviet military preparedness. Patolichev and his aides, including Andropov (who, by this time, was no longer in Yaroslavl), appeared to be in an extremely dangerous position. However, Zhdanov's rivals, notably Malenkov, didn't realize that there had been a change in Patolichev's fortunes: that the son of Stalin's friend during the civil war had become a Stalin favorite.[26] But though Patolichev and his entourage, including Andropov, were immune at this time from Malenkov's drive against Zhdanov, Malenkov did fully succeed in undermining Zhdanov and in ousting some of his other associates in early 1941. Thereby Malenkov became the most powerful of Stalin's lieutenants.[27]

With Zhdanov's temporary eclipse, Andropov got the message, namely to get off the Zhdanov bandwagon. Subsequent events demonstrated that Andropov had, indeed, disassociated himself from what might have become a serious political liability. His work in the Karelo-Finnish Republic in 1940–41 and later, as recorded in published documents, memoirs, and historical accounts, demonstrates a minimum of cooperation with Kupriyanov, Sorokin, and other local Zhdanovite party leaders. The evidence available suggests that instead he worked with such team members as Andreyev and Vershinin, the NKVD chiefs, and their local colleagues, Mikhail I. Baskakov and V. I. Dyomin. There are definite indications, as stated earlier, that Rappoport, the NKVD construction boss, and Gulag deputy chief, and Andropov's patron, had also been in the Karelo-Finnish Republic from mid-1940 until the fall of 1941. It should be remembered that a significant territorial part of the Republic was a huge NKVD enterprise, the White Sea-Baltic *kombinat,* a chain of forced labor camps. The chief of the *kombinat,* Timofeev, was a key figure in the Republic's party administration.[28]

Such a concentration of high-ranking NKVD officials in the same confined area at the same time indicates that something big and important was afoot, over and above the routine timber production in the forced labor camps. Something indeed was.

Two decrees, the texts of which are unpublished to this day, were promulgated in the name of the Central Committee of the Communist Party of the Soviet Union (CPSU) and All-Union Council of People's Commissars, i.e., the Soviet Government, within three months of each other. Both decrees were devoted to a single territory, the Karelo-Finnish Republic. These decrees, one dated May 28, 1940, and the other August 21, 1940, ostensibly dealt with the constitution of an economy in the newly incorporated territories of the Karelo-Finnish Republic and Leningrad province and major resettlement of the rural population.[29] Nothing could have sounded more innocent. It wasn't.

The measures taken to implement these decrees evidently included three operations to be carried out consecutively. One operation was the forced resettlement of urban ethnic Finns from Leningrad and vicinity to the northern areas of the Karelo-Finnish Republic. Their status approached that of inmates of a concentration camp except, perhaps, that families were not broken up.[30]

The second operation affected ethnic Finns and a number of Karelians, altogether tens of thousands of people, who were deported to the north and to Siberia, to places unsuitable for human habitation. Many of them—how many is unknown—perished.[31]

Now it may seem irrational to move some ethnic Finns from the Leningrad area to the Karelo-Finnish Republic while simultaneously ethnic Finns in the Republic are moved out to the far North and Siberia. From Stalin's standpoint, however, he was punishing the Karelo-Finnish peoples because he had lost the war, so they were sent out of the province. In addition, since people were needed to inhabit the now emptied Republic and no Soviet citizen would willingly live in the northern area, he could also punish the Leningrad Finns by sending them to the northern Karelian territories.

The third operation encompassed the habitable areas of the Republic from which the Finns and Karelians were deported to Siberia and the North. Forty thousand rural families from the Ukraine, Byelorussia, and central Russia and eight thousand urban blue-collar families from Leningrad were settled in these areas to replace the expellees.[32] At least 320,000 people were involved in this turnover of population in all three resettlement operations.[33]

The enforcer of these operations was, naturally, the NKVD. However, as the official history of the Karelian Communist Party reports, the Karelo-Finnish Komsomol establishment was, in the official phrase, "the fighting organizer" of these operations.[34] The first secretary of the Karelo-Finnish Komsomol was Yuri Andropov.

7

The Mysterious Death of an Adversary:

1941-1944

WITH the German attack on the Soviet Union on June 22, 1941, the depth of Andropov's connections with the state security apparatus increased. This apparatus, called the NKGB (People's Commissariat of State Security), was in charge of all covert operations, partisan actions, and underground behind-the-lines sabotage in the large part of the Karelo-Finnish territory seized by the Finns. Andropov, who throughout the war remained in the unoccupied area and never crossed the line into the enemy-occupied areas, was charged with the selection of personnel for the NKGB covert operations.

Andropov himself never participated in any military actions, either as part of the regular army or in guerrilla operations. All men of his age were drafted, except those deferred for medical reasons or those whom the Party leadership needed.

During the war, Andropov was also a leading participant in forced labor construction work, which helped make possible the functioning of a new railroad used to carry Allied Lend-Lease supplies from Murmansk. The secret police system thus helped bring about a Soviet victory and, therefore, an Allied victory over Hitler's Reichswehr. Coalition war, like politics, makes strange bed-comrades.

Whatever military events did take place in the Karelo-Finnish territories from 1941 through 1944 were hardly an integral part of World War II or, more specifically, of the Soviet-German War. At no time did the Reichswehr maintain troops in the area, which was solely occupied by the Finns. Within three months of the outbreak of the Soviet-German War—July, August, and September 1941—the Finnish army regained territory in this area that it regarded as originally belonging to Finland. Having done so, they engaged in no further significant combat throughout the war until the Soviet counteroffensive in the summer of 1944. After a cease-fire September 19, the Finns withdrew their troops and then signed an armistice on November 15, 1944.[1]

In February 1941, during the 18th Communist Party Conference in Moscow, Gennadi N. Kupriyanov, first secretary of the Karelo-Finnish Republic Party and Andropov's formal superior, warned Stalin that the Karelo-Finnish territory would be difficult to defend in case of any future war because of the insufficiency of men and materiel. Stalin, of course, then promised Kupriyanov that reinforcements would be sent quickly to the territory.[2] However, what Kupriyanov did not know was that his recommendation contradicted Stalin's grand strategy, namely, in no way to provoke Hitler's suspicions by making any kind of military preparations anywhere.

The Finns started their campaign on Karelo-Finnish territory on June 29, 1941 (a week after the Nazis began their march through the Soviet Union) and by September 1, 1941, they had restored their pre-1939 borders. Even worse for Stalin, the Finns marched deeper into the Karelo-Finnish Republic and on October 2, 1941, they took the Republic's capital, Petrozavodsk. After only three months of war, the Finns had recaptured two-thirds of what had been the Karelo-Finnish Republic.[3] In fact, the entire Republic ceased to exist, and what was left unoccupied by the Finns overlapped with the White Sea-Baltic *kombinat,* the chain of forced labor camps. The Soviets established a new capital in the remnants of the Karelo-Finnish Republic in Belomorsk, which at the same time was the administrative headquarters of the *kombinat.* The Soviet military headquarters also retreated to Belomorsk.[4] In other words, the central committee of the Karelo-Finnish Republic Communist Party, the government of the Republic, the Supreme Soviet, the Komsomol, and the military leadership for three years until 1944 resided within the territory of the prison camp.

This military disaster was to prove the undoing of Kupriyanov, not because he was wrong, but because he was right. He was right in his prophecy to Stalin that the Karelo-Finnish territories were indefensible without substantial reinforcements; and for Stalin, Kupriyanov was wrong to have been right. In wartime, Stalin avoided purges, but the time would come and it did. What was to make life especially difficult for Kupriyanov was that Stalin's animus toward him would eventually become known to other leaders of the Karelo-Finnish Republic, including Andropov.

The leaders who knew of the Stalin-Kupriyanov conversation. and were sophisticated enough to discern its dire implications for Kupriyanov should have distanced themselves from him. Reading Kupriyanov's memoirs, published in 1975, one can see that Andropov followed exactly this line of retreat from Kupriyanov. Although, by statute and custom, the first secretary of a party unit and the first secretary of the respective Komsomol organization would work together hand in hand, as part of the Soviet tradition, like two brothers, the elder and the younger, there is no instance of any concrete collaboration between Kupriyanov and Andropov during the war years. According to numerous published sources, both were responsible for military and partisan resistance, yet they worked separately.[5]

Kupriyanov, Andropov, and other Soviet officials in the Karelo-Finnish Republic were living in a special environment, which they shared throughout the war years, one quite different from that of other party officials. They were living in a prison camp with forced laborers. Unlike other party officials who knew of the Gulag archipelago from a distance and who, ideologically, accepted forced labor camps as necessary, Andropov lived side-by-side with the Gulag system and saw it in operation each day.

Some German Nazi officials claimed, after the horrors of the death-camps were disclosed to the world, that they had known nothing about these camps, or that they had dimly suspected their existence but hadn't known the full extent of their inhumanity, or had known but could do nothing about it. In the same way, many Soviet party officials could make similar claims. But Yuri Andropov was one Soviet official who could make no such claims. He had been connected with the Rybinsk camps and the NKVD and from 1941 to 1944 actually lived and worked on a day-to-day basis within a *kombinat,* a network of forced labor camps. Some party leaders, including Stalin, visited Gulag camps, but none of them except camp administrators actually lived in them as Andropov did.

The NKVD and its troops played an especially important role on the 900-mile Karelian front that extended from Norway to Leningrad. In the Soviet-German war, this was the longest front.[6] Actually there was no front except by formal definition. Just as Western Europe in 1940, had a "phony war," so the line between the enemy troops in the Karelian territory was a "phony front." Neither the Finns nor the Soviets had enough troops to man it. A stalemate finally settled over this line in October 1941. In fact, even the new capital of Belomorsk, where the Karelian military headquarters were located, was unguarded.[7] The Finns simply made no effort to attack Belomorsk. If they had, Belomorsk would have fallen. In the spring of 1942, for example, the Soviets had only 400 machine guns for 900 miles of line.[8]

Since the Karelian front was marginal to the war and since the Republic itself had been dismembered by the Finnish victory, there was little for Party and Komsomol leaders to do. This lack of activity was especially a problem for Andropov since half the Komsomol membership, the males, had been drafted, which meant that mostly female Komsomols remained.[9] What remained for Andropov in the way of official duties was largely bureaucratic routine. He organized small meetings of the remaining Komsomol membership. In fact on one occasion he told the members that because of the urgency of the war effort, the meeting would be a short one—no more than three hours.[10]

Andropov tried, however, to maintain the routine despite the war blazing outside the Karelo-Finnish Republic. In an article Andropov wrote for the Komsomol magazine in 1942, he describes how a young man, one of the few remaining Komsomol members who hadn't gone off to battle, kept pleading to be allowed to volunteer for the army. On five different occasions, says Andropov, his application was blocked. Finally, Andropov said that the young man could go if he would organize another Komsomol unit consisting of the young women who worked on his collective farm.[11]

Andropov's contribution to the war would have continued to be bureaucratic make-work schemes had not the NKVD co-opted him into some real work assignments. Immediately upon the outbreak of the war with Germany, the NKVD organized on June 26 what were openly called "extermination battalions"

(Istrebitel'nye Batal'ony).[12] In July 1941 there were, in the Karelo-Finnish Republic, 38 such units with a total of more than 4,000 men.[13] The responsibilities of these battalions included guarding strategic infrastructures like railroad junctions, canals, Party headquarters, and NKVD enterprises. In the Karelo-Finnish Republic, some of the NKVD battalions were assigned to the White Sea-Baltic prison camp and canal.[14] They were also responsible for killing Soviet political prisoners if they could not be evacuated in case of retreat before an enemy offensive. Such was the practice in other parts of the USSR, as well. The most notorious case known is the NKVD massacre of political prisoners in Orel, a large city in central Russia 200 miles south of Moscow.

Those in charge of forming these battalions in the Karelo-Finnish Republic were V. A. Andreyev, Commissar of Internal Affairs; M. I. Baskakov, Commissar of State Security, and Andropov. Three such battalions in the capital city of Petrozavodsk were organized by Andropov himself from the local population.[15]

On July 4, 1941, the local NKVD was ordered by the Party to organize guerilla warfare detachments. A month later, August 6, a command staff comprising Party and NKVD chiefs was established in the Karelo-Finnish Republic. However, the joint leadership proved to be ineffective, so on October 25, 1941, the NKVD was put completely in charge of this project.[16] Only two non-NKVD persons remained in the upper echelon of the administrative staff on a day-to-day basis and were immediately involved with the NKVD. They were I. V. Vlasov, head of the Organizational Instruction department of the Republic's Central Committee, and Andropov, first secretary of the Republic Komsomol. Both were jointly responsible for the personnel of the partisan detachments and the maintenance of individual records, assignment, and transfers.[17]

Soviet historiography has attempted to depict the guerrilla

warfare as a popular upsurge of the masses in the form of a liberation movement. Except for special Soviet academic and bureaucratic publications, which have been extensively used in preparing this volume, the official party histories of the war years gloss over the role of the State Security institution with respect to the partisan movement. Actually, as has been noted above, the entire Soviet guerrilla warfare campaign during the war from 1941 to 1944 against Nazi Germany and its allies was a State Security operation, administered and led by the NKGB, the forerunner of the present-day KGB. (The NKVD was split in 1941 into two institutions, one still called NKVD, the other the NKGB.)

Although Soviet leaders have avoided crediting the State Security organs with creating the guerrilla movement, one Soviet leader who was directly involved in the movement gives full credit openly to the State Security's leading role in this campaign. He is Yuri Andropov.[18]

As a guerrilla recruiting sergeant, Andropov had many problems. Within the Republic itself lived many Karelians who had not been deported. They felt an ethnic identification with the Finnish army, which occupied two-thirds of what had been the Soviet republic. In addition, there were no German troops, no German atrocities in the area, and the Karelian population was hostile to the Soviets because of the earlier war and deportation.

More importantly, the concept of guerrilla warfare in the Karelo-Finish Republic relied on the recruitment of people and the establishment of bases on the Soviet-occupied part of the territory. Those who were recruited were sent across the lines to sabotage Finnish installations and then to return to their permanent bases on the Soviet side of the line.[19] With this strategy, Andropov and the NKGB could be certain of the loyalty of the partisans since they always had to return because the partisan families were living in Soviet-controlled areas.

Since this strategy and the circumstances precluded the

recruitment of a popular and numerous partisan movement, the NKGB was stymied by a shortage of fighters. What the NKGB and Andropov managed to do was to establish between fifteen to eighteen guerrilla detachments totalling between 1,500 and 1,800 guerrillas. In August 1941, there were fifteen detachments totaling 1,771. At the beginning of 1943, there were 21 detachments and 1,800 partisans. In 1944, there were nineteen detachments for a total of 1,540.[20]

Because of military manpower needs, Andropov sent out an SOS to Komsomol committees in other parts of the USSR for recruits to fight in the Karelo-Finnish areas. In response, Komsomol members were brought in from East Siberian cities like Irkutsk and Kranoyarsk and from Central Asian centers like Tashkent. Out of these levies, Andropov created a detachment which he named "The Karelian Komsomolets," one way of concealing the fact that he had failed to attract sufficient numbers of local people for these detachments.[21]

We now come to a strange event, which occurred on October 4, 1941, during Andropov's career as Komsomol leader and his work with the NKGB in the Karelo-Finnish Republic—the mysterious death in an air crash, if indeed there was an air crash, of Toivo Antikainen, one of the founders (with Otto Kuusinen) of the Finnish Communist Party.[22] The details of his death are contradictory and misleading.[23]

Antikainen seems to have been a genuine idealist ready to accept the notion that class struggle and revolution sometimes lead to errors and even injustice. He seems also to have accepted the notion of proletarian internationalism, namely, that the Soviet Union, because it was the country of the revolution, must be defended at all costs, even if his own country, Finland, suffered as a result. He seems also to have been a maverick, a deviationist, and a romantic who wanted to conduct guerrilla warfare against his fellow-Finns even though it meant disagree-

ing with and discarding the official Party line on guerrilla warfare in the Karelo-Finnish area.[24] The party wanted permanent
bases to be on Soviet territory not on Finnish-held land.

Antikainen had been jailed by the Finnish government in
Finland from November 1934 until May 1940.[25] It was fortunate
that he was imprisoned in Finland because those of the founding
members of the Finnish Communist Party who were in the
USSR during the Great Terror, like Gustaa Rovio and Edward
Gülling, were arrested in 1937. Rovio was shot in 1938, and
Gülling died in prison in 1944. A similar fate was visited upon
other Finnish Communists who had preferred a Soviet sanctu-
ary to their native Finland.

Antikainen came to the Karelo-Finnish Republic after his
release from the Finnish jail, where he had first heard about the
fate of his comrades who had elected the USSR as a place of
exile. He then learned what he had earlier regarded as anti-
Soviet propaganda, namely that the purges of the Finnish communist leadership, were true. He then made his first error. He
sought to overturn the verdict against his comrades in defiance
of what obviously was universally accepted as Stalin's infallibil-
ity. He demanded explanations from Stalin and from the NKVD
for what he openly proclaimed were injustices against good
Party comrades. Stalin refused to receive him, but he was so
loud in his protestations that the NKVD said they would reex-
amine the cases of the Finnish communist leaders and change
the verdict. He even had the audacity to write letters to imprisoned Finnish comrades telling them that they would soon be
freed.[26]

Antikainen's second error was to disagree with the Stalin-
directed conduct of guerrilla warfare in the Karelo-Finnish
areas, a disagreement that reflected upon Stalin's strategy on
guerrilla warfare in the rest of the USSR. Antikainen rejected
the idea of Soviet-based, NKGB-controlled operations. Instead,

he favored recruiting Finnish POWs and sending them to Finnish territory where they would establish permanent bases and incite the Finnish masses to joining the revolutionary forces. It was the kind of strategy that another revolutionary romantic, Che Guevara, employed unsuccessfully in South America a quarter-of-a-century later. Further compounding his error was Antikainen's insistence that he would be the leader of such operations.[27]

For the local NKGB leaders and Andropov, who were in charge of Soviet-based operations, Antikainen represented a threat to their position. He demanded openly the right to organize his own guerrilla battalion and this one battalion, to use Antikainen's own words, "will show up [the NKGB], and show how to make warfare and how to fight the Fascists in the north."[28] To further his demand, he went to Moscow to request approval for his own guerrilla program. By his statement and by his activities he actually put the Karelo-Finnish leadership, including Andropov, into real jeopardy because he was accusing them of being incapable of fighting the Fascist enemy.

Earlier, Antikainen had interfered with Andropov's jurisdiction over the political education of the Komsomol members. From his release in Finland and arrival in Petrozavodsk in 1940, he began a campaign to train Komsomol members to become guerrillas on skis for future combat.[29] This campaign was in direct violation of Stalin's line to do nothing to provoke Hitler and, therefore, complicated Andropov's position as the responsible official of the local Komsomol. It was a nightmare for Andropov because, first, he couldn't accede to Antikainen's demand without going against Stalin, and second, it was supremely difficult to resist the demand of a leading Comintern personality who was upsetting bureaucratic procedures and protocol.

Antikainen's trip to Moscow coincided with the departure of

the Karelo-Finnish leadership also to Moscow to attend what may have been an unrecorded Plenum of the Party Central Committee in October 1941. At this point, the available Soviet sources are contradictory, so much so as to raise valid suspicions about how Antikainen met his death at the age of 43.

One Soviet source says that Antikainen went by train for part of his journey. Another source says that he went entirely by plane. One source says that the weather was extremely bad for flying and that it was high wind velocities that caused the plane to crash. Another says that the weather was fine in the area of the crash and that it was due to pilot error. One source says that Antikainen went by plane because he insisted on flying, while another says that he was urgently summoned to Moscow and because of that he had to fly.[30]

Curious events followed the crash. When Antikainen first came to the Soviet Union, he had gone to live in the same dwelling with Kuusinen. The two were the only important unpurged survivors of the Finnish Communist movement. However, neither Kuusinen nor any other Finnish Communist nor any other Karelo-Finnish Party official was present at Antikainen's secret funeral and burial, which occurred in a tiny village called Kepostrov and which cannot be found on available maps. Orders were also given at the time that Antikainen's death should be kept secret. It was not announced until years later.[31] In addition, all his papers, archives, and four manuscript copies of an autobiography disappeared.[32]

In any murder mystery, one must establish motive, opportunity, and weapon. The motive in the death of Antikainen, if it was not an accident, is quite clear. He embarrassed Stalin, threatened the Karelo-Finnish NKGB and other functionaries, including Andropov, involved in organizing guerrilla warfare. As far as opportunity is concerned, one can infer from the very fact that accounts of his last hours contradict each other in so many

61

details that not one but many opportunities existed for Stalin's state security police to eliminate Antikainen one way or another.

Whatever did happen to this Finnish Che Guevara, this much is true:

Those who gained most from Antikainen's timely disappearance were those who were in immediate charge of the Karelo-Finnish partisan movement.

In the summer of 1943, another strange event occurred in the Karelo-Finnish Republic, an event whose significance went unnoticed until 1975.

In 1975, Gennadi N. Kupriyanov, Andropov's former boss in the Karelo-Finnish Republic, published his memoirs. In them, he made a statement that can only be understood by being aware of the following background:

In addition to the partisan operation, there was also an underground Party and Komsomol operation in the Republic. The partisans were recruited, as has been noted above, from a wide assortment of individuals regardless of their affiliation or lack of affiliation with Party organizations. Recruitment for the underground organizers was made entirely from the established cadres.

There were 121 underground organizers sent behind the Finnish lines by the Republic Central Committee.[33] These organizers, their activities, contacts, aliases, places of residence, everything about them was under the direct control of two men—I. V. Vlasov, head of the Organizational-Instruction department of the Republic's Central Committee, and Andropov.[34]

In the summer of 1943 when it appeared to the Soviets that they would win the war, it was decided to restore Party organizations in occupied territory by the establishment of underground cells. Andropov was still Komsomol first secretary. His second secretary and deputy was F. F. Timoskainen, who in July 1943 was promoted to first secretary of the Party in the capital city of Petrozavodsk, still occupied by the Finns. Timoskainen's position was now higher than that of his former boss, Andropov, even though the capital city was yet to be recaptured.

Timoskainen successfully entered Petrozavodsk and began his underground assignments. He established an underground party cell and then started to recruit people from various professions, even some Finnish soldiers. Very soon, his activities expanded, and he established several groups of Party sympathizers and through them disseminated propaganda leaflets among POWs and civilians. In August 1943, he reported that he had even succeeded in recruiting two important Finnish military officials. His work was suddenly interrupted just as he had established himself as the underground Party leader of Petrozavodsk and was gaining great prestige among the Party leaders in the Republic.

The interruption consisted of his execution by Finnish authorities at the end of August. Regarding the circumstances of the killing, Soviet sources disagree. The most widely disseminated report is that Timoskainen and a group of his underground workers ran into a Finnish patrol near the village of Dereviannoe. There was a short battle and he was shot and killed.[35] However, Kupriyanov, who by his past position should be regarded as the most knowledgable, mentions no fight at all and no Finnish patrol. According to his account, Timoskainen was arrested in Solomennoe, a suburb of Petrozavodsk, and later killed.[36]

Kupriyanov insists that "there were no cowards, no deserters, no traitors" among the underground workers. He emphasizes that there were few arrests of underground activists. And it is in this connection that for no logical reason, Kupriyanov implies that Timoskainen was betrayed from outside his personal network. He then adds that one cannot blame Andropov and Vlasov as responsible for failure by betrayal. Kupriyanov uses a Russian word, *proval,* which means failure by betrayal.[37]

What Kupriyanov has done in his memoirs is to bring up an accusation that had never before publicly been made against these two men, or if not an accusation, then a suspicion against them. He is, in short, acquitting them of a charge publicly unheard of before his memoirs. It must be kept in mind that, in 1975, Andropov had already been head of the KGB for eight years and was a full member of the Politburo. Mentioning Vlasov was really a cover for Kupriyanov because Vlasov was nobody in 1975. Had Kupriyanov wanted to implicate only Vlasov, he would not have dared to mention so powerful a Soviet figure as Andropov. To put it simply, Kupriyanov in the tradition of Aesopian language, is accusing Andropov of having betrayed the underground leader to the Finns. Timoskainen was competition for Andropov's future promotion in the Party. Timoskainen was a rival to Andropov and not to Vlasov.

The Timoskainen tragedy remains a mystery, deepened by the unwillingness of one writer to give any details about how the underground leader was killed and another who denies an accusation that was never made. It would be as if a biographer of John F. Kennedy, in discussing the assassination, were suddenly to exonerate Richard M. Nixon from complicity in the crime when no one has ever made the accusation. In a normal, open, democratic society such irrationality would be regarded as irrational. In the Soviet Union, a Kupriyanov "exoneration" is an accusation. And when other reports simply cloud the entire story, there is every ground for suspecting the man who had the motive, the opportunity, and the means.

8

Storming—Women and Children First:

1941-1944

IN Soviet revolutionary rhetoric, "storming" was a method of exacting free labor from working people. A major project would be announced with a great fanfare in the press, and workers would be exhorted to assemble at a given site to contribute their labor until the project was fully underway. Workers were expected to "storm" the project by working seven days a week with long hours of overtime, no holidays, no rest periods. Storming was also a communist custom during the closing days of a building project so as to ensure completion on some particularly significant day—November 7 (the anniversary of the Revolution), May 1, or a Party Congress. Workers would then "contribute" their labor sometimes for 48 or 72 consecutive hours. Prison labor, of course, had no option at all and was also routinely used for storming projects.

From 1941 to 1944, there were three storming operations in the Karelo-Finnish Republic. Andropov was one of the important manpower organizers for these projects, in which the NKVD was involved.

The first construction project was undertaken following a resolution of the Karelo-Finnish Republic Central Committee of September 1, 1941. The resolution declared that it was urgent to build a defense line of wooden blockhouses and trenches against what was believed to be an imminent Finnish counter-offensive.[1] The legal authorization for this resolution was an all-Union government decree permitting the mobilization of civilians for forced labor.[2]

Within a few days after passage of the resolution, the various Party and Komsomol organs, together with the NKVD, descended upon towns and villages in the Soviet sector of the republic and gave the inhabitants two to three hours to pack and leave for the construction site.[3] More than 20,000 civilian workers were mobilized.[4] As first secretary of the Republic Komsomol, Andropov issued a special order on September 1, 1941, signed by him, which mobilized 2,000 Komsomol members, mostly teenagers.[5]

The work crews were given nothing more than axes and shovels with which to dig miles of trenches and to construct thousands of blockhouses and shelters. There was no machinery, no tractors, just hand tools.[6] Most of the "manpower" consisted of women, old people, and adolescents.[7]

Since such a crew couldn't remotely fulfill the military objectives of the construction, the NKVD had to bring in more people, most likely actual forced labor prisoners, some 19,000, to complete the job.[8] Living conditions for these thousands of people were gruesome, according to even official Soviet histories of the period. When it wasn't raining, it was snowing. There wasn't enough warm clothing to go around, not enough food and, above all, not enough shoes and boots. They worked days and nights in the forests and swamps, and they slept in the trenches or, if they were lucky, in tents in the arctic cold.[9]

As if these forced laborers didn't have enough trouble, the Party leaders and Andropov established political departments to control and drive them on. These departments were organized for extraordinary situations, and dragooning these workers into military battalions was just such a situation. Eighty Party cadres and 100 Komsomol officials sent by Andropov, all of them young or middle-aged males who had been exempted from military service, were assigned to supervise these workers.[10]

In November 1941, it became clear that there would be no Finnish offensive. Having captured the Republic capital of Petrozavodsk and two-thirds of the Republic territory, the Finns were satisfied to call it a day. The defense line was, therefore, unnecessary, and it was abandoned. The Soviet sources do not say when it was abandoned or how much work had been done during the storming.

The second project, in which Andropov played a leading role, became of extreme importance to the Soviet Union as soon as Hitler denounced the Nazi-Soviet Pact on June 22, 1941. This construction project involved building a 220-mile railroad line from Belomorsk, site of the White Sea-Baltic *kombinat,* to the station, Obozerskaia, near Archangel. There was a railroad line from Murmansk via Belomorsk and Petrozavodsk to Leningrad, Moscow, and other parts of the USSR. However, it was obvious that the existing rail-line would inevitably fall to the German-Finnish onslaught. Such an event would have been calamitous to the Soviets because it would have been extremely difficult to move Lend-Lease supplies from Murmansk to the battlefronts and industrial centers in central Russia, the Urals, and Siberia, where industry had been removed. By December 1941, a stretch of some 250 miles between Petrozavodsk and Leningrad had indeed been captured by the invading forces.[11]

Actually, the rail-line between Belomorsk and Obozerskaia had been started during the winter of the Finnish war in 1939–1940. For construction of the line, an autonomous prison-camp system was established in that 1939–1940 winter called GULZhDS, the Chief Administration of Camps for Railroad Construction. It was a department of the NKVD paralleled by the Gulag, the Chief Administration of the Prison Camps. Stalin appointed as the head of GULZhDS, the new forced labor administration, Naftaly A. Frenkel, a notorious labor camp administrator, who is described in detail in Solzhenitsyn's *Gulag Archipelago,* Volume II.[12] When the Finnish war ended in March 1940, construction was still in progress, but Stalin no longer needed the line so it was abandoned for the time being.[13]

The reinstated construction of the rail-line from Belomorsk to Obozerskaia was started sometime in August 1941 by Frenkel's department of railroad prison camps. There are indications that Yacub D. Rappoport, Andropov's long-time patron, was the executive in charge of this railroad project.[14] From the Karelo-Finnish administration, the two persons in charge were N. I. Krachun, a new secretary of the Karelo-Finnish Party, evidently assigned to the project by Stalin, and Andropov himself.[15]

In order to conceal the human hardships involved in building a railroad in sub-arctic temperatures—at the 64th parallel!—through permafrost along the shores of the White Sea during one of the most severe winters in years, the official Party history claims that the railroad was finished in September 1941.[16] The true story, however, is that work continued throughout the winter, and it was barely finished in late February 1942.[17]

The Soviet reports at this time are of snowstorms and blizzards, the worst in contemporary memory.[18] Amidst these temperatures, the worker-prisoners mined rock for ballast and eventually produced four million cubic meters of split rock, a volume equal to 100,000 railroad freight cars.[19] The work continued 24 hours a day. Almost the entire population of the Soviet sector of the Karelo-Finnish Republic, again, mostly women, older persons, and adolescents, were mobilized during that winter to lay down this volume of ballast, after which skilled railroad workers completed the job.[20] Long after Andropov had left these construction projects, Soviet sources recalled approvingly what a superb job he had done as one of the top-ranking organizers.[21]

The main assignment of the Karelo-Finnish party apparatus, the Komsomol organization, and the NKVD was the reestablishment of the timber industry in the Soviet-occupied areas.[22] At the beginning of 1942, a large part of the USSR's productive coal areas had been seized by the Germans. What remained was insufficient to fulfill the country's war needs, and this insufficiency was magnified by the lack of available manpower.

Because of the coal shortages, the rail system, including the branch line that carried Lend-Lease supplies south from Murmansk, was converted from coal to wood.[23] A special decree of the State Defense Committee, the supreme wartime authority headed by Stalin, ordered the Karelo-Finnish Republic to concentrate its entire economy and manpower on producing wood for the northern branch and other railroads.[24]

To be sure, before the war, the timber industry had been the major component of the Karelo-Finnish economy. Timber production comprised 60 percent of the Republic's net material product.[25] If one takes into account infrastructure and auxiliary production—tools and equipment and horse management, for example—then it is clear that the Republic was a one-industry economic area.

Among economic regions in the USSR, before the German war, the Karelo-Finnish Republic had been the fourth largest producer of timber, after Archangel province, Byelorussia

69

Republic, and Sverdlovsk Province. Within the Karelo-Finnish Republic, at least 32 percent of timber was produced by the White Sea-Baltic *kombinat* of the NKVD. Within the all-Union NKVD forced labor system, this *kombinat* alone supplied 30 percent of water-transported timber. This one *kombinat* of the NKVD produced and transported an amount of timber equal to 5 percent of the entire USSR timber output by civilian and forced labor.[26]

During the first few months of the German war, the entire timber industry, including both civilian and prison labor enterprises, was nearly destroyed by the Luftwaffe bombardment and the Finnish offensive. Three-quarters of the prewar industry was located in the area captured by the Finns.[27] Of 28 civilian (non-NKVD) enterprises that, before the war, had produced about two-thirds of the Karelo-Finnish timber output, only five remained in the Soviet-occupied territory.[28] As for the NKVD sector of the timber industry, the *kombinat,* that, too, was razed by the aerial attacks. In addition, horses, the primary means of moving timber from the outlying camps to the central receiving stations, were taken away for military needs. Without horsepower, whatever timber was felled lay on the forest floor. Only a few tractors and autos remained in the entire Republic. Timber industry manpower fell to a few percentage points of what it had been before the war.[29] As a result of all these factors, timber output in 1942 in the Republic was a small fraction of what it had been in 1940.[30]

The leadership of the Republic had to start from scratch in order to meet Stalin's order for restoration of and increase in timber output. The Komsomol leadership headed by Andropov and the party apparatus made a radical rearrangement of labor force recruitment. They replaced male workers, horses, tractors, and autos with women and adolescents of both sexes. In 1942, females in the Republic timber industry comprised about 60 percent of the work force.[31]

At this point, Andropov and other functionaries had a serious problem to solve. As noted earlier, the first two storming projects—strengthening a battleline and building a railroad line—meant enlisting the female population of the Republic since most of the male population had gone off to war. These projects had some kind of terminal date. When you built a trench or a blockhouse, it was built. When you laid down the ballast for a railroad, it was laid down. The task could be completed, and then you could go back to your town or village. But once this storming work-force was disbanded, it would be almost impossible to reassemble them for the timber production project. The original civilian workers had been told that they could expect to be finished with the storming in a few months, and since they had been enlisted or dragooned into the labor service in late summer and fall, they had only light clothing.

The leadership was aware that whatever patriotic feeling had animated the civilian workers on the first two storming projects was no longer a possible inspiration for further work assignments. If word got out that the Party and the Komsomol were planning a new operation, an open-ended one at that, the disbanded work force would probably flee from the Soviet areas for the Finnish-occupied land or else would disperse themselves to remote villages where they would be unreachable by the NKVD or other Party organs. Many of the women were mothers who had been forced, willy-nilly, to leave their children for several months. To expect that these mothers would allow themselves to be mobilized once more, for years ahead, was highly unreal. No mobilization order would be obeyed, especially when no one could predict how long the war would last.

The Party, Komsomol, and NKVD leadership solved the problem, by doing what they always did best.

As each contingent completed the work on either the defense line or the railroad, they were herded together and marched off to the thick forests in the north, known as *taiga,* where there

71

was no human habitation. Although it was winter and they were in their summer clothes and shoes, they were not allowed to return home for winter clothing lest they disappear. They were ordered first to build trenches in which to live while they chopped wood.[32]

During 1942 and 1943, these ill-clothed, ill-housed, ill-fed women's brigades failed to meet the timber quotas assigned them by the leadership. Output in 1942 was miserably low. It doubled in 1943 from its low base. In October 1943, the Party and Komsomol leadership decided to raise production by infusing the entrapped workers with a spirit of sacrifice in honor of the 25th anniversary of the founding of the Komsomol. The sacrifice would be based on production norms. The original norms set before the war were based on healthy males with warm clothing, with horse power, machinery, and motivated by wages.

In 1942 and 1943, the leadership increased the norms from the prewar base for the women recruits.[33] In honor of the Komsomol anniversary, Andropov, in his capacity as first secretary of the Karelo-Finnish Komsomol, raised the norms to a new high: the workers would produce in 145 days what had hitherto been an already unbearable quota for 200 days. The 145 days of storming extended from October 1, 1943 until April 1944.[34] At the height of the winter (and it is really winter most of the year in the *taiga*), these girls and women were expected to exceed by at least *one-third* the quotas that had been laid down for experienced male forest-workers.

As we have seen, it was all quiet on the Karelian front. There were no German land forces, and the Finnish soldiers sat quietly in the land they had seized from the Soviets. In terms of war, this was the forgotten front, and so were the people. To this day, there are no statistics as to how many of these girls and women perished in trying to meet these unachievable quotas.

This was Andropov's last project for the Komsomol after eight years of work as an organizer and leader.

9

Andropov's Career Falters:

1944–1945

YURI Andropov's prewar alliances with prominent Party officials like Nikolai Patolichev, who helped bring Andropov to the top leadership of the Karelo-Finnish Komsomol, were broken during the war years only because of the geographic isolation of the Republic to which he had been assigned.

Patolichev, Andropov's influential patron, had been promoted at the end of 1941 from Yaroslavl to the Ural industrial province of Cheliabinsk, where he was responsible for organizing the Soviet tank industry. A. A. Andreyev, a Politburo member and a CPSU Secretary, who was a friend of Patolichev, had been evacuated to Kuibyshev, on the Volga, which would have become the capital had Moscow been lost to the Germans. At war's end, Andreyev had lost most of his influence in Party affairs and never really regained it after the war. So, by the end of the war, Andropov appeared to be alone, without a protector against his antagonist, Kupriyanov, the Karelo-Finnish Republic Party boss. Even worse for Andropov, he was vulnerable both to Malenkov and Zhdanov, both of whom in the early postwar years decided the fates of junior members of the apparatus like Andropov.[1]

During the war years, Malenkov was the assistant closest to Stalin. By the end of the war, Malenkov had achieved enough influence to expand his power base in all branches of the Party apparatus. He accomplished this expansion in the traditional Communist fashion: by colonizing different parts of the Party apparatus with his own clients and by breaking the hold of rivals for power within the Party apparatus. Malenkov's man in the Karelo-Finnish Republic, as mentioned earlier, was A. S. Varlamov, who reported to Malenkov all during the war through Malenkov's deputies in the Central Committee apparatus, M. A. Shamberg and N. N. Shatalin.[2]

All available Soviet records suggest that Andropov's work during the war years did not cross with that of Varlamov, that there was little working contact between them. Considering that Andropov's prewar career had been outside the Malenkov circle, with the war's end Andropov became a lowly Party official on the outside looking in.

To make matters worse for Andropov, in 1944–45, Zhdanov suddenly outmaneuvered Malenkov and thereby became Stalin's heir-apparent. His rise to power was based on the issue of ideology, which Malenkov had allegedly neglected.[3] The chief postwar ideological problem, which Stalin charged Zhdanov in 1944 to solve, was how to unify the traditional Marxist-Leninist strategy of Communist revolutionary internationalism with Russian patriotism, a phenomenon that had emerged and that had been exploited by Stalin during the war.

Andropov's standing with the once again influential Zhdanov was even worse than with Malenkov. There were several reasons for this:

First, as a result of Andropov's poor working relationship with Kupriyanov, who was Zhdanov's leading representative in the Karelo-Finnish Republic, Andropov was blocked either for promotion within the Republic or for assignment to a higher post outside the Republic.[4]

Second, in the eyes of Zhdanov and his followers, Andropov was regarded quite rightly as a client of Patolichev. Since Patolichev was not trusted by Zhdanov and his machine because of Patolichev's split with Zhdanov in 1940–41, the Zhdanov mistrust extended to Andropov and all other Patolichev clients.[5] Since Andropov was fully connected with the Zhdanov machine through the second half of the 1930s, but thereafter and during the war had worked separately from the Zhdanov machine in the Karelo-Finnish Republic, Zhdanov and Company regarded Andropov as a turncoat.

Third, in 1944–45, Patolichev was not strong enough to prevent a Zhdanovite move against Andropov.

In order to solve the problem of reconciling Communist revolutionary internationalism with Russian patriotism, Zhdanov and his ideological cohorts developed and legitimized an incoherent concept of Communist or Soviet patriotism, an abstraction on a par with democratic communism which Leszek Kolakowski once said was the equivalent of fried snowballs. Soviet or Communist patriotism was self-contradictory and not easily comprehensible by the Party rank-and-file. Numerous deviations from this idea were noted by Zhdanov's "thought police." It was rather difficult to explain what should be the relative share of each component of Communist patriotism—Communist internationalism and Russian patriotism—and even more difficult to establish a fixed criterion. As conditions changed on the international scene, the percentage of the ingredients of this patriotism changed. Woe to a party apparatchik who failed to anticipate the change of line because yesterday's virtuous statement could retroactively become tomorrow's sin. The only way to teach apparatchiks what "Soviet patriotism" was, was to teach them what it was *not*. And the way to teach was by punishing the Zhdanov-defined deviationist.

One of the cardinal sins of this ideological fabrication was parochialism or, in Russian, *mestnichestvo*. This sin meant overemphasis of regional loyalties at the expense of loyalty to world communism and the USSR as a whole.

Unfortunately for Andropov, he had fallen into the sin of parochialism with the publication in Moscow of an article in the national Komsomol newspaper, *Komsomolskaya Pravda,* on June 13, 1943, with a provocative title, "About the Love for a Native Domain."[6] The first part of the 3,500-word article, which extended over three columns, had at its head an even more provocative subtitle, "Motherland, Domain, Home."

Andropov's essay is most interesting as affording an unusual sidelight about a Soviet leader who in February 1983 was described by the French Foreign Minister, Claude Cheysson, after their meeting as "lacking in human warmth," as being a "non-romantic" and working like "a computer."[7] Andropov, on the contrary, emerges from the pages of the Komsomol newspaper, as effusively sentimental about traditional folk melodies and medieval dances. The article is, therefore, worth examining both as to content and ideology and for what might appear today, in the light of Andropov's history, as a youthful naiveté. The very opening sentence must have been read by the Zhdano-vite cabal as confirming any mistrust they may have had of Andropov:

> Before the war we educated our youth insufficiently and didn't emphasize in political education the love for native domain [*krai*], native town and native village.

Here was a truly risky statement for a young and ambitious careerist to make, for what he was doing was accusing those in charge of ideological training before World War II of having erred badly. And who was in charge of this teaching before the war? Zhdanov, himself, as the Central Committee secretary in charge of ideological indoctrination. Andropov, however, went even further in his attack:

> We didn't satisfy the legitimate interests of our young men and women to learn about their native places. A young fighter on the battlefront is actually defending his native domain, his native home and hearth.

Andropov then quotes from a letter he purportedly received at the Karelo-Finnish Republic Komsomol Central Committee, a letter from the front at Stalingrad signed by a number of Karelians drafted for the Stalingrad battle. The letter, as reprinted by Andropov, had the soldiers saying: "Fighting for Stalingrad, we always see before our eyes, the forests and lakes of our native Karelia."

Here Andropov adds a lyrical commentary:

> Going into battle, the young Karelians brought with them memories about shady birch groves of Karelia, about the wonderful songs which their grandmothers and mothers used to sing, about a quiet street in their native hamlet and about a familiar bower in which the first tender words to a beloved damsel were uttered.
>
> To love one's native domain, one's native republic means, among other things, to know and to appreciate folk songs, medieval sagas and traditional dances. Somehow it is no longer in fashion to sing folk songs. We asked some young people in one town which folk songs they knew. Only two answered. They said they knew some romantic songs about bandits but not in full. The songs of the people of our country which celebrate heroic battlefield deeds of our own ancient warriors are often unknown to our youth.

The problem of folk dances is even worse. Somewhere you will find some wise guys who are inclined to think that to dance in the crouching Russian style or a Karelian quadrille is not appropriate for serious people.

One of the startling revelations about Andropov's avocations after his accession to the chieftaincy of the Communist Party in November 1982, revelations which were to be found only in the Western press, was that he likes to tango. Thus it is interesting to read in the 1943 article that Andropov doesn't think much of the tango. Criticizing the "wise guys" who sneer at folk dancing, Andropov writes:

Well, they say, go and tango—that's another thing. . . . One looks at such people and does not see any youth in them. . . . In order to popularize folk songs and Soviet songs, we compel our Komsomol officials to go to villages with a phonograph and records.

Andropov's concluding sentences must have compounded his deviationism because he writes:

These, then, are the issues which should be incorporated into the political education work among young people. . . . All this will undoubtedly serve its great service [sic] to the pursuit of political education of Soviet youth.

These opinions, even if seen as frivolous aperçus tossed off by a young man, were not to be forgotten in that young man's maturity. Andropov included this article in a collection of writings and speeches that he published in 1979, 36 years later.[8] It is difficult to believe that such sentimentalizing on a personal level on the one hand and such dissenting from the Party line on the other would be suitable for reprinting, especially when set against a backdrop of a life-and-death struggle on the Stalingrad front. Was all so quiet on the Karelian front that folk songs and quadrilles became an ideological question for Andropov?

Yet what else could Andropov do? Here he was a Russian amidst a group of people, Karelians, who identified with the Finnish army. The Karelians didn't want to fight the Finns and wouldn't have cared had the Finns taken and occupied the entire Republic. Andropov had to show that he was able to get Karelians to fight, to convince Karelian youth that when they fought the Germans they were fighting for their own homes in the Karelian-Finnish Republic. The line of his article was the only possible one for him to pursue. The pseudo-romanticism of his prose wasn't Andropov's problem. His problem was that as the official in charge of political education, *inter alia,* of Karelian youth, he had somehow to translate the localist patriotism into some kind of national patriotism and, if possible, to the Communist patriotism of the Zhdanovites.[9]

To say, however, that in fighting for Stalingrad, Karelian youth were not really fighting for the USSR but for bowers and quadrilles, for home and hearth, was perhaps effective propaganda for Karelian youth but dangerous deviationism for Andrei Zhdanov. Therefore, as Andropov pressed his localist home-and-hearth patriotism while Zhdanov in 1944 pressed his Communist patriotism line, Andropov became a sinner in the eyes of the powers in the Kremlin, ever fearful of any centrifugal nationalist forces.

In 1944, the time came for Zhdanov to settle old scores with his rivals and their clients. Andropov was an easy target because he was a man with liabilities and no assets, a political bankrupt. On June 28, 1944, Petrozavodsk, the capital of the Karelo-Finnish Republic, was recaptured by the Red Army, and by September 19 the entire territory of the Republic had been regained from the Finns. Finland was, effectively, out of the war.[10]

In mid-1944, Zhdanov was transferred from Leningrad to Moscow. This transfer meant that as a Politburo member and as a secretary of the Central Committee, second only to Stalin, he could now concentrate his power where it mattered most, in the Kremlin, and no longer have to exercise this power from a distance. Zhdanov immediately began his ideological attack against the Malenkovites and other potent groups in the Party.[11] At the same time, Zhdanov was also assigned the task of dealing with a postwar and still independent Finland.[12]

With two such assignments—one, ideology, and two, Finland —Zhdanov couldn't possibly overlook Andropov because both assignments met at one geographical point—the Karelo-Finnish Republic, which for Zhdanov could be defined as an ideological anti-Soviet morass. Such a disaster couldn't be the fault of Gennadi Kupriyanov, Zhdanov's ally in the Karelo-Finnish Republic and first Party secretary, nor the fault of Kupriyanov's deputy in charge of ideology, Iosif I. Siukiiainen. This left Andropov as the scapegoat for the putative failure in the Republic's ideological performance.[13]

In the same period, the Central Committee of the CPSU in Moscow issued two resolutions, undoubtedly at Zhdanov's prompting, criticizing the Party and ideological work in the Karelo-Finnish Republic. The first, dated August 31, 1944, was titled, "About the Shortcomings of Mass Political Work Among the Population of the Regions of the Karelo-Finnish Soviet Socialist Republic Liberated from Finnish Occupation." The second was a little shorter and more innocuous-sounding, "About the Work of the Central Committee of the Communist Party of the Karelo-Finnish Socialist Soviet Republic." The texts of the resolutions, like many Party documents, are unavailable. However, summaries of their contents would indicate that they dealt with deficiencies in the ideological and organizational work.

One of the many issues referred to, insignificant in itself but significant for Andropov, was the emphasis placed on the poor personal training and educational background of certain leaders of the Karelo-Finnish Republic.[14] (One of the consequences of this criticism was that Andropov went back to school as an external student at the Petrozavodsk State University. The record shows that he entered as an undergraduate but did not graduate.)[15]

With the passage of the first August resolution, Zhdanov sent a task force from the Central Committee of the Soviet Party in Moscow to reactivate the propaganda effort in the Republic. There are certain indications that the task force, during its two months in the Republic, concerned itself, among other things, with the Party press and the work of the Republic's Komsomol apparat, which was still headed by Andropov.[16]

During December, 18-20, 1944, a special Plenum of the Karelo-Finnish Republic Communist Party met to finalize the results of the two made-in-Moscow resolutions. What the results were in detail was not made public but one result is known. Sometime between the first Moscow resolution of August 1944 and the December Plenum, Andropov was fired as the Komsomol first secretary of the entire Republic and demoted to the position of second secretary of the city Party Committee of Petrozavodsk.[17]

Andropov was fortunate. Under the circumstances, his demotion was light punishment. But for the long run, his hopes seemed to be in ruins. There he was for the indefinite future sidetracked in a remote area of the USSR, in the smallest Republic of the country, doomed to an inferior position in a provincial capital. Other young party leaders were moving forward and upward. Andropov's career seemed to have come to a full stop.

There was a particular problem for Andropov. He hadn't served in the war as had other future leaders like Khrushchev, Brezhnev, and even Suslov, the later chief ideologist, all of whom were on the battlefront.

Perhaps this divorce from the reality of large-scale war would account for a strange difference between the speeches of Andropov and Kupriyanov, who had been on the battlefront. On May 9, 1945, V-E Day, a huge assembly of some 20,000 people came together in Petrozavodsk to celebrate the victory. Andropov spoke first, and it was the kind of rodomontade that seems to characterize his oratory. He said:

> History has never known such a majestic, sublime, grandiose victory as the Soviet people have won. We now rejoice in incredible days of ascendancy and triumph.

Missing here as he spoke to a throng, most of whom had suffered in the war, either as soldiers or else had lost relatives and friends, was any sense of the sacrifice that the war had entailed. Contrast Andropov's words with those of Kupriyanov:

> The victory we celebrate today was achieved by endless bloodshed on the field of battle and by unprecedented hardships of the people behind the lines. We gained victory at the price of huge sacrifices and countless victims. Today when the people celebrate we must remember those who gave up their lives, for this victory.[18]

10

The Brotherhood:

1945-1953—Part I

WE can explain a great deal about Andropov's past if we postulate the existence of a loosely organized hierarchical group within the Party, one with its own rules, its own traditions and aspirations, a Marxist-Leninist brotherhood of power and strategy. We are not postulating some shadowy, primitive conspiracy of the Illuminati or Freemasons but rather a group of Communist leaders of high and low degree who, as beneficiaries of Stalin's purges during the late 1930s, became Stalin's acolytes. The Brotherhood, whose power greatly increased until Stalin's death, in later years provided from within the Communist Party the future ruling class of the Soviet Union.

During 1939–1940, with the emergence of Andropov's personal relationship with Patolichev and with the emergence of Patolichev's personal relationship with Stalin, Andropov may be discerned as having joined the new, though as yet uncrystallized political force that was destined to rule the USSR for decades to come. This force consisted of a new generation of Communist Party *vydvizhentsy*, activists who had not participated in the inner-party political struggle of the 1920s and the early 1930s. They began their ascent during the 1937–38 purge but belonged to none of the competing group of party elites, neither to Zhdanov's group, nor Malenkov's, Kaganovich's, or Beria's.

To be a member of the Brotherhood certainly helped in getting ahead in the Party. Whether one had or hadn't a university degree or engineering degree or managerial experience or war decorations or a proleterian background was of little moment. What mattered was the strength of patron-client relations within the Brotherhood and the closeness to Stalin of the patrons, particularly as he planned the last party purge just before his death.[1]

The Brotherhood, for the most part comprising first secretaries and sometimes ranking secretaries of provincial party committees after the 1937–1938 purges, could cooperate with any group that enjoyed Stalin's favor at any given moment and on any given issue. It was these secretaries who became Central Committee members after the Eighteenth Party Congress in 1939 and after the Eighteenth Party Conference in 1941. A few of them, like Brezhnev, entered the Central Committee later in 1952, but most of them belonged to the age cohorts—born between 1902 and 1908—with the junior members, like Andropov, born between 1908 and 1914.

The best-known names of the Brotherhood are Mikhail A. Suslov, Brezhnev, Patolichev, Semyon D. Ignatiev, Vassily M. Andrianov, Aleksandr N. Larionov, Averkii B. Aristov, Nikolai G. Ignatov, Frol R. Kozlov, Panteleymon K. Ponomarenko, Nikolai A. Mikhailov, Leonid G. Mel'nikov, Boris N. Ponomarev, Aleksei A. Yepishev, and Andropov. Having witnessed the great 1937-1938 purge, these men learned from that experience that the purgers of one Stalin purge could easily become the purgees of Stalin's subsequent purge.[2]

Therefore, they saw the need to establish a large, strong group of permanent purgers, independent of intra-leadership rivalry, loyal to each other, whom Stalin would need no less than they would need him and who, after Stalin's death, would become rulers of the Communist world. During the last months before Stalin died, these men became the apparatus for what would have been Stalin's final purge. It was the sudden death of Stalin that prevented them from seizing power as early as the mid-1950s. Actually, they achieved their aims anyway since they won out over Stalin's successors, including Malenkov and Khrushchev.[3] It is these men and later entrants into the Brotherhood who have ruled the USSR since the fall of Khrushchev in October 1964.

Available sources suggest that it was Andrei A. Andreyev, a powerful Soviet official in the pre-World War II era, who brought together the senior members of the Brotherhood during 1937-1941.[4] The pattern for such an organization Andreyev most probably adapted from his revolutionary underground experience in Petrograd (the name of St. Petersburg during World War I). From 1915 until the Revolution, Andreyev participated in conspiratorial groups that worked independently of Lenin's Central Committee.[5] The Brotherhood's principle then and in the Stalin era was: the Brotherhood's group goals were more important than the personal goals of various leaders.

Prior to World War II and especially during the aftermath of the war, Stalin had incorporated Andreyev's institution into his own schemes to counterweight or counterbalance ascending leadership groups such as those of Malenknov or Zhdanov.[6] Stalin found his counterbalancing force in the strongly interconnected group of middle-level leaders such as Suslov, Patoli-chev, Andrianov, and Ignatiev among others. Schematically, the design can be put this way: Zhdanov was a force to be reckoned with, so was Malenkov, and both were rivals for power in the future. Therefore, organize or accept a third force in addition to the usual two-force rivalry of powerful leaders.

Stalin's method was congruent with the Brotherhood's own group goals of gradual ascendence. For Stalin, the Brotherhood was a handy group to have about especially since, in his view, they were no more than a group of temporarily interconnected individuals.

World War II had interrupted Stalin's complicated power game, but immediately after the war, Stalin began to consider his inevitable departure from the scene and his mistrust of his closest associates in the Politburo came to the surface.[7] To guarantee his own security and undisputed supremacy, Stalin first undermined Malenkov and Beria (who from his standpoint had each concentrated too much power during the war) by depriving them of their power bases: in the case of Malenkov, in the party apparatus, in the case of Beria, in the state security organs. At the same time, Stalin promoted Malenkov and Beria into full Politburo membership as a counterbalance to the rising Zhdanov and his Zhdanovites.[8]

Second, Stalin promoted Zhdanov and his closest deputies, Alexei A. Kuznetsov and Nikolai A. Voznesenskii, to the highest positions in the leadership. Zhdanov became Stalin's second in command, Kuznetzov became chief supervisor of the party apparatus and the state security organs, while Voznesenskii became acting head of the government and economy.[9] At the same time, Stalin arrested Aleksei I. Shakhurin, Zhdanov's close associate and Andropov's former boss in Yaroslavl. The arrest was intended to implicate Zhdanov, Voznesenskii, and other leaders who were responsible for development of Soviet aviation.[10] The Shakhurin arrest put a restraint on the political expansionism of the Zhdanov clique.

Third, Stalin moved to establish for the "third force" a strong power base in such crucial Party institutions as the Orgburo (Organization Bureau), second only to the Politburo, the Secretariat, and the Central Committee Department in charge of all Party appointments. For these institutions Stalin co-opted middle-level leaders such as Patolichev, Suslov, Ignatiev, Andrianov, G. A. Borkov, N. M. Pegov, and Mikhailov.[11] They, in turn, began to promote their personal clients, men like Andropov.

For Andropov's career, the decisive fact was that, through the Brotherhood establishment, Andropov went from being solely Patolichev's client to being a client integrated into the entire Brotherhood as a tight grouping. In other words, whether or not Patolichev's personal fortunes went up or down, Andropov could no longer be damaged. He was on the promotion ladder—or so it seemed—and success was inevitable. Whatever might happen to Patolichev as an individual from 1946 on, Andropov was on the list for patronage and other services from members of Stalin's "third force" brotherhood.

During the 1951-53 period, when Patolichev worked outside of Moscow and therefore was unable to make Central Committee appointments in the apparat, Suslov, Ignatiev, Mikhailov, and Pegov constituted a powerful group close to Stalin. Since they were at the core of the Central Committee apparat, they could act in accordance with the principle of collective obligation and patronage for junior members.

There was an important reason for the maintenance of such a network greased by patronage. The senior members of the Brotherhood needed loyal associates for the purge they were preparing under Stalin's guidance. Because they needed such loyal juniors for the unpleasant days ahead, Andropov's career approached its peak in 1951–1953 when he was finally promoted to the position of the head of a sub-department of the Party's Central Committee at the age of 38.

The line between success and failure in politics and in political leadership is thin; in a totalitarian society the ambitious party careerist knows the razor's edge and is frequently the victim of plots, counterplots, premeditated "accidents," invisible conspiracies, unexpected victories, and just as sudden defeats. The years between the end of World War II and the death of Stalin were crucial in the life of Andropov. It is these eight years also that are the most obscure in Andropov's history.

There were dramatic swings in Andropov's fortunes during these years. In 1944, he fell from his rather lofty position as first secretary of Karelo-Finnish Republic Komsomol into the trifling position as second secretary of the party machine in Petrozavodsk.

On his own and minus any Brotherhood connections, Andropov would have had slim pickings in the 1944–51 period. So long as he was a party official in the Karelo-Finnish Republic or second secretary of the Petrozavodsk party, there was little likelihood of any advancement to an all-Union post.

From 1944 to 1947, Andropov was the second-string party official in Petrozavodsk with an estimated 50,000 population and no significant industry.[12] The politico-economic marginality of his place of work meant an even deeper decline in his future prospects.

In 1945, Andropov was charged with reconstruction of industrial facilities and roads in Petrozavodsk. Both the task and the methods used to fulfill the task were familiar to Andropov from past activity. The city's entire population, including women, the elderly, and schoolchildren were mobilized for this work on weekends when people were available. For those who were already working full-time, it meant forced labor during what might be called their days off.[13] What else Andropov did in the Petrozavodsk apparatus during 1944–1947 is not known.

Trying to fathom what happened from 1945 to 1953 cannot be done by reading the official Andropov biographies. On November 13, 1982, the day following his election as general secretary of the Soviet Communist Party, *Pravda* referred briefly to these mysterious years. Yet its terse report raised, as we shall see, more questions than it provided answers. The official biography published on the day of Andropov's triumph tells us that from 1944 through some unspecified time in 1947, he was second secretary of the Petrozavodsk party in the Karelo-Finnish Republic. In 1947, says *Pravda,* he was promoted to second secretary of the Republic's party. Then, to quote the official biography, came an even higher promotion:

> In 1951, Yu. V. Andropov, according to the decision of the Central Committee of the Communist Party of the Soviet Union, was transferred to the apparatus of the Central Committee of the Soviet Union and was appointed inspector and later the head of a sub-department of the Central Committee of the Communist Party of the Soviet Union. In 1953, the party assigned Yu. V. Andropov to diplomatic work.[14]

Another official biography, published in the *Soviet Military Encyclopedia* in 1970, provides a few more details about the same period. To the foregoing data it adds the fact that sometime between 1951 and 1953, when Andropov received his appointment as an inspector and head of a Central Committee sub-department, he was also enrolled as an undergraduate in the Moscow Higher Party School. In 1953, he was transferred to diplomatic work, but it was only in 1954 that he was appointed ambassador to Hungary. From 1950 to 1954 he had been a deputy of the Supreme Soviet of the USSR, but he was not reelected to this post in 1954.[15]

The chronology of Andropov's educational experience adds a further confusion to an assessment of Andropov's career. The

Yearbook of the Great Soviet Encyclopedia, published in 1981, states that, during some unspecified years between 1945 and 1953, he studied at the State University at Petrozavodsk then, later, in the Higher Party School of the Central Committee in Moscow.[16] Still a fourth source, the *Directory of Deputies of the Supreme Soviet of the USSR* states that Andropov did not finish his undergraduate education (*obrazovanie nezakonchennoe vysshee*).[17]

A number of questions emerge from these data:

1. Promotion from second secretary of the Petrozavodsk party, a local position, to second secretary of the party of the entire Karelo-Finnish Republic is a significant upward move since the normal intermediate appointments did not occur. Kupriyanov, Andropov's longtime antagonist, was still first secretary of the Karelo-Finnish Party, and Andropov was nevertheless assigned to be Kupriyanov's deputy, his second-in-command. Zhdanov, to whom Andropov owed his demotion in 1944, was still in power in 1947 when Andropov was suddenly named to the second highest Party position in the Republic. It is not unreasonable to ask why and how such a meaningful event occurred.

2. As noted previously, Andropov became an external undergraduate at the Petrozavodsk city university in 1944 or 1945. Why didn't he graduate and get his degree? Should one assume that during this period in which he was stigmatized by his demotion from first secretary of the Republic Komsomol, he needed a higher education degree to improve his status and that as soon as he was appointed second secretary of the Republic party he no longer needed the degree since he had been promoted without it? Yet if this is the case, why did he enroll in the Higher Party School in Moscow when he was promoted to his Central Committee position from 1951 to 1953 and why did he once more leave school without a degree? These questions aren't intended

to suggest that Andropov's lack of formal education necessarily means anything in evaluating Andropov's skills and qualifications for leadership. Rather, these questions are an attempt to establish whether the volatile pattern of his schooling from his earliest years has any correlation with his party career.

3. At the end of 1949 Kupriyanov, first secretary of the Karelo-Finnish party, was dismissed and arrested. Nothing, however, happened to Andropov's career at this time even though he was Kupriyanov's deputy as second secretary. Whatever Kupriyanov's "guilt," it didn't spill over on Andropov. He was neither demoted nor promoted as Kupriyanov's replacement, even though as second-in-command he would have been the natural successor. Why was he neither punished by those who arrested Kupriyanov or, if he was "innocent," why wasn't he given the job of the unfortunate Kupriyanov?

4. Why, a year-and-a-half later was Andropov transferred to the Central Committee apparatus in Moscow? If he wasn't good enough in 1950 to become first secretary of the small Karelo-Finnish party machine, why was he good enough to become head of a sub-department of the Central Committee, a much higher all-Union position?

5. The biography says he was transferred to the Central Committee, by the decision of the Central Committee. However, there is something peculiar about this statement because the Central Committee, according to the Party's published records, was never convened between February 1948 and August 1952, while Andropov was transferred to the Central Committee apparatus sometime in 1951. In the absence of a Central Committee meeting, whose decision was it to move Andropov into the very heart of the Party apparatus, and who promoted him from the position of inspector to a much higher position as head of a sub-department of the Central Committee? In fact, what did the position of "inspector" signify since the position, as such,

doesn't exist in the Party statutes? Even further, in which department was Andropov an inspector and then head of a sub-department and what were his duties?

6. If Andropov was qualified sufficiently to occupy a high Party position as head of a Central Committee sub-department in 1952, what happened to him in 1953 that he was sent packing to a minor diplomatic post in Budapest instead of being appointed right away, as he was a year later, as ambassador to Hungary?[18] What did this sudden demotion mean?

7. Why was he dropped from the Supreme Soviet in the 1954 elections after having been elected to the Supreme Soviet in 1950? If he was being prepared for an ambassadorship, why was he not reelected to the Supreme Soviet since it is normal Soviet practice for such a diplomatic post to be paired with that of a Supreme Soviet deputy?

8. What was the connection between Andropov's career and the State Security organs during these eight years? What was his relationship with M. I. Baskakov, referred to in Chapter 7, who was removed from his position as NKGB chief of the Karelo-Finnish Republic in 1943 shortly before Andropov's demotion and who later reemerged as Minister of State Security in the Byelorussian Republic where Nikolai S. Patolichev, Andropov's long-time patron, was Party First Secretary? What was Andropov's relationship with Semyon D. Ignatiev, Patolichev's onetime deputy, whose tenure as Minister of State Security of the USSR coincided with Andropov's subsequent promotions in the Central Committee apparatus and whose fall in 1953 coincided with Andropov's fall in the same year?[19]

These questions no longer need puzzle us when we understand Andropov's position in the Brotherhood.

With the end of World War II and the unchecked Soviet march into Eastern Europe, Stalin became acutely aware of the thrusting power, stemming from the war, of the military-industrial establishment that, because of the needs of the war campaign, had undermined the Party apparatus.

Quite correctly, Stalin perceived that the Central Committee's supervisory power over the Party network throughout the USSR had collapsed, an event that could in time threaten Stalin's one-man dictatorship. To the outside, non-Communist world, the USSR seemed like an unbreachable monolith, but Stalin knew better. Perhaps that is why he allowed Finland to go its own way, why he waited until 1948 to instigate the coup d'etat against Czechoslovakia, why he didn't incorporate the Soviet-conquered Balkan lands into the Union of Socialist Soviet Republics. For Stalin it was more important to restore and to reinvigorate the Party's power over his own country than to engage in further territorial expansion for the sake of the international communist revolution. That could wait for later.

Whether or not ordinarily vigilant Communist leaders like Zhdanov, Kuznetsov, and Patolichev perceived the debilitation of the Party apparatus to the degree that Stalin did is not known. However, Stalin told these men during one of his proverbial midnight dinner meetings, on May 4 and 5, 1946, that "it is necessary to restore the rights of the Central Committee to control the activities of party organizations. . . . The work of the Central Committee will have to be reactivated and new organizational forms will have to be introduced into the Central Committee structure so as to implement our tasks more successfully." Said Stalin:

> Let us create the special Directorate in the Central Committee and call it the Directorate for checking party organs. . . . You [Patolichev] we will appoint to be the chairman of this Directorate. . . . We will appoint as the inspectors of the Central Committee the best secretaries of provincial and territorial party committees. . . . Now we face new tasks. 1946 is the first postwar year. . . . The new stage of Soviet construction begins. . . . Write down

another point of the Central Committee decision: approve Comrade Patolichev in the position of Secretary of the Central Committee. . . . Well, shall we eat our supper?[20]

Stalin's dramatic while private admission that the Party network and Party control over the country and Central Committee control over the Party had actually collapsed during the war years (the same collapse occurred in Hungary, Czechoslovakia, and Poland in subsequent years) tells us a good deal about the fragility of the Party machinery under the pressure of war or other crisis.

Stalin's disclosure had sinister implications for his closest lieutenants who, since he regarded himself as blameless, were responsible for this collapse of the Party machine. Obviously, Zhdanov and Malenkov and their entourages, as well as other leaders, were not capable enough to run the Party and country. From 1945 on, Stalin began to look for new sub-lieutenants, his successors, in whom he could repose the future of communism and revolution.

What Stalin had in mind for his underlings could be seen in the fact that Zhdanov, his second-in-command and presumably a rising leader in 1946–1947, was not consulted by Stalin in the crucial administrative decision of May 1946. During Stalin's enunciation of the decision, Zhdanov and Kuznetzov were silent. Evidently, it was only Patolichev who participated in the conversation with Stalin.[21] Zhdanov was still number two and would still be number two for the next couple of years, but he was a doomed man. Malenkov, who had concentrated most of the administrative power during the war years in his hand, was promoted to full Politburo membership in March 1946, but was dismissed from organizational Party work in May 1946 and even exiled, if only temporarily, from Moscow.[22] Actually, it was Malenkov's place in the heirarchy that Patolichev had taken over.[23] Later Malenkov returned to become the number two man after Zhdanov's downfall and mysterious death in August 1948. However, before Stalin's own death in March 1953, Malenkov was once more in a threatening situation.[24]

What Stalin was doing from the end of the war years until his death was collecting around him an entirely new leadership, predominantly, we can say, from the members of the Brotherhood. Most of these newcomers were appointed as inspectors of the Central Committee and were supervised by chiefs of the inspectorate called heads of departments and sub-departments. During 1951-1953, Andropov was one such inspector and a sub-department head.

What is striking about the position of Central Committee inspector is that immediately after Stalin's death, March 5, 1953, the positions disappeared and the occupants of these positions were dispersed to various low-status local positions or low-status diplomatic posts.

The institution of inspectors and their supervisors was extraordinary and supra-party. Only high-ranking party officials were selected by Stalin during 1946-1953 to fill these positions. Usually these positions went to the first secretaries of the most important provincial party machines or high standing professionals on the Central Committee itself.[25] Even for high Party officials, the position of Inspector of the Central Committee was a promotion. They had the power to select, rule, purge, and inspect all party leaders at the republican and provincial level. Their omnipotence stopped at the Politburo level.[26] Some of these inspectors and their superiors were men like N. N. Shatalin, Andrianov, Pegov, Patolichev, Suslov, Mikhailov, Aristov, Ignatiev. Some were even members of the Orgburo of the Central Committee from 1946 to 1952 and of the enlarged Presidium (the Politburo name from 1952 to 1966) in 1952-53 during the last months of Stalin's rule.[27]

The inspectorate and their supervisors were granted extraordinary powers by Stalin so that they could replace Party leaders in the provinces or republics who had been censured. Heads and deputy heads of departments would be sent out on short-term assignments to take over from an outcast Party leader and then, victorious, would return to the Central Committee headquarters to run the apparatus once again.[28] One of the inspectors, N. I. Gusarov, defined the position as "the personal representatives of Stalin." He considered his status great enough to attack even such a Politburo member as Khrushchev.[29]

In his memoirs, Patolichev cites Stalin's other name for the inspectors—he wanted to call them "the agents of the Central Committee." Patolichev, however, reminded Stalin that the word "agent" had a sinister connotation in the Soviet vocabulary; therefore Stalin agreed to the job designation "inspector."[30]

These agents or inspectors were Stalin's most trusted watchdogs and henchmen, whose job it was to rule and purge the party apparatus or the country at large at Stalin's orders. During the 1946–1953 period there were 20 to 25 inspectors at any given time.[31] Andropov was one of these inspectors from 1951 to 1952 and one of the inspectorate chiefs in 1952–1953.

11

The

Brotherhood:

1945-1953—Part II

ENCOURAGED by Stalin, the Brotherhood took over the newly reemerged power base in the Party, namely the Organization Bureau (Orgburo) of the Central Committee, and thereby diminished the authority of the Politburo. Since Stalin had successfully established his one-man dictatorship, he no longer needed the Politburo as a legitimizing institution for his rule, especially since the Politburo consisted of an old guard, which—it having aided him in establishing his dictatorship—he was now determined to discard. In 1946, then, Stalin dismantled the Politburo as a permanent institution and replaced it by temporary "committees of six" or "committees of seven." Stalin created these committees on an ad hoc basis from among Politburo members and assigned them to deal with various sets of issues.

For Stalin's lieutenants and his later successors, the under-mining of the role of the Politburo was one of Stalin's major sins for which he was bitterly criticized at the Twentieth Party Congress in 1956.[1] For a while there had been three groups—Zhdanov's, Malenkov's and Khrushchev's—acting as mutually balancing powers independent of the Politburo structure and personnel. Under these circumstances, the Politburo lost its institutional function as an appointing power for local Party leaders and Central Committee apparatchiks. Instead, Stalin delegated the appointing power to the Orgburo and thus fabri-cated the Orgburo and the Central Committee inspectorate into an acting Politburo.

Judging from the recently officially published secret Party materials covering the post-war period, one sees that it was the Orgburo that in the 1946–1952 period acted in the name of the then powerless Central Committee and that actually ran Party and country.[2] In October 1952, the Orgburo as a formal institu-tion was abolished, but its core was incorporated into the enlarged Presidium of the Central Committee so as to fashion a *coup* from within and thereby to oust the old Politburo members who had earned Stalin's displeasure.

In August 1946, the Orgburo was endowed by Stalin with the statutory power to make all Party appointments from top to bottom.[3] Patolichev's secretariat in 1946–1947 and the inspec-torate headed by Patolichev, Andrianov, Shatalin, Ignatiev and Pegov from 1946 to 1952 successively became the impelling force of the Orgburo.[4] The official biographies state that Andropov was promoted to the Central Committee apparatus to be an inspector and, later to be the head of a sub-department. These facts, however, should be read to mean the following if they are to have any substance:

During 1946–1947, the Orgburo selected its own trusted people to control and check the local Party leadership and to oust the old leaders. Thus Andropov was promoted in 1947 to be second secretary of the Karelo-Finnish Party. He was promoted again in 1951 by the same institution to the inner rank of inspectors. His success as an inspector boosted him further in 1952 to the position of a sub-department head, i.e., Andropov himself became a member of the small circle of men around Stalin who, unknown to the country and to the world at large, became the real power, under Stalin, within the USSR.

In 1946, when Patolichev and other Brotherhood members had begun to accumulate power and with this power had begun to promote their own associates, Andropov still had to wait his turn. The Brotherhood was not yet strong enough to overcome a Zhdanovite obstacle to Andropov's hope for advancement. Zhdanov and his followers were still strong both in the Party Central Committee and in the local party apparatus of the Karelo-Finnish Republic.

Zhdanov and his group from 1944 to 1946 exploited the issue of weakened Marxist ideology as a weapon against their competition.[5] As discussed earlier, Andropov who was demoted in 1944 during the Zhdanov-instigated ideological campaign, was still vulnerable on the issue of political education. This vulnerability precluded any promotion for Andropov before 1947 when the balance of power was altered so that the defeat of the Zhdanovite forces in the Karelo-Finnish Republic loomed as a possibility.

Andropov's was only one of other on-going promotions and transfers elsewhere in the USSR arranged by the Brotherhood. Andropov was needed as an "agent-in-place" in the Karelo-Finnish Republic when the time would come for the future purge of the Republic Party apparatus.

In 1946 and in 1947 the Brotherhood began to take over key positions in the Party apparatus. In March 1946, Patolichev, Suslov, Andrianov and Mikhailov became their Orgburo members, which meant that they held four seats against three seats—Zhdanov, Kuznetsov, M. I. Rodionov—for the Zhdanovites and three seats—Malenkov, Shatalin, G. F. Aleksandrov—for the Malenkovites.[6] Khrushchev was not on the Orgburo probably because he was not powerful enough to merit a seat. In the same month, Patolichev took over from Malenkov's associate, M. A. Shamberg, as head of the Central Committee's department in charge of the party apparatus. Andrianov became Patolichev's first deputy, Ignatiev his second deputy and Suslov, supervisor of the Central Committee on unspecified international and ideological affairs with Boris N. Ponomarev as his associate.[7]

The evidence suggests that Suslov and Ponomarev were preparing to implement Stalin's decision to create the postwar Cominform—a successor to the prewar Comintern organization that Stalin, in the interests of Allied unity, had for public relations reasons ostensibly dissolved in 1943. From later events one can see that Suslov and Ponomarev were also aided by Otto W. Kuusinen, then nominal President of the Karelo-Finnish Republic and the Central Committee member whose rivalry with Kupriyanov and whose connection with the Brotherhood became, from 1946 onward, important in the advancement of Andropov's career.[8]

The next step occurred in May 1946 when Stalin greatly increased Patolichev's power. The Organizational Instructor Department of the Central Committee was restructured into the "Checking Directorate," which supervised the Party organs. The Directorate received enormous authority and held the inspectorate institution under its jurisdiction. As head of the Directorate, Patolichev was appointed a secretary of the Central Committee, in charge of the party apparatus, instead of Malenkov, whom Stalin dismissed. Malenkov was also dismissed as head of the Cadres Department of the Central Committee with Suslov, apparently, taking over this department. Sharing de-

partmental supervision was Patolichev and the Zhdanov supporter, Kuznetsov.[9]

In August 1946, the power of the Orgburo and of the Patolichev "Checking Directorate" was even further increased,
replacing to a large extent Politburo authority. Shatalin, Malenkov's closest associate, was dismissed as a deputy head of the
Cadres Administration and reassigned to Patolichev's apparatus as a ranking inspector. One of the Brotherhood, A. N. Larionov, was appointed as deputy head of the Cadres administration
to assist Suslov and Patolichev.[10] The authority of other Patolichev associates, such as Andrianov, Ignatiev, Borkov, and Pegov
was also increased. At the same time, Malenkov, having lost his
post as a Central Committee secretary, was relegated to a lower
position, that of a ranking deputy to the Chairman of the Council of Ministers.[11]

Patolichev, Andrianov, Suslov, Ignatiev, and their supporters, together with their old ally, Andreyev, made the bid for
power at the end of 1946 and the beginning of 1947 on the
incongruously combined issues of agriculture and cadres. The
Brotherhood's real goals, of course, were, one, to weaken the
Politburo members, such as Zhdanov, Malenkov, and Khrushchev; two, to purge the existing middle-level Party apparatus;
and, three, to form a vast network of new Party cadres.

On the local level, in the case of Andropov in the Karelo-
Finnish Republic, for example, Brotherhood members purged
clients of Politburo members and replaced them with their own
supporters. Stalin, however, evidently didn't want to alarm his
old Politburo prematurely. Therefore, the need to establish
cadres for the new economic tasks of the postwar Five Year Plan
and the need to halt the failures of the country's agriculture
became a twofold justification for the purge and for the continuing rise of the Patolichev group.[12]

The country's agricultural misfortunes—the poor 1946 harvest, the starvation in the Ukraine, and in the western parts of

the Russian Republic and other Soviet areas formerly occupied by the German forces—represented a great opportunity for Stalin to press the collectivization issue even further than in the days of the 1930's terror. He blamed the Soviet agricultural failure on the collapse of collective farming during the war when the peasants, paradoxically liberated from Soviet Party control by the invading armies, took back the collectivized land.[13]

The reality, which was admitted 17 years later, was that the leadership deliberately caused the 1946 starvation and the famine the following year. As revealed at the December 1963 Central Committee Plenum, Stalin seized whatever grain had been harvested during 1946 and sold it abroad while people in the Western Russian provinces like Kursk and in the Ukraine perished of hunger.[14] In his memoirs, Khrushchev describes the horrors in great and terrible detail.[15]

Stalin, according to recent Party historiography, saw the need not only of another purge against the ever recalcitrant peasantry but also of a special Party purge in the Western areas of the USSR recaptured after the German occupation.[16]

Stalin had set before himself these goals: creating a famine in order to subdue a truculent population, reestablishing socialized agriculture, and purging the old—and to Stalin, useless—party apparatus and replacing it with a new apparatus. These tasks were entrusted by Stalin to the Patolichev group in the 1946-1947 years.

In September-October 1946, a new institution, the Council of Collective Farm Affairs was set up to supplement the Council of Ministers of the USSR and to lead the terror. Andreyev headed this new Council, Patolichev was made his first deputy, Andrianov a deputy, and Ignatiev, evidently another deputy. At the same time, Malenkov was put in charge of agriculture as a ranking deputy Chairman of the Council of Ministers—a position somewhat lower than that of Patolichev.[17]

The terror against the peasants, the Party apparatus purge,

and the promotion of the new apparatus, under Patolichev and Suslov, began in many Soviet areas, including Moscow, the Ukraine, Byelorussia, the Baltic Republics, Moldavia, and the Karelo-Finnish Republic. And here we have an interesting innovation in the Party bureaucratic management, the establishment during mid-1946 through mid-1947 by the Brotherhood of a new institution called *nomenklatura* of the Central Committee of the CPSU.

Nomenklatura referred to a network of 40,000 newly promoted officials and newly approved old apparatchiks like Andropov. They received their training during the combined mass terror, man-induced famine, and party purge. As junior members of the Brotherhood they benefited from the redistribution of the cadres so that most of them remained in the apparatus for the rest of their lives. All the Brotherhood members, senior and junior, benefited from an agreed-upon job and personal security, unlike the apparatchiks who emerged during the 1937–1938 purge who didn't know whether or not they might be the next victims. The new network operated on the principle that so long as the recruits maintained a mutual loyalty to each other and to the Brotherhood as an unofficial institution, they would remain in the coveted *nomenklatura*.[18] Andropov's personal experience proved the efficiency and security of this Stalin-Patolichev-created system.

The Brotherhood and its *nomenklatura* escalated the 1946–1947 purge. Many officials, charged with divers ideological and cultural assignments, were dismissed; these were the lucky ones. Others were accused of spying for the British and arrested.[19] Suslov was evidently the man behind this part of the purge. More than sixty first secretaries of provincial party committees were removed from office during 1946-1951. Fifty of these were purged, i.e., arrested, disgraced, or expelled from the party. Of these fifty, however, only nineteen could be regarded as definitely of the Zhdanov camp.[20] The fall of the remaining provincial party secretaries can be attributed to the much broader purge organized by the "third force" Brotherhood.

In March 1947, Patolichev together with his enemy, Kaganovich, was sent on a special mission to open a terror campaign against the Ukrainian peasantry and to purge Khrushchev's party apparatus and "nationalist" Ukrainian intellectuals. Ignatiev and another Brotherhood member, Gusarov, a Central Committee inspector, were assigned to a similar bloody task in Byelorussia. Throughout the USSR, similar campaigns were launched.[21]

The fact that Patolichev and Ignatiev had been transferred out of Moscow to the Ukraine and Byelorussia respectively did not mean any undermining of the Brotherhood. Suslov merely replaced Patolichev in May 1947 as a Central Committee secretary, and Andrianov evidently took Patolichev's office as the leading Orgburo spokesman, chief of the Inspectorate and head of the "checking Directorate" over the Party subsidiaries. Pegov was brought to Moscow as Andrianov's deputy.[22]

Andropov's time had now come. After the Central Committee Plenum on agriculture in February 1947, when the position of the Brotherhood was at its zenith and when Patolichev was still in Moscow, Andropov was promoted from the position of second secretary of the Petrozavodsk Party organization to the second secretary of the entire Karelo-Finnish Party. Andropov thus became, formally, the first deputy of his major antagonist in the local Party, Kupriyanov. The official Party historiography says that the work of the Karelo-Finnish Party organization immediately became more vigorous.[23]

As noted, in the Karelo-Finnish Republic and in other areas of the USSR during the war years, Communist control either disappeared or else slackened vis-à-vis farm collectives. Land was retaken by the peasants for their private use. Socialized agriculture as part of the Soviet economy existed only on paper. On the eve of the 1947 February Plenum and Andropov's appointment as the Republic Party second secretary, which really meant he was the all-Union Central Committee's secret watchdog, it was clear that the Karelo-Finnish Party leadership had failed to restore the prewar collective farm system in the Karelo-Finnish Republic.[24]

The extent of Andropov's achievement in the Republic's agriculture can be seen in the following figures: Before Andropov's promotion in 1947, of the Republic's Party membership, only 5 percent or 486 Party members were employed or otherwise involved in agriculture. In other words, the 486 were so widely dispersed over the vast areas of the Republic that 85 percent of the Republic's collective farms had no Communists at all as leaders or supervisors.[25]

In 1947–1948, Andropov managed to engage 2,600 new recruits as Party members in the Karelo-Finnish economy outside of the city of Petrozavodsk, hundreds of whom were assigned to agriculture.[26] Under Andropov's leadership in 1947–1948, the collective farm system had been restored and spread throughout the Republic (1) through the expropriation of peasant lands; (2) enforcing collective work programs; and (3) establishing a party network in the rural areas.[27]

Restoration of the collective farms was one thing; making them produce after their restoration was another. In actual fact, agriculture in the republic had collapsed in 1946–1947 because administrative and repressive methods were no cure for one of the major problems agriculture faced in the Republic—a lack of manpower to deliver the grain quotas prescribed by the State. Andropov solved the problem of manpower by forcing the non-working age part of the population, whether urban or rural, into the fields to harvest or perform other agricultural tasks without pay. The forced laborers were mostly schoolchildren who were taken away from their homes for several weeks at a time, sometimes even for months, to toil on the collective farms.[28]

In addition to organizing these children's brigades, Andropov became the main Karelo-Finnish Party spokesman on ideology and the disciplinarian within the Party apparatus and government cadres.[29] In the meantime, during 1948, Zhdanov's power gradually evaporated in the USSR as a whole and in the Karelo-Finnish Republic in particular. Local Karelo-Finnish Zhdanovites were undermined. Andropov's rise as the Party ideologist in the Republic came at the expense of Iosif I. Siukiiainen who was dismissed from the position as the Republic Party secretary in charge of ideology and transferred to an inferior position in the government.[30] And, naturally, Kupriyanov's power gradually weakened over the course of Andropov's rise in 1947 through 1949.

Back in Moscow, where the big decisions were made, events continued on their dramatic course of leadership changes, which—for those who understood the maneuvers and saw through the camouflage—were a warning of evils to come. In February 1948, the Zhdanovites reached the apparent peak of their influence at the secret Plenum of the Central Committee, a meeting whose agenda is still unknown.[31] But while they were reaching this peak of influence, the actual influence of Zhdanov and his followers was declining. They were being outmaneuvered on all sides—by Beria, by Malenkov, and by the "third force" Brotherhood.[32] Beria was pressing hard to eliminate Kuznetsov, then in charge in the Central Committee for supervision of security, and he was trying to persuade Stalin to restore Malenkov to power.[33]

Suslov, a charter member of the Brotherhood, one might say, was moving up first by becoming a Central Committee Secretary in May 1947 and then, in the fall of 1947, official head of the Central Committee's Ideological Department or Agitprop. The latter position enabled him in 1948 to reorganize Zhdanov's ideological apparatus.[34] Together, Malenkov and Suslov overpowered Zhdanov in June 1948 and then, still united, had implemented, on Stalin's orders, the Soviet-Yugoslav split.[35]

The following month, July 1948, Malenkov became the number two Central Committee secretary and thus was back in the saddle.[36] Ponomarenko, one of Malenkov's allies but at the same time a close associate of the Brotherhood, was promoted to the position of a secretary of the Central Committee in October 1948. This promotion can be viewed as Ponomarenko replacing Kuznetsov and taking over supervision of the security organs.[37]

And now we come to one of several climaxes in the course of Andropov's career. On August 31, 1948, Zhdanov died at age 52, under mysterious circumstances, reportedly a hunting accident. The Moscow rumors were that several leaders went hunting boar in a forest near Moscow. At the end of the hunt, Zhdanov was dead. The cause of death was never revealed. Whatever it was, soon after the event, his closest associates, Voznesenskii, Kuznetsov, Rodionov, and others were, starting in 1949, dismissed, arrested, tortured. A year later, they were tried and shot.[38]

The general purge of the Party apparatus in the Karelo-Finnish Republic in 1948 and then the special purge of Zhdanovites in 1949–1950 became the most important events in Andropov's party career until that time. Andropov's power was increasing while that of Zhdanov's ally and the Republic's Party First Secretary, Kupriyanov, was declining. In 1948 alone, one-third of the entire Karelo-Finnish apparatus was purged.[39]

The various ceremonials of a purge—arrests, interrogations and executions—were under the Ministry of State Security (MGB). However, the supervising power of the purge in the Karelo-Finnish Republic undoubtedly rested with Andropov since he was the second Party Secretary in charge of cadres, Party structure, and ideology and, most importantly, he was the leading anti-Zhdanov representative in the Republic.

In April 1949, the purge accelerated in the Karelo-Finnish Republic. The Karelo-Finnish Party Central Committee plenum became the scene for raising the issue of Party cadres. In his speech at the Plenum, Andropov attacked the industrial managers for their supposedly poor performance. Andropov skillfully exploited the anti-Zhdanovite line that there had been too much emphasis on political education and that this emphasis had been made at the expense of technical training, which led to serious shortcomings in industrial production.

Andropov implicated the local party apparatus in the Republic and the Central Committee itself, i.e., Kupriyanov, whom he held responsible for these deviations, without mentioning Kupriyanov by name. Andropov's remarks at the Plenum had a particularly ominous ring because he kept repeating that the new Republic Central Committee should take care of "mistakes" of the old committee.[40]

Andropov was speaking, not as the Republic Party's second secretary and, therefore, as someone who shared a certain responsibility for the "mistakes" that had been made. He was speaking as someone assigned to check up on subordinates and as someone with a mandate from Moscow. But from April 1949 on, Kupriyanov was most probably deprived of his power. By January 1950, he had been formally dismissed and replaced by one Aleksandr A. Kondakov.[41] According to the official Party history, Kupriyanov had ceased being First Secretary in 1949.[42] However, Solzhenitsyn has found evidence that Kupriyanov had already been arrested in 1949. Solzhenitsyn had described Kupriyanov's interrogation at the hands of persecutors:

> Some of the teeth they knocked out were just ordinary ones, of no particular account, but others were gold. At first they gave him [Kupriyanov] a receipt that said that gold teeth were being kept for him. And then they caught themselves just in time and took away his receipt.[43]

Despite the beatings and tortures, Kupriyanov survived and, after Stalin's death, was even "rehabilitated," Soviet jargon for acquittal of crimes after the fact. (There is no indication as to what happened to his gold teeth.) Kupriyanov published his war memoirs in 1975. They are discreetly silent about what happened to him after the war.

With Kupriyanov gone and the new First Secretary not yet on the scene, Andropov became the acting First Secretary of the Karelo-Finnish Party. On January 10, 1950, the Republic Party was summoned to Moscow to report to the Central Committee apparatus about the results of its work, particularly on the issue of the cadres. The leadership was censured and Kupriyanov, already in jail, was dismissed. However, the censure did not apply to Andropov, who was the rapporteur for the Republic Party apparatus. All the derelictions and shortcomings and deviations and other crimes were blamed on the Zhdanovites, especially on Kupriyanov, while Andropov remained in office as Party second secretary.[44]

Toward the end of January 1950, the Karelo-Finnish Central Committee Plenum, with lots of new faces, convened to elect the new leadership. First, however, it was necessary to excoriate Kupriyanov and his associates, a task that fell easily upon the shoulders of Andropov who reported to the Plenum the punishments meted out to the miscreants of the old apparatus by the all-Union Central Committee.

However, it was not Andropov but a complete outsider with no significant Party record, Kondakov, who was appointed as First Secretary and Andropov's new boss.[45] Here was a definite, tangible setback to Andropov, perhaps even unexpected. How had it happened? The matter of appointing a Karelo-Finnish Party First Secretary was in the hands of the all-Union Party organs. Since the issue was the cadres themselves, only the negative attitude of Malenkov can explain why Andropov failed to get the appointment in 1950. Malenkov, who was back in power, did not want Andropov for exactly the same reason that Zhdanov didn't want him: Andropov was somebody else's man.

During 1949–1950, as in 1946, the Brotherhood was strong enough, in terms of the positions its adherents held, to lay the groundwork for future successes. It was not, however, strong enough to promote their people right then and there against the wishes of a powerful and rising leader, like Malenkov, whose closest associate, Shatalin, was during the first half of 1950, head of the Central Committee Department of Party Organs. Patolichev's ally, Andrianov, who had held this strategic post was transferred in 1949 to Leningrad as the Party First Secretary.[46] In addition, Andrianov also became a member of the Presidium of the Supreme Soviet, which was an important gain for the Brotherhood. Another gain consisted in the fact that Suslov was able to consolidate his authority over all Soviet foreign policy and ideological questions.

It was not, however, all smooth going for the Brotherhood. A temporary loss occurred with the demotion of Patolichev and Ignatiev to party positions in the northern Caucasus and Central Asia respectively. Pegov and Larionov were also removed from the Party Organs department, although Pegov remained in the Central Committee apparatus.[47]

In Stalin's Soviet Union, his subordinates were like mountainclimbers who, no sooner do they reach the crest of the mountain, than they start down, the descent in some cases being gradual, in others swift. Such was the case of Kaganovich in the mid-1930s, of Yezhov in the spring of 1938, of Molotov in the early 1940s, of Beria in the aftermath of the war, of Zhdanov at the beginning of 1948, of Malenkov in 1950 and the beginning of 1951. Nobody ever lasted too long at the crest except Stalin.

During the second half of 1950, precisely at the moment of Malenkov's zenith, the opposition force of Patolichev, Suslov, and others in the Brotherhood began to increase its influence once more, and this time to Andropov's great advantage. On July 5, 1950, Patolichev was promoted to the position of First Secretary of the Byelorussian Republic Party. Another important

Brotherhood member, Mel'nikov had been First Secretary of the Ukrainian Republic Party since the end of 1949.

With the dismissal of Foreign Minister Molotov and the demotion of Dmitri T. Shepilov as head of Agitprop in 1949, Suslov was left without any real opposition in the area of international and ideological policy. In fact, Suslov and Andrianov were the only surviving Orgburo members who were responsible for foreign affairs, while Suslov again and Mikhailov remained the only surviving Orgburo members responsible for ideology. Both of these key issues—foreign affairs and ideology—were now in the hands of the Brotherhood, always keeping in mind, of course, that Stalin had the last say, if not worse.

Even more important than this concentration of power, sometime at the end of 1950 or at the beginning of 1951, Shatalin, Malenkov's right hand in the Party apparatus, was demoted from his position as head of the Party Organs department to that of deputy head. Pegov became at the same time another deputy head to counterbalance Shatalin while Ignatiev evidently became head of this most important Central Committee department.[48]

During these developments at the Moscow center, the Karelo-Finnish leadership was shaken once again. Andropov's new boss, Kondakov, can be presumed to be an anti-Brotherhood appointee of the Malenkovites in January 1950. In September 1950, he was dismissed as First Secretary of the Karelo-Finnish Republic.[49] A year later, at the age of 43, he was dead.[50] Nothing is known about his last months of life after he was fired. Although one cannot rule out something like a heart attack, his dismissal and providential death some months later justify other suspicions.

To replace Kondakov, one of Patolichev's long-time associates, Aleksandr N. Yegorov was appointed as the Republic Party First Secretary.[51] Yegorov was the typical member of the Brotherhood and a long-time colleague of Andropov. In 1936–

1937 he was First Party Secretary in Rybinsk, where Andropov had started his Komsomol career in the forced labor project. Yegorov was demoted by the Zhdanovites in 1938, but promoted by Patolichev in 1939 to a higher position in the Yaroslavl provincial apparatus. During the war Yegorov was promoted to the Central Committee apparatus and after the war was evidently in Patolichev's inspectorate. From September 1950 to 1955 he ruled the Karelo-Finnish Republic. In 1955, in the dark period of the Brotherhood that followed Stalin's death, Yegorov was dismissed and disgraced.[52]

Andropov's last appearance as second secretary of the Karelo-Finnish Republic Party is recorded on April 12, 1951 when he published an article in *Pravda* on an already familiar subject: intensifying Party control over industrial enterprises. In this article, Andropov, inter alia, quoted Stalin's remarks about the necessity of a mass espionage network to aid the Party apparatus in supervising the activity of industrial executives and managers. In the context of the Andropov article's attacks on the former Karelo-Finnish establishment, the implication of his words must be read as a call for a new purge with the remaining Malenkovite managers as one of the prime targets.[53]

Soon after the *Pravda* article, Andropov was called to Moscow to become part of the inspectorate, which became the core of the apparatus assigned to prepare a new purge, to be directed by Ignatiev, Suslov, and Pegov. During the next three years, Andropov's name disappears from the newspapers or other public records. Only what is known of the records of his superiors and the general flow of events in these three years can help to reconstruct Andropov's work career in the period of 1951–1953.

12

The

Brotherhood:

1945-1953—Part III

THE period from the middle of 1951 through February 1953 saw the consolidation and elevation of the Brotherhood "third force" above all other factions and alliances. The old Politburo members who were the Brotherhood's major competitors were gradually undermined and deprived of any real power. In September 1951, Stalin made sweeping changes in the key security apparatus, which aided the Brotherhood's triumph, temporary though it was to be.

Ignatiev was promoted from the Central Committee chieftaincy of Party Organs to become the powerful Minister of State Security (MGB). Aleksei A. Yepishev, who was appointed by Patolichev in May 1946 to be Secretary of the Ukrainian Party Central Committee in charge of cadres and who was dismissed by Malenkov and Beria in 1950, was, in September 1951, brought back to Moscow and promoted to Deputy of the all-Union MGB, i.e., as Ignatiev's right hand.[1] It is important here to note that:

1. Ignatiev and Yepishev were dismissed immediately after Stalin's death in March 1953 at the time of Andropov's fall. Yepishev and Andropov were subsequently dropped from the Supreme Soviet.

2. In 1955, Yepishev was appointed ambassador to Rumania when Suslov became a full member of the Central Committee Presidium.

3. In 1962, when Suslov had evidently started his preparations to oust Khrushchev, Andropov was appointed a Central Committee secretary and Yepishev was appointed head of the Military Department of the Central Committee and head of the Main Political Directorate of the Soviet military forces.[2]

Yepishev's assignment to the MGB was a bad omen for some Politburo members, especially Malenkov, Beria, Kaganovich, and Khrushchev. In 1947 Kaganovich had removed Yepishev and attacked Patolichev. So now the time had come to settle old scores.[3] Yepishev, whose cruelties as a purger were notorious, was evidently responsible for providing Stalin's personal secretariat with secret reports about Khrushchev as an alleged "softy" who had foresaken a sense of vigilance while in the Ukraine. Yepishev's reports led to Stalin's attacks on Khrushchev.[4] Such back-channel personal reporting to Stalin by his omnipresent watchdogs about his top lieutenants was one of the more important duties of the Brotherhood. In fact one of the reasons that Stalin tolerated and encouraged his "third force" was precisely so that he could have people, slavishly dependent on him, to keep a watchful eye on possible competitors.

Ignatiev's promotion to the MGB's top position in 1951 was a terrible blow for the then alliance of Malenkov and Beria. It was Malenkov who had demoted Ignatiev in 1949 from, first, a high position in the Central Committee apparatus and, second, a high position in the Byelorussian Republic and had exiled him to a post as Central Committee representative in Central Asia, the very post Malenkov himself had held during his disgrace in 1947. It was Malenkov's right-hand man, Shatalin, who had to step down in 1950 and thereby relinquished his position as head of the Party organs department of the Central Committee to make room for Ignatiev's appointment to this critical position. Now, in September 1951, having risen to the strategic post as head of the MGB, Ignatiev transferred the position as head of the Party organs department to his and Patolichev's long-time deputy, Pegov.[5]

The assumption by Ignatiev of the MGB chieftaincy meant, among other things, the dismissal of Viktor S. Abakumov from this powerful post. According to available evidence, following Abakumov's dismissal, he was then arrested on Stalin's personal orders. He had failed to understand the meaning and scale of Stalin's preparation for the new terror he was about to inflict on this tortured land.[6]

Abakumov, who had been the MGB minister from 1946 to 1951, was not as close to Beria, as Abakumov's predecessor, Vsevolod N. Merkulov, MGB minister from 1941 to 1946, had been. Abakumov's degree of cooperation with and subordination to Beria during 1946–1951 had a certain significance.[7] Ignatiev, by contrast, did not report to Beria but to Stalin personally. And with good reason, for the first part of the programmed terror that Ignatiev was to arrange as MGB chief was the persecution and extermination of the Georgian Republic Party leadership closely connected with Beria. This action is known as the so-called "Mingrelian Affair."

For ethnocentrists who believe that tribalism is confined to sub-Saharan Africans, it should be noted that the "Mingrelian case" was as arrant a case of bellicose tribalism as between Yoruba and Hausa, between the Shona and the Ndebele or between Xosa and Zulu. Georgia consists of three ethnic tribes: Imeretians, Kartvels, and Mingrelians. Stalin was a Kartvel, Beria a Mingrelian.

In the 1930s, Stalin wiped out the old Georgian Party leadership who were mostly Imeretians. The new Georgian leadership in the 1940s were, like Beria, Mingrelians. This tribal aspect of Soviet power struggles, at least in Georgia, has been overlooked by scholars. In November 1951 and in March 1952, Stalin personally dictated the Central Committee resolutions that accused the Georgian leaders of organizing a Mingrelian nationalist anti-Soviet conspiracy in the interests of Turkey. These resolutions were kept secret from the Politburo and Beria himself.[8] In 1952, 427 Georgian Party functionaries were arrested. Not only was the Communist leadership destroyed but, according to Khrushchev's secret speech, "thousands of innocent people fell victims of willfulness and lawlessness."[9] Beria had not yet been accused, but the time was not far off for, as Khrushchev says, "this was an action directed by Stalin against Beria."[10] Since Malenkov, in the last years of Stalin, had allied himself with Beria in a bid for power, the Mingrelian "conspiracy" case undermined Malenkov as well.

With this background, stitched together from Soviet sources, it is clear that the attack against the old guard in the Politburo was to be launched by Stalin's new executioners, headed by Ignatiev in the MGB and Pegov and Suslov in the Central Committee's inner core. The most important aspect of the Brotherhood campaign during 1951–1953 is the complete merger, obviously with Stalin's approval, of the Central Committee Inspectorate, the ideological apparatus, and the MGB under Pegov, Suslov, and Ignatiev respectively. Stalin concocted this blend of ideology, internal espionage, and secret police to give the impetus for the new wave of terror. By now, Andropov was deep in the heart of Stalin's secret conspiracy.

As mentioned earlier, Ignatiev, Suslov, and Pegov brought

Andropov to the Central Committee inspectorate in the Party organs department some time in spring or summer of 1951, just before Ignatiev's and Pegov's further rise in the Stalin entourage. For a better understanding of how the Brotherhood's "mutual welfare society" code worked then—and still works—it is to be noted that Pegov, after his dismissal following Stalin's death and during the Khrushchev era, was brought back to high positions in the 1970s. In April 1973, immediately after Andropov, now the KGB chief, was promoted to full Politburo membership, Pegov became a deputy Foreign Minister of the USSR. In 1975, Pegov was appointed head of the Central Committee's Cadres Abroad Department, one which is, of course, most closely connected with the KGB.[11]

Pegov was not the only Brotherhood member dismissed after Stalin's death who reemerged later, thanks to other members who had retained their power. After Stalin's death, Brezhnev lost his post as Secretary of the Central Committee, but from 1955 on, he rose steadily after Suslov's ascendancy to the Politburo. The same applies to Andropov and Yepishev. Mikhailov was dismissed in 1953 but reemerged in the 1960s and kept rising through the 1970s. There are more notorious cases. For example, the Ukrainian party boss during 1950-1953, Mel'nikov, Stalin's personal appointee and the unyielding enemy of Beria, Malenkov, and Khrushchev was ousted and disgraced in spring 1953 together with Ignatiev. Mel'nikov was sent to Rumania as ambassador, as Mikhailov was assigned to Poland and Andropov to Hungary. After Khrushchev's ouster in October 1964, Mel'nikov reemerged—this time as a member of the USSR Council of Ministers in charge of workers' safety.[12]

This was, of course, a suitable job for a Soviet official who, according to Khrushchev's memoirs, had implemented Stalin's suggestion that, to quote Stalin, "the good workers at the factory should be given clubs so they can beat the hell out of those Jews at the end of the working day."[13]

Even so notorious a Brotherhood leader as Andrianov, who was arrested soon after Stalin's death, tried for the political murders of the Zhdanovites, and evidently executed, was, during the Brezhnev-Suslov-Andropov era, posthumously rehabilitated. In the Patolichev and A. S. Chuianov memoirs he is described as one of the best Communist Party leaders.[14] The Brotherhood "mutual welfare society" code has from the beginning transmuted criminality into proleterian duty and guaranteed posthumous glory to any Brotherhood member who might suffer a fatal reprisal at the hands of conspirators masquerading as revolutionaries.

In 1952, when Stalin's and the Brotherhood's preparation for the new wave of terror and Party purge were in full swing, Andropov was promoted once more, his second promotion in one year, this time within the Central Committee apparatus itself. From the position of a Central Committee Inspector, Andropov became head of a sub-department. This meant that he was now chief of a group of inspectors. In terms of real power, the position of overlord in a Central Committee subdepartment in 1952 was one of the most powerful in the Party machinery. It was during 1952–1953 that the inner Party apparatus, namely, the Brotherhood, took over all administrative and policy decision-making in the USSR as a whole, leaving little influence and power to the governmental leadership below Stalin.[15]

One sure sign that Stalin had shifted the center of gravity to the inner Party apparatus was the fact that in August 1952, for the first time in eleven years, Stalin himself signed the resolution of the Central Committee Plenum as the Central Committee secretary.[16] Before that date, Stalin always signed the decrees as Chairman of the government and either Zhdanov or Malenkov signed them as the Central Committee Secretary. Now as the reestablished Central Committee signatory, Stalin's reappearance as head of the Central Committee also meant that he wanted the Party world to know that even though he had entrusted the Central Committee report to the Nineteenth Party Congress in October 1952 to Malenkov, there was no sharing of authority, no premonitory laying on of the hands on a potential successor.

Later, Khrushchev explained in his memoirs that some events, which might have looked at the time as if Malenkov was being elevated to the second spot in the Soviet hierarchy, were in reality purely contingent. Malenkov and not Stalin made the report to the Congress simply because Stalin could not physically stand and speak for more than a few minutes. While Stalin was ready to allow Malenkov to deliver the report, he did not permit Malenkov more significant tasks such as preparing the agenda and the issues for the Congress and preparing the personnel composition of the Party leadership.[17]

Equally important, all preparation for the Party Congress, the shaping of Party activity in 1951-1952, had been made under Stalin's personal guidance in the secret inner core of the Central Committee apparatus, which now, more than ever, was alienated from the Politburo Old Guard, including Malenkov. With no position in the apparatus, without Shatalin's leverage in the Party Organs department, Malenkov was just a senior Politburo member, which did not mean much since, in Khrushchev's words, the Politburo was "little more than a rubber stamp."[18]

Suslov and Pegov in the recesses of the Central Committee, Ignatiev in the MGB, and all their associates, like Andropov, were now at the levers and pushbuttons of the party machine. Andropov's swift rise to within the Central Committee apparatus itself meant that Pegov, Suslov, and Ignatiev were highly pleased with Andropov's performance. Stalin himself must have approved of Andropov, because his earlier appointments necessitated, if only procedurally, Stalin's assent either directly or indirectly. But the 1952 sub-department appointment needed Stalin's consideration personally before such a promotion could be made. The MGB and the Brotherhood core in the vital Party organs stood behind Andropov, but Stalin himself had to examine Andropov's credentials for so important a post. Since Andropov got the job, we can assume he passed Stalin's scrutiny with flying colors.

It is widely accepted in the Western academic community that the second Great Terror that Stalin had been preparing was stopped only by Stalin's providential death on March 5, 1953. Khrushchev's secret speech bolsters that belief. On what date, had Stalin lived, the mass terror and the party leadership purge would have been launched, remains unknown. Solzhenitsyn suggests that a Jewish holocaust was planned early in March about the time that Stalin had his fatal stroke.[19] Since the purge and massacres did not occur, scholarly analysis has attempted to reconstruct the plans, steps, and dimensions from various threads of evidence. Andropov, Pegov, and Patolichev are now perhaps the only living men on earth who could reveal what Stalin's Second Great Terror envisaged and what Stalin had in mind after his Second Great Terror was finished.

Andropov's official biography and his personal connections in the 1940s and 1950s may help further to support as true that the new Great Terror was being readied at the 19th Party Congress in the fall of 1952.

From Soviet history we know that the important individual for Stalin's purges was the man to carry out the purge, the State Security head. The purger-in-chief was always appointed on the eve of the purge. Yagoda, for example, was appointed in May 1934, a half year before Serge Kirov's murder, which had launched a purge. Yezhov was appointed in September 1936, half a year before the February-March 1937 Central Committee Plenum that turned a purge into the Great Terror. Ignatiev was appointed in September 1951, on the eve of the "Mingrelian Affair" and the great purge in Czechoslovakia, climaxed by the

Slansky trial, which might well have been a dress rehearsal for what was to happen in the USSR.

Keeping this pattern in mind, let us now turn to the Soviet republic of Byelorussia in the fall of 1952. As of the end of September 1952, the chief of State Security in Byelorussia for thirteen uninterrupted years, was Beria's close friend and associate, L. F. Tsanava. Sometime toward the end of the month, Tsanava was dismissed from the position of MGB minister in Byelorussia. He disappeared, and after Beria's downfall, he was shot without public trial.[20]

Tsanava's dismissal was, of course, another nail in what would have been Beria's coffin had Stalin lived. It is quite possible that after he was dismissed, Tsanava may even have been arrested and interrogated in preparation for an anti-Beria case. Far more interesting, however, is the fact that Tsanava was replaced by Mikhail I. Baskakov as MGB chief of Byelorussia. Baskakov was Andropov's old-time comrade-in-arms from the good old days in the Karelo-Finnish Republic where Baskakov served as deputy head of the then NKVD in 1938–1941 and from 1941–1943, as chief of the NKGB. (The joint activities of Baskakov and Andropov were described in chapters 6, 7 and 8.)

At the end of September 1952, Baskakov was appointed the MGB minister of Byelorussia, one of the highest MGB positions in the USSR.[21] Besides Stalin, three other people had to approve Baskakov for such an office—Ignatiev, the all-Union MGB Minister, Pegov, head of the Central Committee cadres, and Patolichev, the First Secretary of the Byelorussian Republic Party.

According to the available evidence gathered by a study of their biographies, none of the three men had ever known Baskakov before his name came up for the Byelorussian vacancy. On the other hand, what was needed was someone trustworthy in the Byelorussian MGB office on the eve of Stalin's purge.

Only one person knew Baskakov and at the same time knew Ignatiev, Pegov, and Patolichev and was trusted by them—Andropov. It was, therefore, Andropov who recommended Baskakov to all three and through them to Stalin. In other words, Andropov was a man who in 1952 was in the position to be trusted by Stalin on so important and crucial an appointment as a republic MGB minister. Obviously, Andropov was in the center of the purge preparations. He not only knew what was going on in Stalin's office but actively participated in the launching of the terror itself, including the MGB sphere of activity. He not only would have supplied nominees for vacancies caused by the terror, but in the case of Byelorussia he supplied a nominee in advance of the purge.

Andropov's advice on Baskakov to Ignatiev, Pegov, and Patolichev must be seen as more than an informal bit of name-dropping by a trusted associate. Andropov's sub-department must also have been in direct charge of MGB cadres, and, therefore, he was someone who could recommend Baskakov for so strategic a police position—indeed, one of the six most important in the USSR. Andropov very likely had become Pegov's assistant for state security matters, and in such a case Andropov's place in the preparations for the 1952–1953 terror was among the highest in the hierarchy. Andropov's involvement in the key State Security appointments in 1952–1953 suggest that it became an important qualification on his record when he was approved as chief of the later KGB in 1967.

Baskakov's later story is not without interest. On the day of Beria's downfall at the hands of Malenkov and Khrushchev on June 27, 1953, Baskakov was summarily dismissed as Byelorussian State Security chief. Baskakov had nothing to do with Beria, was actually an anti-Beria man and had been recommended for the Byelorussian police post by anti-Beria forces. One month later, July 24, 1953, Baskakov was reinstated in his full capacity including membership in the Bureau of the Central

Committee of the Byelorussian Party, and served until April 1958.[22] His final fall and disappearance came after Patolichev's removal from Byelorussia in the summer of 1956, i.e., after the Twentieth Party Congress disclosed Stalin's plans for the new Great Terror.

The Nineteenth Party Congress, which convened on October 5, 1952, was given the gloss of a victorious Party led by party leadership greats. The atmosphere resembled the so-called "Victors" Congress, the Seventeenth, in June 1934, a half year before Kirov's murder, which launched the purge and the subsequent Great Terror. Stalin's modus operandi was much in evidence.

Stalin designated Malenkov an acting Party first secretary and made Molotov and Voroshilov look like distinguished elder statesmen. Molotov opened the 19th Party Congress ceremony, Voroshilov closed the Congress with another ceremony on October 14. And then two days later, October 16, at the Plenum of the Central Committee that followed the Congress, Stalin accused Molotov, Voroshilov, and Anastas Mikoyan of being British spies and leveled other charges against them.

Stalin kept most of the old members of the Politburo, except Andreyev and Aleksei N. Kosygin, in the newly enlarged Presidium of the Central Committee. (The Presidium was the new name for the Politburo by Stalin's orders.) However, he also insisted that the old Politburo members should in time be replaced by the new ones.[23] He could have dismissed these Politburo veterans at the Congress and replaced them then and there, but he did not. In fact, he kept them on the Presidium after having leveled his espionage accusations against them. The clear implication of this behavior is that Stalin was going to have his purge of incumbent leaders right in the Politburo-Presidium, a foreign intelligence service plot right in the heart of the Party apparatus.

At the Nineteenth Congress, Stalin deprived the old guard,

even those with the highest standing in years of service and position, of any influence or leverage in the Central Committee. Beria's closest associates, Merkulov and V. G. Dekanozov, long-standing Central Committee members and former State Security chiefs, were dropped from the Committee.[24] Malenkov's right hand in the party apparatus, Shatalin, was kept out of full membership in the Committee. It was only after Stalin's death that Malenkov promoted Shatalin into Committee membership and made him Committee secretary in charge of cadres.[25]

The new Central Committee established after the Nineteenth Congress consisted of many Brotherhood members. The highest leadership in the Party, the Central Committee Presidium, and the Secretariat included the hard-core of the Brotherhood who, it was clear, would be the future Politburo after Stalin's purge of the old guard.

Of the 25 full members of the now enlarged Presidium, Malenkov had four seats—himself, Maksim L. Saburov, Mikhail G. Pervukhin, and V. A. Malyshev; Khrushchev had two seats—himself and D. S. Korotchenko. Beria and other veterans had nothing more than their own individual seats. The Brotherhood now had at least nine seats: Andrianov, Aristov, Ignatiev, Kuusinen, Mel'nikov, Mikhailov, Ponomarenko, Suslov, and D. I. Chesnokov. And with Stalin that made it ten—obviously the future Politburo.

In reserve for future promotions was the list of candidate (or non-voting) members of the Presidium. Of the eleven candidate members, two were Malenkovites—I. F. Tevosian and A. G. Zverev; one was a Zhdanovite leftover, Kosygin; another was A. Ia. Vyshinskii, former State prosecutor and known to many Americans as the rebarbative Soviet spokesman at the UN during the late 1940s. The remaining seven were all Brotherhood members—Brezhnev, Ignatov, I. G. Kabanov, Patolichev, Pegov, A. M. Puzanov, and Yudin.[26] Of the ten members in the powerful Secretariat, the top three were Stalin, Malenkov, and

Khrushchev and the remaining seven were familiar names: Aristov, Brezhnev, Ignatov, Mikhailov, Pegov, Ponomarenko, and Suslov.[27] It is important to note that of the new establishment, at least seven—Andrianov, Ignatiev, Ignatov, Mel'nikov, Patolichev, Pegov, and Suslov—were personal enemies of Malenkov, Beria, and Khrushchev. Immediately after Stalin's death, the Malenkov-Beria-Khrushchev coalition dropped the Brotherhood leaders from the Central Committee Presidium and from other powerful positions. This counter-purge will be discussed in more detail later.

Stalin's theoretical writings on economic issues, prepared several months in advance but published on the Nineteenth Party Congress opening day, dealt with the framework into which Stalin would fit future all-encompassing social changes in the Soviet Union. He spoke vigorously against what remained of the supply-demand system. He was referring to the fact that the collective farms allegedly possessed surplus produce after having delivered their compulsory procurement quotas to the State. The collective farms exchanged these surpluses for money at local markets and thus, for Stalin, created an anomaly within the socialist system.

Stalin proposed that this remaining element of the produce-money exchange within Soviet society be gradually but forcefully abolished. There would be established in its stead a pure exchange of agricultural products for industrial goods produced by the State. Stalin implied in this scheme that money as an economic entity would be eliminated.[28] For Stalin such measures would finally extrude the collective farm system from the uniform Communist economy since the collective farm system was nothing more than a transition infrastructure for true socialism.[29]

The Nineteenth Congress immediately pronounced Stalin's proposals as the foundation of the future socio-economic and political direction of the Soviet Union. In actual fact, Stalin's 1952 ideas contained little new. They were the old ideas of the Wilhelmine German command economy that flowered in World War I. The theory had been developed by a Social Democratic group known as *Die Glocke* (The Bell), which was led by Parvus, the revolutionary pen name for Alexander Helfand, and by Paul Leunsch. Lenin adapted and implemented these ideas for a moneyless exchange of products in Russia during the years of War Communism, 1918–1920.

Lenin retreated from this system in 1921 after strong popular resistance. In 1930, Stalin tried to establish the same system during his collectivization campaign. Like Lenin, he also failed because of peasant resistance. Now, in 1952, Stalin was going to give it another try, regardless of human cost. His decision meant that the second stage of deeper socialization and communization of agriculture would be implemented once more by mass terror.

The first concrete stage of this new campaign was proposed by Stalin in February 1953, sometime between two to four weeks before he died. Stalin proposed to use the same methods he had used in the 1928–1929 campaign before the main collectivization thrust, i.e., taxes on agricultural enterprises, on collective farms, and on the individual tiny subsistence plots of collective farmers. The diabolical nature of these proposals was that these taxes were to be raised so high that the countryside would be unable to meet the payments, according to Khrushchev's "secret" speech at the Twentieth Party Congress. In 1952, collective farms and their members combined received 26 billion rubles for all products delivered and sold. Stalin proposed that they should pay 40 billion rubles in taxes, meaning that there was a deficit against the collective farms and their members of 14 billion rubles.[30] This contrived deficit was, of course, a deliberate provocation that would justify terror and mass persecution of the peasants because of their putative unwillingness to make up the deficit. Stalin would then accuse them of sabotage and unleash a wave of terror that would involve all strata of Soviet society, the peasantry, the Party apparatus, and the old and dislodged Politburo members.

Western scholars have suggested that the Czech arrests and trials during 1951–1952 and the major show-trial in November 1952 were, in reality, a dress rehearsal for the domestic purge that Stalin hoped to stage in 1953.[31] Czechoslovakia was a sort of out-of-town tryout with a local company. In addition to the similarities in the composition of the victims' list, there are two important corroborative items:

1. The new Czech purges began within days after Ignatiev's appointment as the USSR MGB chief during the early days of September 1951. On September 6, 1951, Rudolf Slansky was removed as Czech Communist Party Secretary-General. On November 27, 1951, at about the same time as Stalin's first resolution on the "Mingrelian Affair," described above, Slansky was arrested.[32] Other arrestees included Foreign Minister Vlado Clementis; Bedrich Reicin, a political general; Eugen Loebl, the Minister for Foreign Trade, and leading party apparatchiks, like Bedrich Geminder and Joseph Frank.

2. The newly created Czech MGB was expanded with the inclusion during 1950–1951 of Soviet MGB officers who suggested that Slansky be included as a defendant in the upcoming trial. The veiled suggestion became a command, despite the veto of Klement Gottwald, the Czech Party chairman and the country's President.[33] In January 1952, Ladislav Kopriva, the Czech MGB Minister, was himself arrested.[34] For every arrested Czech official, there was a Soviet homologue who was a visible target of Stalin's oncoming purge: Slansky-Malenkov, Kopriva-Beria, Clementis-Molotov, Reicin-Voroshilov, Loebl-Mikoyan, Geminder and Frank-Kaganovich.

A number of economic managers, equivalent to Malenkov's associates in the Politburo, were also on the purge roster. In November 1952, after two weeks of the show trial, all the accused were condemned. Eleven were hanged and three sentenced to life imprisonment.[35]

Two aspects of the Czech purges must be singled out here for comment:

First, the majority of the accused were revolutionaries of Jewish origin who had long been involved with the Comintern's international activities, with long-time connections with Beria's apparatus and the Soviet MGB. The Jewish Communists were, among other things, accused of involvement in a U.S.-inspired world capitalist-Zionist conspiracy.

Second, The Soviet-Czech MGB included in its cast of traitors and conspirators, a Jewish physician, Dr. Haskovitz, who was accused of medical malpractice in attempting to shorten the life of Gottwald—a pilot plot before the Soviet Jewish "Doctors' Plot."[36] In November 1952, a group of Soviet doctors, most of them Jews, were arrested, several days before the opening of the Slansky trial in Prague.[37]

It is a valid conclusion from this evidence that the new Great Terror being readied in the USSR in 1952–1953 by Stalin, Ignatiev, MGB Deputy Minister Mikhail Riumin, and their Party apparatus collaborators, Suslov, Pegov, Andrianov, Aristov, and others—including Andropov—would have involved the following groups:

1. Party veterans like Molotov, Mikoyan, Voroshilov.

2. Diplomats like the former Soviet Ambassador to Britain Ivan M. Maisky.

3. State Security chiefs like Beria and Merkulov.

4. Military leaders and political generals like Nikolai A. Bulganin and eventually, perhaps, Marshal Georgi K. Zhukov, since he was not named in a list of loyal generals published in *Pravda* on January 13, 1953, whose deaths could have been attributed to the alleged malpractice of the "Zionist" doctors.

5. High- and medium-level economic executives and managers.

6. The highest leaders of the Party apparatus, like Malenkov and Khrushchev.

7. Medical elites, most of Jewish descent.

8. The Jewish population at large.

9. The Soviet population, particularly peasants.

Stalin's new Great Terror had a cast of thousands, perhaps millions—who knows? Under Stalin, a purge developed a life and a momentum of its own—and his scenario involved everybody from Malenkov, the acting Party General Secretary, to the peasantry. In passing, one should note that a similar party purge and mass terror, which only his death prevented Stalin from carrying out, was effectuated in China during the bloody years of the Cultural Revolution. Mao Zhedong's scenario also involved all levels of society, from the Party General Secretary Teng Xiaoping and President Liu Shaoqi to millions of ordinary Chinese.

Malenkov, Beria, and other Soviet Party leaders were aware of Stalin's purge program for 1953 although they apparently did not know the full details. In his main report to the Nineteenth Congress in October 1952, Malenkov spoke carefully against the new Great Terror. Socialist ideology rules in the USSR, he said, while only some remnants of bourgeois ideology and psychology remain. Of course, foreign enemies could exploit unhealthy attitudes of some Soviet people and defeated anti-Leninist groups, well-disguised, could penetrate branches of ideological apparats. However, the remedy against such disorders, to Malenkov, was not a purge but strengthening the political education of party cadres.[38] Malenkov, in other words, was singling out for criticism not real individuals or strata but rather attitudes or ideological derelictions.

The Stalin campaign of attack, implemented by the Brotherhood in January 1953 following the announcement of the "Doctors' Plot," subsumed a different analysis. This analysis, stressed by Suslov, Mikhailov, Kozlov, and others as well as the

Soviet press, argued that the class struggle once more, as in the 1930s, was sharpening in the USSR and that it was not some abstraction called a remnant of bourgeois ideology but real enemies, "live people," social groups who were the carriers and bearers of the hostile ideology and that the target ought to be real people connected with imperialist circles abroad.[39]

Andropov's involvement in what would have been the purge and leadership changes can be noted, in addition to Baskakov's case, in the sudden rise of Otto W. Kuusinen after the Nineteenth Congress and before Stalin's death. As discussed in earlier chapters, in 1940 Kuusinen lost his important position in the Comintern and was exiled to the Karelo-Finnish Republic as the nominal president. Kuusinen's position, for what it was worth, was about on a par with the young Komsomol apparatchik, Andropov.

In 1941, however, Stalin changed his mind somewhat about Kuusinen and promoted him to full membership in the all-Union Central Committee at precisely the same time that Patolichev and Suslov were promoted. It was, even for Stalin's USSR, strangely anomalous that Kuusinen was made a full member of the Central Committee while Republic Party First Secretary Kupriyanov was but a candidate member.[40]

Stalin, however, did not appoint Kuusinen to the position of the Karelo-Finnish First Secretary in 1949 when Kupriyanov fell, a post that would have been appropriate for this aging Finnish Communist and full Central Committee member. Evidently, the Malenkov forces, still strong in the apparatus, checked Kuusinen's rise since he was regarded as a dangerous rival for the existing Party establishment. But with the aftermath of the Nineteenth Congress, Kuusinen was not only promoted to full membership in the Presidium but was even appointed to the eleven-man commission to write the new Party program.[41] While Kuusinen still technically remained in the

Karelo-Finnish Republic as chairman of the meaningless Supreme Soviet, it was obvious that he was destined to be the head of Soviet foreign policy and leader of the international Communist movement, with Suslov as part of the duumvirate.

However, Kuusinen's career was not so smooth between 1952 and 1957. Immediately after Stalin's death, Kuusinen was dropped from the Central Committee Presidium. And after the Twentieth Party Congress and Khrushchev's destalinization speech, Kuusinen was dismissed even from his nominal chairmanship of the Karelo-Finnish Supreme Soviet.[42] In actual fact, from August 1956 until the end of June 1957 he had no position at all.

In June 1957, when Molotov, Malenkov, Kaganovich, and other veterans were ousted by Khrushchev from the leadership, Kuusinen, along with senior members of the Brotherhood, again became a full Presidium member and a Central Committee secretary.[43] And exactly at that time, in May 1957, Suslov promoted Andropov to the position of head of the Central Committee department in charge of liaison with the ruling Communist parties of socialist countries.

The ups and downs in Kuusinen's career dovetail, chronologically, with those of the Brotherhood.

In chapter 11, we noted that Kuusinen had worked with Suslov and Ponomarev sometime in 1946 to set up the new Cominform. Kuusinen's involvement with that project contributed, later in 1952, to Stalin's decision to include him in the new Presidium and what would become the new Politburo after the purge of the old leadership. However, it would not seem that in the case of so controversial a figure as the veteran Cominternist Kuusinen, Suslov's recommendation would alone suffice in 1952 for a promotion. After all, Kuusinen was the same international apparatchik type that Stalin had rid himself of in 1937–1938, and he was preparing to deal with the existing apparatchiks in the same summary fashion in 1952–1953. And there was, of course, Kuusinen's fall in 1940 on the public record.

For Kuusinen to be promoted to the Central Committee Presidium would have required the support of the Central Committee Department of Party Organs and of the new heads of the MGB. Pegov and Ignatiev, however, did not know Kuusinen. Andropov, most probably was the connection, the "Karelo-Finnish Connection," between Kuusinen on one side and Ignatiev, Pegov, and Suslov on the other. It should be remembered that Andropov had already in 1951 been in the core of the Central Committee apparatus while Kuusinen was still wasting away in the Karelo-Finnish Republic with his honorific title. Without Andropov's support, it is difficult to imagine that Kuusinen could have returned to the top.

Reconstructions of this kind from fragments of data are obviously subject to correction as more precise information becomes available, if ever. However, it is clear to us that the relationship on the one hand between Andropov and Kuusinen and Andropov, Pegov, Ignatiev, and Suslov on the other, suggest Andropov's deep involvement in the Stalin-determined process of selection of Soviet leaders, purgers, and future "social engineers" of Soviet society on the eve of the planned Great Terror.

In February 1953, the investigation of the doctors' connections with Politburo members and the international imperialist-Zionist conspiracy was in full flower. Stalin presented Ignatiev with a rather persuasive argument to come up with results: "If you do not obtain confessions from the doctors, we will shorten you by a head."[44]

Khrushchev in his memoirs describes how the hapless Ignatiev worked himself up to the edge of collapse:

> He had had a near-fatal heart attack. . . . Stalin used to berate him viciously over the phone in our presence. Stalin was crazy with rage, yelling at Ignatiev and threatening him, demanding that he throw the doctors in chains, beat them to a pulp, and grind

them into powder. It was no surprise when almost all the doctors confessed to their crimes."[45]

After the doctors' confessions came the disclosure of an alleged connection between the old Politburo members and the international Zionist conspiracy, a connection evidently established through intermediate links, middle-level officials.

In February 1953, an arrest full of foreboding was made in Moscow. Ivan M. Maisky, former Soviet Ambassador to Britain in the 1930s and 1940s, a former deputy foreign minister of the USSR, and a close associate of Molotov, was arrested as an alleged British spy.[46] Maisky's arrest was clearly intended to implicate Molotov himself. Stalin had already begun an inquiry into Molotov's alleged recruitment by U.S. and British intelligence during Molotov's trips to the U.S. and England in the 1940s. Molotov's Jewish wife was already in jail as a participant in the Zionist conspiracy.[47]

Maisky's arrest may have been the signal that the final stage had arrived for Stalin's grand opera of plot and counterplot, conspiracy and exposé, espionage and counterespionage. The Brotherhood was making the last arrangements for the twilight of the fallen gods, a drama that would then be followed by the mass terror in every corner of the Soviet Union. Publicly Stalin said nothing and was little visible in those final days. His last signed document was dated February 3, 1953. It was a decree issued in his position of Chairman of the Council of Ministers, a decree in which he dealt with strangely minor, almost trivial matters, hardly of moment to the Leader of the Soviet peoples.

The decree commands that a special publishing house be created for publishing artbooks of high quality and with excellent color reproduction. In the same decree there is included the transfer from place A to place B of two engineering experts on aniline dyes and two other engineering experts on varnish lacquer, and a final command for the provision in 1953 of eight cauldron steel boilers and five kneaders for mixing paint.[48]

Suddenly on March 5, 1953, Stalin died. Now the Brotherhood was on its own with no Big Brother to watch over and protect it. The survivors of what would have been Stalin's new Great Terror—Malenkov, Beria, Khrushchev, Molotov, and other veterans—were not down and out, they were up and in, very in. And now it was their time to decide the fate of the Brotherhood—Ignatiev, Andrianov, Pegov, Suslov, Patolichev —and lowlier figures like Andropov.

13

No Room at the Top?

THE sudden death of Stalin spelled disaster for Andropov and his Brotherhood associates. Stalin's successors—Malenkov, Beria, Molotov and Khrushchev—on March 6, 1953, the day after Stalin's death, launched a thorough purge of Stalin's apparatus, so carefully culled and selected by the late *Vozhd* in the last years of his life. Brotherhood members were thrown out and even barred from entering their offices in the large buildings of the Old Square, occupied by the Central Committee apparatus, and Dzerzhinsky Square, occupied by the MGB.

However, with the crisis in the new "collective leadership" that began immediately on Stalin's death and with the rising power of Khrushchev, the Brotherhood gradually reemerged from exile during the period from 1954–55 to the 1960s. This development should explain Andropov's fall in 1953 and his gradual rise in 1954, 1957, and in 1962.

From the powerful position of a sub-department chief and head of the Central Committee Inspectorate, evidently acting as liaison between the Central Committee Party Organs and the MGB, Andropov was assigned to insignificant diplomatic work compared to his former position. First, in 1953, he became head of the Fourth European Department of the Soviet Foreign Ministry, the one in charge of diplomatic relations with Poland and Czechoslovakia.[1]

Then came another demotion in the same year—assignment as counsellor in the Soviet Embassy in Hungary.[2] Such an appointment was about as low on the *nomenklatura* totem pole as one could go. Another blow came in 1954 when the session of the Third Supreme Soviet, 1950–54, expired. Andropov, who had been a deputy to this largely honorific body, was dropped for renomination by the Party at about the same time that he was promoted to be ambassador.[3]

Then Andropov hit the comeback trail. On July 14, 1954, a day not without significance in revolutionary history, he was appointed Soviet ambassador to Hungary.[4] He held that position through the Hungarian Revolution in 1956 until March 8, 1957.[5] At that time Andropov was recalled to Moscow and reassigned to the Central Committee apparatus from which he had been fired after Stalin's death. What exactly Andropov did from March to May 1957 is not known. However, available data suggest that he was at first put in charge of the Party Cadres department that covered the peripheral Soviet republics, excluding the largest Russian republic, the Russian Soviet Federal Socialist Republic, which produces more than 60 percent of Soviet GNP. It was an important assignment.[6] In May 1957, came another step upward within the Central Committee appointment as head of the department concerned with Communist Parties in socialist countries.[7] Andropov was to supervise relations with ruling Communist Parties, those in countries that were Soviet satellites and those Communist countries, like North Korea and China, which, if only by geography alone, couldn't be regarded as satellites. Since these were ruling parties, Andropov could deal with them not as institutions separate from the country they were in, as he might with the Communist Party of Great Britain, but with the Party as the impelling monopolistic force in the entire country.

It must be assumed that whatever he was doing in his capacity as departmental director of liaison with Communist bloc countries met with Politburo approbation because of his subsequent promotions. In October 1961 Andropov became a full member of the Central Committee, thus hurdling over the routine procedure of first being a candidate member.[8] In November 1962 Andropov became Secretary of the Central Committee in charge of Communist bloc parties and countries, a position from which he could supervise the work of the department from a higher and policy-making level.[9]

Andropov's steady rise from 1954 to 1962 in the context of the revival of the Brotherhood's fortunes, especially those of Mikhail Suslov's, will be discussed in a later chapter. Here special consideration will be given to Andropov's precipitous but short-lived decline and fall in 1953 and recovery in 1954.

Stalin's death came as a shock for the divers leadership groups. Dmitri Z. Manuil'sky, a veteran Cominternist, Ukrainian foreign minister 1944–1952, a U.N. delegate in 1948, reacted to the news in a way that might seem strange to a Westerner but wasn't at all to anyone who had lived through the Soviet environment of purge and terror. Manuil'sky reportedly said that the announcement was sheer provocation.[10] He, obviously, meant that Stalin had hidden himself somewhere while his death was announced so as to create the proper mood for launching a total massacre.

The death was real. The old guard immediately assumed what in U.S. military strategy is called C^3—command, control, and communication. The committees and other institutions set up by Stalin and filled by Brotherhood members for handling the purge collapsed. On March 6, 1953, the day after Stalin's death, both the enlarged Presidium of the Central Committee, which was to be the nucleus of the future leadership, and the MGB were abolished. The Presidium became the old Politburo although the new name "Presidium" remained for a while longer.

Soon after Stalin's death, Beria started his own destalinization campaign on a much muted level with none of the shock value that Khrushchev produced three years later with his "secret speech." It was a Beria ploy against the Brotherhood and in particular against Ignatiev, one of the purgers-to-be.

After Stalin's death the MGB was merged with the Ministry of Internal Affairs (MVD) as one of the departments of the MVD. The MGB leadership was dismantled and Ignatiev and Yepishev fired.[11]

Of 25 Presidium members, 15 were dropped including Andrianov, Aristov, Ignatiev, Kuusinen, Mel'nikov (who unaccountably remained for another two months as a candidate member), Mikhailov, Ponomarenko (who remained for several months longer as a candidate), Suslov, Chesnokov, i.e., all the Brotherhood members were dropped. Of 11 candidate Presidium members, all 11 were dropped, including Brezhnev, Ignatov, Patolichev, and Pegov. On March 6 and again on March 14, 1953, of ten Secretariat members on the Central Committee, seven were dropped, including Aristov, Brezhnev, Ignatov, Mikhailov, Pegov, and Ponomarenko. Suslov was the only Brotherhood leader who remained a Central Committee Secretary after the March 1953 purge, but he lost his seat in the Presidium. Ignatiev, having lost his MGB ministry and his seat in the Presidium, was brought into the Secretariat on March 6, 1953 but was expelled shortly thereafter, April 6, 1953.[12] From that day until the beginning of 1954, he dropped out of sight. His disappearance might be explained by the possibility that he was under arrest. In any case, he reemerged in February 1954 as First Secretary of the Bashkir province, a very insignificant position.[13]

Other leading Brotherhood members lost positions in the Central Committee apparatus as department heads and supervisors. Pegov and Aristov lost their power in the Party Organs department where Andropov had served as their closest associate. Pegov was dumped into the powerless, largely ceremonial post of Secretary of the Supreme Soviet. Aristov was exiled to the Far East city of Khabarovsk as chairman of the territorial Soviet, a trifling position for the once high and mighty.[14] The network of the department of Party Organs was evidently eliminated and its apparatchiks, like Andropov, suspended.

The ideological and foreign policy apparatus in the Central Committee, headed by Suslov, also ceased to function. From June through December 1953, Suslov's apparatus did not issue a single ideological instruction, although it routinely did so about once a month before Stalin's death and resumed such guidance after December 1953.[15] In May 1953, a secret Central Committee Plenum was convened, which ousted Mel'nikov from candidate membership in the Presidium and from his post as Ukrainian Party first secretary. He was probably under arrest during the weeks before Beria's downfall.[16]

This Plenum evidently censured Suslov and Patolichev as well. Patolichev's Byelorussian Central Committee apparatus was strongly criticized by the all-Union Central Committee resolution of June 18, 1953 for its political and ideological shortcomings.[17] In short, the more than nine months from Stalin's death was a debacle for the Brotherhood.

However, the Politburo that succeeded Stalin refrained from using terror against oppponents except in the case of Beria and Beria's paramilitary gang of state security professionals. The new leading group of Malenkov, Khrushchev, and Molotov, were afraid that Beria and his gang were capable of acting on their own against them. After all, Beria had under his personal command thousands of his own MVD troops, which he could use.

The case of Andrianov, in which violence was used, was another exception. He was arrested and probably shot as part of Khrushchev's budding plot to rid himself of Malenkov and also Beria.[18] Since Andrianov had participated actively in the anti-Zhdanovite purge instigated by Malenkov, Andrianov was elected by the new leadership to be the fall guy.

In the case of the Brotherhood, however, Stalin's successors did not see them as able to do anything without Stalin and his protection. Therefore, demotion, dispersion, and purge without bloodshed was the method the new leadership chose in dealing with them.

Terror against Party leaders and members of the apparatus was largely abolished by an unspoken consensus among the new leadership that if they didn't call an end to terror, the time would come when the revolution would once more devour its children. Stalin's successors evidently accepted the Brotherhood's rule that loyalty to one's own was a venial sin to be rewarded by condign punishment but no "final solution."

In addition, the Brotherhood had developed a particular kind of strength. As a trained network of high- and middle-level apparatchiks and an available force of unyielding ideologists ready to deal with any faction seeking battle against another faction, it had a value in the *kto-kgo,* who-whom, environment of post-Stalin Kremlin politics. Malenkov and Khrushchev needed the Brotherhood network in support against Beria and his agents in the local republics' apparatus in 1953. Khrushchev, looking ahead, could see that he would need help from the same network against Malenkov and his clients in party, government, and management during 1954–55. And later Khrushchev would need the Brotherhood to fight and expel Molotov, Kaganovich, Malenkov, Voroshilov, and Bulganin in 1956–1957.

The Brotherhood quickly recovered from the blows against its existence because its strength was such that any Soviet leader who had vaulting ambitions needed them. Gradually, the Brotherhood increased its strength, in large part because its own institutional arrangements were congruent with a Communist one-party political structure.

The year 1953, however, was a time of disarray and unpredictability even in this unpredictable tyranny. Having decided to abolish and disperse the Suslov-Ignatiev-Pegov network and having decided against a policy of bloodletting, the collective leadership had to find places for dozens of Brotherhood functionaries, like Andropov. Shoving them unceremoniously into the Foreign Ministry seemed like a good idea to the new leadership in the Politburo of how to get rid of this crowd. The fact that the influx of all these newcomers into the Foreign Ministry exceeded existing posts didn't bother the Politburo; they had issued the orders, let somebody else worry about the consequences.

The consequences were that some professional diplomats lost their jobs and others remained unassigned to new posts while the new boys were given the positions and told to settle in. Andropov's predecessor as head of the Fourth Department was a certain P. F. Strunnikov, who was not an unimportant figure in the Soviet Foreign Service. He was in charge of personnel selection for the Foreign Service from 1948–1952 before he moved to the Fourth Department.[20]

Since room had to be made for Andropov in the Foreign Ministry, Strunnikov was dismissed and given no other assignment. When Andropov soon after left for Budapest, Strunnikov's job was given to another Brotherhood member, one from Patolichev's entourage. Strunnikov was still jobless. Finally something had to be done because of Strunnikov's prominence; so he was appointed in 1954 to the position of Party secretary within the Foreign Ministry apparatus in Moscow. Andropov's interposition interrupted whatever momentum poor Strunnikov had going for his career, and he ended up during the late 1950s and 1960s as a counsellor in the Soviet Embassy in Canada.[21]

So Andropov went to the Foreign Ministry and then to the Soviet Embassy in Hungary. Mel'nikov was sent to Romania as ambassador in August 1953. Yepishev followed him there in August 1955. Mikhailov went to Poland in March 1954 as ambassador. Ponomarenko followed him there in May 1955. Aristov landed there in February 1961.[22] Pegov was sent to Iran in August 1956 after he had the audacity to refuse, in his capacity of Secretary of the Supreme Soviet, to implement the decree to rehabilitate victims of Stalin's terror enacted during the destalinization campaign after the Twentieth Party Congress.[23] It should be noted that while senior Brotherhood members were given the rank of ambassador in their diplomatic appointment, Andropov, a junior member, was first appointed as a mere counsellor of the embassy in 1953. Only a year later was he promoted to be an ambassador.

A pattern of Party leadership behavior was emerging in the post-Stalin aftermath. Brotherhood members removed from the highest Party positions should be exiled from Moscow to satellite countries where they could be watched and controlled by the Soviet and local KGB, just in case. Malenkov and Khrushchev wanted to take no risks during 1953–1955 with their onetime rivals and would-be purgers. A Soviet ambassador to a satellite borderland is no diplomat at all; in fact, he couldn't be, since probably every Soviet embassy has the concealed KGB station-chief who undoubtedly exercises power equal to, if not greater than, that of the Ambassador. The Soviet ambassador to a satellite represents the Communist Party of the Soviet Union and actively participates in the activity of the national Party leadership, passing on Kremlin orders to the local party.

After Beria's fall in June 1953, the Brotherhood's position began to improve. Suslov reemerged as a ranking Secretary of the Central Committee in charge of ideology and foreign relations. In 1954, Suslov added another important post to his office, chairman of the foreign policy commission of the Supreme Soviet, a post previously occupied by Zhdanov and then Andrianov.[24] Thus Suslov once again emerged, as he had during Stalin's reign, as Molotov's competitor in dominating Soviet foreign policy.

At the same time in 1954, Suslov's closest associate, Ponomarev, became head of the Central Committee's International Department.[25] This department was actually established in 1943 after the ostensible dissolution of the Comintern. Ponomarev had worked in that department as a deputy head since 1944. In July 1949, the department was split in two—one section as a foreign policy commission, the other section for cadres for diplomatic and foreign trade organs. In 1954, both sections were reunited into the Central Committee international department with Ponomarev as its head.[26]

For Andropov's future career, the important aspect of these bureaucratic changes was that Ponomarev in 1954 had become responsible for administering not only Soviet foreign policy but foreign service cadres as well. As senior supervisor of foreign policy in the Central Committee apparatus, Suslov was now also more closely involved in personnel matters. It was during the Suslov-Ponomarev takeover in 1954 that Andropov, already in Budapest, was promoted to the rank of ambassador.

The Brotherhood's restoration in 1954 as a functioning power structure—not dominant but coming along—and in particular the rise of Suslov was the source of Andropov's personal recovery after demotions in 1953 that might have destroyed the career of a less fortunate apparatchik. The new period had begun for

ANDROPOV

Andropov's career and, obviously, with friends at court like Suslov and Ponomarev, Andropov would not be long for the world of diplomacy. Where would he land? There was time. After all, Andropov was only 40 years old.

14

Hungary: Revolution and Counterrevolution

YURI Andropov celebrated his fortieth birthday as counsellor of the Soviet Embassy in Hungary. It was probably his first journey beyond the Soviet borders. However, while Hungary was technically foreign soil, it was only a little more independent than the Karelo-Finnish Republic or some other territorial sub-division of the USSR.

It should be remembered that Hungary's contact with communism in the period after World War II was not its first. In early 1919, following the Bolshevik Revolution, the Communist Party in Hungary seized national power under the terrorist dictatorship of Bela Kun, himself in later years executed on Stalin's orders during the Great Terror. Kun's reign lasted only

133 days. The Hungarian people overthrew Communism again in 1956 but this time it was a different—and bloodier—story.

The Hungarian uprising began on or about October 22, 1956. Revolutions never have an exact moment when they can be said to have begun, especially lost revolutions, because the defeated cannot, as victors can, select one moment as the sacred event that unleashed the revolution.

Perhaps, the symbolic moment when it can be said the Hungarian Revolution was officially launched came when, on the evening of October 23, crowds assembled around a huge statue of Stalin. One of the demands at a student convocation a day before had called for removal of that statue. Hungarians, with the secret police looking on, "climbed the huge monument and set to work on it." At 9:30 that night the Stalin statue fell from its pedestal.[1]

The rebellion had been coming a long time, for the eight years since the Communist Party seized power under the direction of Mátyás Rákosi, a Moscow-trained Communist.

The postwar election in 1945, authorized by the Allied Control Commission, revealed how small actual support of the Communists was. Of 409 Parliamentary seats, the bulk—245—went to the Independent Smallholders, 69 to the Social Democrats, 23 to the National Peasants, two to the Democratic Party. The Communists won 70 seats of the 409 or just 17 percent.

The four major parties formed a coalition, but Communist influence steadily increased. By 1948, leaders of the non-Communist parties had been silenced, including the Social Democrats, whose pro-Soviet leadership had formed an alliance with the Communists. Other non-Communist spokesmen had fled into exile or had been arrested. In 1949, Hungary officially became a "People's Democracy," and real power rested with Rákosi and Moscow.[2]

Under Rákosi, Hungary was modeled closely on the Soviet pattern. Freedom of speech and individual liberty ceased to

146

exist. Arbitrary imprisonment became routine, and there were purges, including the execution of Foreign Minister László Rajk in June 1949. The State Security police, the AVH, used classic Stalinist terror methods against the population.

Khrushchev's anti-Stalin speech at the 20th Party Congress in February 1956 had a profound effect on Hungary. Rákosi announced in March that Rajk had been condemned on "fabricated charges." In July, Rákosi was dismissed and succeeded by Ernö Gerö, who quickly proved he was no better than the hated Rákosi. Early in October 1956, there was a ceremonial reburial of Rajk in the presence of a huge crowd and things began to pop among the writers, the students, and workers.

The evening of October 22 certainly set the revolutionary wheels in whirring motion. Some of the students asked Budapest Radio to broadcast a list of 16 demands, but the censor refused to broadcast those for withdrawal of Soviet troops and for free elections. The students wanted all their demands publicized or none.

The following day a large crowd assembled at the Radio Building in Budapest, and a student delegation entered the building to negotiate with the director. The students seemed to be inside for a long time. Suddenly at about 9 P.M., teargas bombs were tossed out from upper windows of the building and a few minutes later the AVH secret police fired on the crowd, killing a number of people and wounding others. As a result, what had started out as a peaceful demonstration turned into an uprising against the government. When Hungarian troops were called out, they sided with the crowd. A revolution against the Soviet-controlled regime was underway. It was led by Imre Nagy and military men like Pal Maleter and Bela Kiraly, supported by a coalition of workers, students, intellectuals, writers, soldiers, and officers.

With Hungarian soldiers as well as students and common citizens allied against the Soviet occupiers, obviously Moscow felt only Soviet troops could cope with the uprising. At 2 A.M. on October 24 the first Soviet tanks rolled into Budapest.[3]

To an experienced Communist Party official like Andropov, one who had seen how dangerous and unstable a Communist society can become when the Party apparatus falls into unsure hands, it must have been a shock to see the almost overnight disintegration of the Communist Party of Hungary in October 1956 after almost a decade of domination.[4] The Hungarian secret police, the AVH, were dislodged in a matter of hours; Hungarian officers and men, supposedly Communists, took up arms against Communism; Imre Nagy, one-time Communist who had been trained in the Soviet Union, became the new Premier of Hungary and announced Hungary's withdrawal from the Warsaw Pact; the trade unions, so long under Soviet control, announced their secession from the Moscow-controlled World Federation of Trade Unions. The revolution had to be stopped.

In a few days—in disregard of world protests and United Nations resolutions—Soviet heavy guns, tanks, and masses of troops overwhelmed the city's defenders. Reconquering pockets of Hungarian resistance in other parts of the country proved to be an extended mopping-up operation for the Soviets. Total resistance did not end until December, but in the end it was purely passive resistance that failed to impress the Soviet invaders. Thousands of Hungarians were arrested and sent to prison camps in the USSR.[5]

Andropov, who was Soviet Ambassador to Hungary throughout the revolution, probably learned as much or more during those bloody days than in any other period of his career. Nothing so concentrates the mind of a Soviet diplomat as to be an eyewitness to a foreign people's uprising against Soviet imperialist power. With guns in their hands, the Hungarians drove—if only temporarily—Soviet troops out of their Soviet-occupied country.

Andropov saw how brute military power, if you were prepared to shrug away outraged world opinion, could crush a popular uprising. The lesson here to be learned was that military power must be credible, meaning that its possessor is ready to use it, and that potential victims of that military power believe that it will be used against them. Having witnessed and been alarmed by an uprising by German workers in East Germany in June 1953 and a Polish uprising in Poznan among auto workers in early summer 1956, the Soviets were now prepared to raze Budapest to the ground to prevent a democracy from springing up alongside Soviet borders. When the Soviet armies marched back into Hungary November 3, 1956, few doubted that the Kremlin had ordered them to prevent the Hungarian defection no matter what the cost. The Red Armies were prepared to create a bloodbath—and they did just that.

Months earlier, Khrushchev had already warned the Yugoslav ambassador in Moscow, Veljko Mićunović, that "if the situation in Hungary gets still worse, we here have decided to use all means at our disposal to bring the crisis to an end." Nor would the USSR "at any price allow 'a breach in the front' in Eastern Europe, and that was just what the West was working for."[6]

So Andropov's assignment to Budapest, which had started out as a demotion, had become, thanks to the strategy imposed upon the discredited Hungarian Party leadership by Suslov and Mikoyan, of major consequence to Soviet politics. The strategy, according to Mićunović, was Suslov's who was doing "his best to deepen and sharpen the crisis, instead of reducing it and making a better solution possible."[7]

In Andropov, the Soviet Union had a masterful representative. General Bela Kiraly, the highest-ranking military leader to escape from Hungary, has described his meetings and experiences with the duplicitous Andropov when, during the uprising, the USSR was pretending to remove its troops from Hungary. Kiraly, who served as Military Commander of Budapest during the October days, says that on November 2, 1956, Nagy phoned him to say that Andropov had sent him "a formal note" that "bands of Hungarians are raging around his embassy." If the

149

Hungarian government didn't do something about that, Andropov, as Ambassador, would have to call in Soviet troops. Nagy ordered Kiraly to go to the Square of Heroes, site of the Soviet Embassy, and restore order.

Kiraly ordered a mechanized infantry battalion and a tank company to move on the Embassy square and then rushed over himself. When he got there, the streets were empty; there was no sign of trouble. Kiraly went to the embassy itself and asked to speak to Andropov. After a 10-minute wait, he was ushered into Andropov's office. Kiraly said that he had "a command from my premier to check the rioting here but I see no rioting." Andropov replied that there had been reports of trouble, but it had stopped. Kiraly quoted Andropov:

> We Russians don't want to mix in your business. We understand your troubles and are on your side. Did you know that we have offered to negotiate with your government? Our government wants to take its troops out of Hungary immediately, and we want a discussion to arrange the details of the evacuation. Will you be kind enough to phone Mr. Nagy immediately and see if he has received our written proposal?

Kiraly says he picked up a phone on Andropov's desk that turned out to be a direct line to Hungarian cabinet members. Nagy himself answered the phone. Kiraly reported that there had been no disturbance and that Andropov wanted to know if Nagy had received the written proposal and that if he had, could Nagy say when the negotiations would begin and could he supply Andropov with a list of committee members? Nagy said negotiations could begin that very afternoon—November 2—at the Hungarian parliament building and that, among others, Kiraly would be a delegation member. That night, says Kiraly, Soviet planes began flying out of Hungarian airfields toward the

150

USSR. Soviet tank columns "moved ostentatiously through the city, asking directions for the best way out of town." Then the Soviets asked that evacuation negotiations be postponed one day, to November 3.

Negotiations began but there were some hitches. Would the Hungarian government please be patient about the evacuation, which would take until January 15, 1957, because Soviet troops were not "prepared for a winter movement." There was a rather priceless request by Andropov, according to Kiraly's source, General Istvan Kovacs, the army chief of staff:

> Lastly, they say the Russian army did not wish to attack the Hungarians but only did what the Hungarian government asked. Therefore the evacuation must be not only peaceful but friendly. The troops must leave in a festive air, and the Hungarians must cheer them as they leave.

And while all these negotiations about the Soviet "evacuation" were going on, Soviet armored divisions were massing into two operational bases along the main highway to Budapest and setting up a vast front-line fighting force of combat-ready troops and 4,000 tanks. Yet at 11 P.M. the Soviets asked the Hungarian commanding general, Pal Maleter, who headed the negotiations, to telephone Kiraly and "say that everything was in good order." It was all so believable—and false. By 4 A.M. on the morning of November 4, Soviet tanks moved into Budapest and started shelling. Kiraly phoned Nagy immediately and told the Premier that Budapest was being invaded and asked for orders to return the Soviet artillery fire. Kiraly quotes Nagy: "No, no. Calm down. The Russian ambassador is here in my office. He is calling Moscow right now. There is some misunderstanding. You must not open fire."

A few hours later, Nagy was broadcasting over the radio that "in the early hours of this morning, Soviet troops launched an attack against our capital with the obvious intention of over-throwing the legal democratic Hungarian government. Our troops are fighting."[8]

The Hungarian Revolution was lost because the Soviet Union, under Khrushchev and, it should be added, Suslov for his unyielding, uncompromising stance, was ready to use all military power to quell the Hungarian resistance. True, the leaders of the Hungarian uprising, some of them Communists who had only recently broken with Moscow, were amateurs when it came to leading a revolution and Suslov, Mikoyan, and Andropov—who watched it all happen before their very eyes—were professional *counter*revolutionaries, men who knew how to use political terror without qualm.

Since Andropov had become ambassador in 1954, he had learned lessons and techniques that would stand him in good stead in later years. His Hungarian experience taught him how to deal with the dangers of counterrevolution and subversion and how to use power, political and military, in a crisis that endangered Soviet interests and the future of Marxism-Leninism. When he left Hungary in 1957, Andropov had lived through a revolution which, by chicanery and duplicity—and ruthless power—had been stopped dead in its tracks.

During his years in Budapest and especially toward the end of his diplomatic stint, Andropov worked closely under a Brotherhood potentate, Mikhail Suslov. With Anastas I. Mikoyan, Suslov had been assigned by the Politburo to keep Hungary in the Warsaw Pact and in the "socialist camp," however unwilling the Hungarian people were to remain in either. Both senior Politburo members were in Budapest during both interventions by the Soviet army.

There is little question that Andropov benefited in a number of ways from his experience in Hungary. In the first place, he was part of a highly successful operation for the maintenance of

Soviet power in Eastern Europe during a crisis whose origins could not be attributed to the Ambassador but the resolution of which could be, at least in part, attributed to him. In the second place, being an intelligent man, i.e., one who learns from other people's experience, Andropov must have been profoundly influenced by all the implications, the "what if's," the "worst case" and the "best case" scenarios dealing with the Hungarian crisis and, not to be ignored, the inept British-French-Israeli attack on Egypt during the same period. In the third place, Andropov was working closely with the man who now appears to have been the Politburo "king-maker," the Communist Warwick, Mikhail Suslov, his old patron who propelled him upward. His experiences during the climactic weeks in Budapest must have taught him a great deal that became useful during his 15 years as head of the KGB and today as the Soviet Party General Secretary.

Among the useful things that Andropov learned in Hungary was the fact that *the Chinese were simply not to be trusted in their relations with the Soviet Union and the East European satellites.* In the critical 1950s, the Peoples' Republic of China (PRC) was represented in Budapest by Ambassador Ho Te-ching, described as "a man of supple intellect and considerable diplomatic experience." He kept in touch with the opposition in Hungary and "had at his disposal an extensive intelligence apparatus that earned the Chinese embassy the reputation of being the best-informed foreign post in the Hungarian capital." Ho's staff, one of whom, the cultural attaché, spoke fluent Hungarian, maintained contact with Hungarian intellectuals, particularly the anti-Soviet Petőfi Circle. The PRC Embassy encouraged the pro-China sympathy among Hungarian intellectuals. It provided Hungarian press and radio with loads of information about the Hundred Flowers movement. So close were relations between China and the Hungarian rebels-to-be that a Hungarian literary magazine during a fit of euphoria stated that "the

West and the East are on our side; America has proclaimed faith in our cause as clearly as have powerful nations like China and India." The article appeared on November 2, 1956 and must have sat badly with Andropov, Suslov, and Mikoyan.

But on November 4, 1956, with the revolution crushed, the Chinese ambassador "appeared on the scene once more, this time offering China's advice and assistance to the new Hungarian regime." The *Peking Review* in 1963 said that "we Chinese insisted on the taking of all necessary measures to smash the counterrevolutionary rebellion in Hungary and firmly opposed the abandonment of socialist Hungary."[9]

There is little question that China's policy toward the Hungarian rebels was an old strategy of trying to dance at two weddings. If the rebellion against Moscow succeeded, the Chinese Embassy would have an inside track with the new government. If it appeared likely that the rebellion would fail, China could appear as the rescuer of the foundering Soviet vessel in the stormy waters of Eastern Europe. Whatever the strategy, "The Soviets on the sidelines eyed the Chinese activity with suspicion," writes Janos Radvanyi.[10]

Andropov also learned that the Yugoslavs were not to be trusted. The expulsion of Yugoslavia from the Cominform and Tito's own purges of "Cominformists" in Yugoslavia had so worsened relations with the USSR that war might have occurred in 1950. Says Kiraly:

> When the Korean war broke out, the East Central European armies were poised to strike against Yugoslavia. Had the United States and the United Nations not resisted in the Far East, preventing the conquest of South Korea, war would have broken out in the Balkans. The United Nations resistance in Korea made it seem likely that an attack on Yugoslavia would also have been resisted, and Stalin was not ready to run that risk. Western

action in the Far East averted an offensive against Yugoslavia by its socialist fellow states.[11]

During Andropov's tenure as Ambassador to Hungary, a series of war exercises took place in which atomic weapons were used as tactical weapons for offensive purposes. These war exercises, which involved the general staffs of Czechoslovakia, Poland, Hungary, Rumania, and Bulgaria were under the personal command of Marshal Georgi K. Zhukov, then Soviet Minister of Defense. The objective of the war games was exploitation of satellite countries as forward bases for projected attacks on Western Europe and Yugoslavia.[12]

Particularly revealing was how the 1946 Paris Peace Treaty concerning Hungary was violated so as to build up "Hungary as a base of aggression against the West," said General Kiraly. According to the treaty, Hungary was entitled to an army of 65,000 men, an air force of 5,000 men with 90 fighter planes. Bombers were prohibited. In 1956, during Andropov's tenure at the embassy, the Hungarian army total strength was 250,000 men, three-and-a-half times the amount permitted under the peace treaty. This figure excluded trained reserves. New units were under continuing formation, suggesting that the strength of the standing army was to be further increased. In 1956, the true strength of the Hungarian air fighter division exceeded 500 planes, including a fighter-bomber regiment with 37 planes. The Hungarian army was also to be used in an invasion of Yugoslavia in a drive through the so-called Ljubljana gate in southwestern Hungary. Earlier war games in Hungary were also directed against Yugoslavia.[13]

The Soviets were probably correct in blaming Tito for the troubles in Hungary, where "the forces for change had been unleashed by Khrushchev's destalinization and the attendant reconciliation with Tito, and the latter was in a sense the godfather of the [Hungarian] revolution," to quote Kovrig.[14]

The hostility to Yugoslavia didn't cease with Stalin's death. In some ways it grew worse even after the Canossa pilgrimage of Khrushchev to Belgrade in 1955. The Soviet hope that Tito would rejoin the Big Brother socialist camp in return for such a generous act of Soviet repentance proved to be in vain.[15] Suslov did much to inflame this hostility. And Khrushchev himself ascribes the problem of worsening relations between Yugoslavia and the USSR to Suslov even though some part of the Soviet leadership wanted a reconciliation between the two countries. Says Khrushchev: "Mikhail Suslov was particularly adamant in resisting the idea of trying to relieve the tension between us and the Yugoslavs. He insisted that Yugoslavia was no longer a Socialist country."[16]

In addition, Andropov learned that intellectuals are not to be trusted. Andropov would have learned a lot about the power of dissident intellectuals in a totalitarian one-party state by watching the activities of writers who "[m]oving from literary and artistic grievances . . . began to express the dissatisfaction and longings of the average citizen."[17] In April 1956, the Hungarian General Assembly of the Writers' Union met to elect its new executives. The Assembly rejected the official Party candidates' list and, by heavy majorities chose others in their stead. Another organization set up at this time emerged out of the League of Working Youth, a Soviet Komsomol clone, and was called the Petöfi Circle. The Circle consisted of young writers, journalists, and composers, and even cadets from the military academies came and joined the discussion meetings. To appease the intellectuals, the Communist Party newspaper, *Szabad Nép,* called the Petöfi Circle a valuable forum and encouraged Hungary's leaders to participate in its debates.[18]

Appeasement will not work. You can't give an inch to counter-revolutionaries. Khrushchev himself reportedly told the Yugoslav ambassador on November 12, 1956 that "there are some people amongst us who think that the new decisions are responsible for everything bad that has happened." The new decisions he was referring to were in the context of the Twentieth Party Congress where Khrushchev had delivered the anti-Stalin speech.[19]

Probably the most important lesson Andropov learned during his tenure in Budapest was how weak and irresolute the Western democracies were in a crisis and how unwilling they were to exploit Soviet weaknesses. Although the Eisenhower Administration had been elected in 1952 on a slogan of "rolling back the Iron Curtain," the East German uprising on June 17, 1953 found the White House strangely inactive and even quiescent.

During the Hungarian crisis, Soviet concerns about U.S. or West European actions to support the uprising vanished when the U.S. "on three separate occasions in rapid succession" gave the USSR assurances that it had no intention of making Hungary a military ally. The first such assurance came the day after the U.N. Security Council meeting, when Secretary of State Dulles addressed a Dallas meeting and said that "we do not look upon these nations [Poland and Hungary] as potential military allies." The following day, October 28, 1956, Ambassador Henry Cabot Lodge called the Security Council's attention to Dulles's speech. On October 29, U.S. Ambassador Charles Bohlen was instructed to tell the Kremlin officially that Dulles's remarks had been approved by President Eisenhower.[20] The invasion of Hungary followed in a few days.

For Andropov the lesson learned, as he watched the Western powers in the United Nations go through the motions of indignation and passionate moral assertions, was that the West was really a paper tiger despite "rollback" threats and anti-Soviet U.N. resolutions. And if the U.S., a superpower in 1956, was willing to ignore the continuing crises in Eastern Europe, why should the Soviet Union, as its military power expanded exponentially, worry about the U.S. today?

Growing out of this experience there is another lesson: the division of the Western Alliance when faced by crisis—the fragility of Western unity. The United States government was ready to impose sanctions on Britain, France, and Israel over their attack on Nasser. It was unwilling to do much more than support resolutions against the Soviet invasion of Hungary and the killing of tens of thousands of Hungarians, especially workers and peasants, who saw their role not as Marx's gravediggers of capitalism but as Lajos Kossuth's gravediggers of foreign imperialism *redidivus*. It would not be difficult in years to come to split the U.S. from its NATO allies. That was what the KGB, inter alia, was for.

It should at this point be recalled that while Andropov was still Ambassador to Budapest, world opinion was outraged by the Soviet-Hungarian violation of a guarantee of safe-conduct to Imre Nagy and a group of dissident Hungarians who, on November 4, 1956, had been granted political asylum in the Yugoslav embassy in Budapest. After protracted negotiations between the new Soviet puppet premier, Janos Kadar, and the Yugoslav embassy, Kadar pledged in writing on November 21 that Imre Nagy and his companions could leave the embassy "and proceed freely to their homes." Obviously such an agreement necessitated Andropov's and Moscow's approval—in this case, Suslov's approval, who was the Politburo ideologue-in-chief, virtually on permanent station in Budapest.

The next evening, November 22, a bus arrived at the Yugoslav embassy, which Imre Nagy and his colleagues boarded. They were followed into the bus by Soviet Army officers who ordered the bus to be driven to Soviet military command headquarters in Budapest. When it arrived, two Yugoslav embassy officials who had accompanied the bus to ensure that the Nagy party, as per the signed agreement, would be allowed to return to their homes, were ordered out of the bus by a Soviet lieutenant-colonel. Surrounded by Soviet armored vehicles, the bus then drove the Hungarian prisoners to a local airport from which they were flown away to an unknown destination.

When the next episode in the drama occurred, June 16, 1958, Andropov was no longer in Budapest; he had risen high in the Soviet hierarchy and was now an executive in the Central Committee apparatus. But his hand must have been in the decision about Imre Nagy. After nineteen months during which little was heard about the Hungarian premier, it was suddenly announced that the People's Tribunal of the Hungarian Supreme Court had found the defendants guilty, after a trial about which no details were given, save that Nagy, Pal Maleter, Miklos Gimes, and Jozsef Szilagyi were sentenced to death, the others to long jail terms. And the final word: "No appeals were admissible. The death sentences have been carried out."[21]

The aftermath of worldwide protests, a statement from the U.N. Special Committee on the Problem of Hungary, and President Eisenhower's statement of condemnation proved to the Soviet leaders that they could move as they wished in Eastern Europe and little would happen. The case of Czechoslovakia in 1968 and Poland in 1981 only confirmed to the Kremlin what it had learned in 1956.

In the Kremlin, where Andropov's future would be decided, strange maneuvers were going on in spring 1957 in the Central Committee. It was on the eve of the ouster of the old leadership, including Malenkov, Molotov, and Kaganovich by Khrushchev. There are strong indications that suggest that Suslov once more had established the independent "third force" that helped Khrushchev against the old guard at the price of restraining Khrushchev's destalinization campaign.[22]

The ouster of the old guard was, of course, in the best interests of the Brotherhood since it would open wide all kinds of new opportunities, from the standpoint of ideology and patronage. In a sense, Khrushchev helped them to achieve in 1957 what the Brotherhood had failed to achieve after Stalin's death.

What the Brotherhood needed was to reinforce its position in the international communist movement. By so doing they would strengthen Soviet control over the East European satellites whose peoples had, between 1953 and 1956, demonstrated their contempt for the "international communist movement." Rebellions like these could happen again. Workers, peasants, intellectuals, students couldn't be trusted to stay in line. One had to know how to deal with them and even with Communist Parties that, outside the USSR, had an unfortunate tendency to fragment, to split, to fly apart unexpectedly. One of the lessons that Brotherhood leaders clearly had learned was the need for a Moscow-centralized network within the Central Committee to avert such disasters. Therefore in 1957 the Central Committee created a special department to supervise—for which read, to dominate—Soviet Party relations with Communist bloc ruling parties.

With his long-standing attachment to the Brotherhood and with his fresh Hungarian experience, Andropov seemed the perfect choice for Suslov to install within the Central Committee apparatus to run this department. Undoubtedly, his reassignment was in part a reward for a job well done during the suppression of the Hungarian revolution in 1956. Thus, in May 1957, at the age of 43, Andropov was appointed to a post of some importance, one that restored his tenure in the Central Committee. Now he would be working with his Brotherhood patron-in-chief, Suslov, whose power in the party was undiminished. Andropov was back on Old Square, Moscow headquarters of the Central Committee.

15

A Decade
of Promise:

1957-1967

THE Hungarian Revolution led to a severe Soviet domestic political struggle, one that altered the course of Andropov's Party career. In 1956, Andropov's standing in the inner hierarchy of the Communist Party was quite low. The Twentieth Party Congress, which met in 1956, had launched, under Khrushchev's goading, a destalinization campaign that gathered momentum for some months after Khrushchev's anti-Stalin speech at that same Congress.

Such a Congress could find no room in any of the Party's ruling institutions for a former Central Committee officer like Andropov, who had been a member of the staff preparing Stalin's abortive second purge. Andropov was neither elected to the Central Committee, even as a candidate (non-voting) member, nor to a Central Auditing Commission. Membership on this commission was relatively insignificant in the Party structure but the institution itself is endowed with some prestige.

Most Soviet ambassadors, who were equal in diplomatic rank to Andropov in 1956, were elected either as full members or candidate members of the Central Committee or at the very least to the auditing commission. But the climactic, highly dramatic anti-Stalin Party Congress was hardly the moment for an Andropov to obtain even a nominal position among a Party elite of some 300 people.

However, no sooner did the negative impact of destalinization on the very foundations of Communist rule become apparent to the Party hierarchs in 1957—thanks to the Polish upheaval and Hungarian revolution in 1956—than Andropov's ambitions for Party advancement seemed realizable. In May 1957, the low man on the Party totem pole was promoted to be head of the Central Committee department in charge of liaison with the Communist Parties of Socialist countries. In October 1961, at the Twenty-second Party Congress, Andropov became a full member of the Central Committee without having been previously a candidate member. In 1962, he regained the seat in the Supreme Soviet that he had lost in 1954. In November 1962, Andropov received another promotion in the Party apparatus as a Secretary of the Central Committee still charged with supervising other communist countries and apparently in charge also of some general ideological issues.

All at once, it seemed, Andropov had become one of the important Soviet spokesmen on issues of international political strategy and on the maintenance of communism in those countries where it had been imposed on the populations. In June 1967, a month after Andropov had been transferred from the inner Central Committee apparatus to the position of KGB chief, he was promoted to candidate member of the Politburo.[1]

Andropov's steady ascent on the Party ladder began during

the seven years of Khrushchev's power, from 1957 to 1964 and continued smoothly after Khrushchev's ouster.

When Khrushchev was the First Secretary (the title was later changed by Brezhnev to General Secretary) of the Central Committee, Andropov was head of a department of the Central Committee and later a Secretary of the Central Committee. On the surface, it would therefore appear either that Andropov was at the time Khrushchev's client or, at least, the client of someone who supported Khrushchev and loyally implemented Khrushchev's program of destalinization.

Such an interpretation would be correct on the assumption that Khrushchev was omnipotent as Party leader, that he had successfully suppressed any remaining opposition forces after he had ousted Stalin's old guard, the so-called "anti-Party group" in June 1957. But in actual fact he had never been *the* powerful leader. In the intervening years since Khrushchev's downfall in October 1964, it has become more and more clear that the entire Khrushchev period in Soviet history was in the nature of a long transition between Stalin and the Brezhnev-Suslov coalition.

Throughout the period that Khrushchev was in office as First Secretary, he was afflicted by a potent opposition within the Politburo and the Central Committee that fought his destalinization program even though, for tactical reasons, they might utter carefully chosen words of criticism against Stalin. These forces, which eventually ousted Khrushchev, were led by Suslov, Kozlov, and Brezhnev, who eventually succeeded Khrushchev. It is ironic that while Khrushchev was the object of a "cult of personality" propaganda campaign during the later years of his term of office, those years were actually marked by collective leadership.

This collective leadership, however, was not based on a consensus but rather on balancing two opposing powers, on perpetual compromises, on the ups and downs in the destalinization campaign, and on accidents and vagaries that on some days meant orating about Stalin's greatness and on others, Stalin's infamies.

Western scholars, like Robert Conquest and Michel Tatu, have uncovered an organized Suslov-Kozlov opposition whose strength was such that Khrushchev had to tolerate its existence throughout his term of office.[2] Khrushchev himself concedes, both directly and indirectly in his memoirs, that more often than not he stood alone in the Politburo trying to juggle and counterbalance the opposing forces of Suslov and others like him. Even on what might seem like trifling matters, Khrushchev acted in response to collective judgment. For example, in his memoirs, he says that when the prewar French statesman Eduard Daladier, passing through Moscow, asked to see him, "I discussed his request with my comrades. (I never received foreign visitors without consulting the leadership first.) We decided I should meet him, and I did so in the Kremlin."[3]

Another example from Khrushchev himself is his admission that he went to the aborted 1960 Paris summit meeting with the approval of the Politburo leadership. It will be recalled that a Four-Power summit meeting had been convened in 1960 in Paris to be attended by the U.S., Britain, France, and the USSR. Because President Eisenhower accepted full responsibility for overflights by a high-altitude reconnaissance U-2 airplane flying across the USSR, Khrushchev demanded an apology from Eisenhower. His demand resulted in cancellation of the summit meeting when Eisenhower refused to proffer the apology. In any case, Khrushchev says in his memoirs that as the date of the proposed summit neared, the time had come "to select members of our delegation." Says Khrushchev: "It had already been arranged that each delegation would be led by the head of government or head of state. Therefore my own name was immediately approved by the leadership."[4]

Suslov, as mentioned earlier, sought to counteract Khrushchev's policy of restoring friendly relations with Yugoslavia. It is obvious from Khrushchev's memoirs that he resented Suslov's resistance to his policy of rapprochement, but was powerless to subdue Suslov, or punish him, or oust him from the Politburo. In Stalin's time or even under the Brezhnev-Suslov coalition later, from 1964 on, disagreement on such an issue of principle as Yugoslavia would have been sufficient reason for all kinds of reprisals, including, under Stalin, summary execution for treason. Khrushchev couldn't mete out summary punishment to Suslov or any other opponent in the Soviet leadership.

Andropov's supervision of relations with ruling parties in Communist countries should be read in the context of Khrushchev's inability to dominate Suslov. Hardening Soviet relations with Yugoslavia, which began in 1958 and lasted through 1961, can be viewed as an important gain for Suslov and a defeat for Khrushchev.

Andropov's appointment as head of a strategic department in 1957, his promotion to membership in the Central Committee in 1961 and to the Secretariat in 1962 can be regarded as part of Suslov's battle against Khrushchev on what policy to pursue toward the satellites and other socialist countries far from Soviet borders. It is obvious that along a Soviet ideological continuum, Khrushchev tended to greater tolerance toward these countries, a sort of crude many-roads-to-socialism approach, while Suslov looked upon such an approach as revisionist and therefore to be suppressed because of its dangers to Party control at home and abroad. As can be inferred from the chronology of Andropov's promotions, he was throughout this period implementing Suslov's, not Khrushchev's, policies.

Suslov's position in the spring of 1957, when he had obtained Andropov's promotion to the Central Committee apparatus, was a very special one. Suslov had managed to establish an independent third force, this time standing between the camp of Khrushchev and his most loyal supporters like Kirichenko on the one hand, and Molotov, Malenkov, and Kaganovich on the other.

Suslov had received his promotion to the Party Presidium in July 1955, simultaneously with Khrushchev's man, Kirichenko, but with a marked difference. Kirichenko kept moving up steadily: candidate Presidium member in May 1953 and full member in July 1955.[5] Suslov had been made a full member of the Presidium a few months before Stalin's death and with Stalin's death he was ousted. Now in July 1955, he was back as a full member without having to go through the ritual of first being a candidate member.[6]

More importantly, the July 1955 Plenum that elevated both Suslov and Kirichenko was devoted, inter alia, to a decision on Soviet-Yugoslav relations.[7] As noted earlier, Suslov strongly resisted Khrushchev's rapprochment policy toward Tito. The Plenum accepted a carefully worded resolution on this question, one that said that the Central Committee had decided "to approve the results of negotiations between governmental delegations of the USSR and Yugoslavia."[8]

The fact of the matter is that the Plenum, with these words, was approving a reconciliation policy between two countries on a strictly government-to-government level, not between two Communist ruling parties. The Plenum was ratifying the work of the Soviet governmental delegation, i.e., the work of the then head of government, Bulganin; it was not ratifying the policy of the leader of the Party, Khrushchev, who headed the Party delegation. Khrushchev's initiative and the work of the Party, under Khrushchev, toward rapprochement with Yugoslavia, was downplayed and not approved by the Party Plenum.

This finding arises from an interesting omission from the Plenum's proceedings. Usually when the Party, through its central organs, backs a leadership decision, the standard phrase that accompanies the endorsement, reads: ". . . to approve fully and completely the policy." This phrase was left out of the final Plenum statement. It was not an oversight.

One can only assume that there had been some kind of compromise in which Khrushchev lost something and Suslov won something. Suslov's partial victory brought about his swift promotion to full membership in the Party Presidium even though he was an opponent of Khrushchev, the First Secretary. From 1955 on, Suslov's position became even stronger, precisely because his promotion had come about without Khrushchev's consent. From 1955 on, Suslov had a strong independent position in the highest echelons of the leadership. This position included policy decision-making and promotion of officials who would back Suslov's restalinization policy. One of the promotions Suslov engineered was that of Andropov.

During the Twentieth Party Congress in February 1956, when Khrushchev delivered his anti-Stalin speech, Suslov openly sided with Malenkov, Kaganovich, and Voroshilov on the question of restricting Khrushchev's personal power because Stalin's old guard was needed to counterbalance Khrushchev.[9]

By the beginning of 1957, Khrushchev had come to the conclusion that the time was ripe to reshuffle the top leadership of the Party, to alter the composition of the Central Committee Presidium and to oust Stalin's old guard and replace them with his own clients. From some of the speeches made at the later Twenty-second Party Congress in 1961, it has become clear retroactively that what Khrushchev had been doing from April 1956 on was to exploit the process he had instituted of posthumous rehabilitation of Party and military leaders purged in 1937–1938 so that he could accuse Molotov, Voroshilov, Kaganovich, and Malenkov as accomplices in Stalin's crimes.[10]

Stalin's old guard in turn tried to use the Hungarian revolution and the earlier Polish upheaval along with Soviet domestic economic problems, as weapons against Khrushchev's policy.

All of them—Molotov, Malenkov, Kaganovich and Voroshilov—evidently stressed that with his anti-Stalin speech, Khrushchev had been guilty of conduct unbecoming a true Communist. His speech had, indeed, endangered them all since they had participated in and benefited from the Great Terror.[11]

For Suslov, an ideological purist, Khrushchev bore the blame for having destabilized Eastern Europe, most notably in Hungary and Poland, by his reckless and imprudent speech. In short, there was no leadership consensus and no established leader to impose a consensus. There were just these two loosely organized adversaries, Khrushchev's group and the "Anti-Party Group" as it became known after the bloodless June 1957 purge. The latter's aim was simple—get rid of Khrushchev and stop his destalinization campaign and the reforms. And they were a powerful lot—Molotov, Kaganovich, Malenkov, Voroshilov, Pervukhin and others. Allied with them but not of them was Suslov, who supported the "Anti-Party Group" until the last minute when he switched sides.

Suslov was not with either faction because his own Brotherhood still existed. He was apparently prepared to play on whichever side seemed politically stronger and, if possible, ideologically purer. It was even more advantageous for Suslov to switch sides at the last minute for a practical reason. To side with Khrushchev meant that with the ouster of the "Anti-Party Group," there would be a lot of high-level job openings for his Brotherhood allies. If they sided with Khrushchev's opponents and they won, the ensuing job benefits would be slim; there was also the uncertainty of who would be Khrushchev's successor and how friendly he might be to the Brotherhood. But to side with Khrushchev meant that there would have to be replacements not only for the "Anti-Party Group" but for all their clients—a great opportunity for Suslov's Brotherhood.

One can speculate even further. Suslov was not so much opposed to Khrushchev as he was to Khrushchev's destalinization program. If siding with Khrushchev could strengthen Suslov, he would then be able to bring Brotherhood members into the Party apparatus who would stand as an opposition bloc to Khrushchev should he insist on further pursuing his program of destalinization. Let Khrushchev be First Secretary of the Party so long as the Brotherhood could snatch the strategic posts in the Central Committee and the Secretariat. In time there could be a settling of scores with Khrushchev himself, if the Brotherhood could take over the Party apparatus before Khrushchev could consolidate his power over the Party.

The fact that Suslov was pursuing his own definitely anti-Khrushchev policy in spring 1957, at the time of Andropov's promotion, was revealed in 1957 at the Twenty-first Congress in a speech by one of the alleged members of the "Anti-Party Group," Maksim Z. Saburov. Prior to the final clash between Khrushchev and the "Anti-Party Group," Saburov said, only a small "healthy section of members of the Presidium" existed, one which included Mikoyan, Kirichenko, and Khrushchev himself.[12] This, of course, means that Suslov did not belong to the "healthy section," i.e., the Khrushchev group.

After an unstable compromise had been reached in the summer of 1957 between Khrushchev and Suslov, Suslov continued to exploit any describable or definable failure in economic or foreign policy by Khrushchev so as to imprint his, Suslov's, view of what the Party line ought to be. By so doing, he could bring up to the leadership his own supporters. Frol Kozlov, who had been promoted to candidate membership in the Presidium in February 1957 (a month before Andropov's recall from Hungary for his promotion to the Central Committee apparatus), became a full member of the Presidium in June 1957. Three years later, in May 1960, Suslov and his allies, exploiting what they regarded as the failure of Khrushchev's policy toward the West after the U-2 episode, were able to oust Khrushchev's strongest supporter, Kirichenko, and to bring Kozlov into the

Party Secretariat.[13] By such a move—making Kozlov a full Presidium member and a Central Committee secretary—Kirichenko was replaced by Kozlov as Khrushchev's heir-presumptive. The significance of this replacement is that Khrushchev's potential successor was not an ally of Khrushchev but one of the members of the anti-Khrushchev cabal.

The new balance—or imbalance—of power in the Soviet leadership reached in May 1960 with the strengthening of Khrushchev's enemies became apparent through an unusual event in the Soviet Union. On May 18, 1960, *Pravda* translated and published, without so much as an altered or omitted word, a column by Walter Lippmann from the *New York Herald Tribune* of the day before. The reason for this remarkable republication of Lippmann's column became evident as one read that the commentator, discussing the U-2 incident, said that because of his handling of the U-2 incident, Khrushchev might have become vulnerable "to his critics within the Soviet Union and to his communist allies" as a leader who might have surrendered Soviet sovereignty.

Such an unprecedented event—the reprinting of an article from the capitalist-bourgeois press, critical of the top Party leader of the Soviet Union—was a clear signal from Suslov and Kozlov to the Party apparatus, from top to bottom, that Khrushchev was not all-powerful. After all, someone had to tell the editor of *Pravda* to reprint the Lippmann column and the editor of *Pravda* had to recognize the legitimacy of the order being conveyed to him.

The special reference to "communist allies" of the USSR as potential critics of Khrushchev undoubtedly meant the Chinese leadership. Kozlov, Suslov, and Andropov, the latter because he was the Soviet official responsible for relations with ruling Communist parties, including the Chinese, thus—by their use of the Lippmann column—were hinting about the Suslov-Kozlov solidarity with those forces at home and abroad in the

Communist world who wanted a more anti-American policy than Khrushchev and his allies presumably did.

By the time the Twenty-second Party Congress convened in October 1961, the struggle between Khrushchev and the Suslov-Kozlov coalition had sharpened. To beat back this coalition and to concentrate what was left of his visibly ebbing power, Khrushchev exploded at that Congress a second and even stronger destalinization campaign than that which he had initiated in February 1956 and one which, by various maneuvers enabled him to subdue the opposition, if only on this issue.

However, the existence of a strong opposition to Khrushchev was openly acknowledged, not by republishing Western reportage, as in May 1960, but through the statement of the then KGB head, Aleksandr N. Shelepin. He said:

> Trying to misinform public opinion . . . bourgeois newspapers write about an alleged "hidden domestic threat" and "domestic difficulties," "about a fracture in the monolithic structure of the Reds," about some "opposition group in the present composition of the leadership" and "the renewed accusations against the Anti-Party Group is aimed at cautioning some hotheads" etc., etc. . . .
>
> We must disappoint the bourgeois propagandists. We are speaking about the Anti-Party Group not because it represents at the present time any danger to the party. No! . . . We are speaking about them in order once more to bare their true faces and to underscore the fact that they are nonentities."[14]

Since it was clear to everybody in the Party apparatus that it was not "nonentities" like Molotov and the other members of the "Anti-Party Group" ousted in 1957 who had inspired the new destalinization campaign, Khrushchev's message in Shelepin's mouth was obviously targeted at the then current Suslov-Kozlov opposition, rather than the past group. Shelepin, using phrases

171

allegedly taken from Western newspapers instead of limiting himself to, perhaps, a few vague remarks, was telling Suslov and Kozlov and their allies that since they were supposedly the most anti-Western forces in the Soviet leadership, all they were doing by opposing Khrushchev was objectively helping the West. Shelepin's message also contained a real warning: if the Suslov-Kozlov cabal didn't wish to join the "nonentities," they had better stop working against Khrushchev and his destalinization program.

As subsequent events demonstrated, Khrushchev's tactics didn't work. His opposition kept promoting its own clients as if there were no Khrushchev. Andropov was brought into full Central Committee membership. Ponomarev, another strong Suslov ally and a colleague of Andropov in the Central Committee apparatus, became a secretary of the Central Committee.[15]

A year later, in November 1962, when Suslov and Kozlov had swung the party back to a program of restalinization, Andropov was promoted to the Central Committee Secretariat. Now the entire structure of Soviet foreign policy and relations with the international communist movements was securely in the hands of that section of the Party apparatus led by Suslov, Ponomarev, and Andropov.

Khrushchev's new defeat and Suslov's new victory, including Andropov's promotion, came as a result of global events, including "the missiles of November," the Cuban crisis of fall 1962, which weakened Khrushchev. In the face of President Kennedy's successful ultimatum calling for the removal of Soviet missiles from Cuba, Khrushchev's retreat strengthened the internal opposition to him. It is possible that Kennedy's success made it possible for Suslov to place his client, Andropov, into a seat in the Party Secretariat, the seat of a ranking secretary, which can be regarded as a first real step to the position of General Secretary.

16

"The KGB Has a Very Long Arm"

A story was recently told about Yuri Andropov when he was still KGB chairman. Seated across the dinner table from him was a Moscow actor. Andropov reached across the table and offered the actor a glass of cognac. When the actor demurred, Andropov joked: "You'd better accept. The KGB has a very long arm."[1]

History does not record whether the Moscow actor, perhaps a teetotaler, was able to persuade Andropov that no insult was intended by his refusal to drink the proferred brandy. Nor will we ever know whether the actor persuaded himself to change his mind and accept the glass of *eau de vie*. And there is no way of telling whether the new Party General Secretary is innately given to such jocosity or whether it was Andropov's feeble attempt to appear as just an ordinary man doing his duty and seeking to belie an unjustly accorded reputation for malevolence. On one thing we can agree: judging from its activities, one might even suggest that the KGB has many, many long arms.

Andropov became chairman of the USSR Council of Ministers' State Security Committee, or KGB, on May 19, 1967. Some five weeks later, June 21, 1967, he was named a candidate (non-voting) member of the Politburo.[2] Six years after that promotion, he was raised from candidate to full Politburo membership following the plenary session meeting of the Central Committee April 27, 1973. Upon Suslov's death in January 1982, Andropov was named by a Central Committee meeting in May 1982 as Suslov's successor in the Secretariat.

Andropov was not the only official to be named a full Politburo member in April 1973. So also were Andrei Gromyko, the veteran Foreign Minister, and Marshal Andrei Grechko, then Defense Minister. Both men were allowed to skip the customary but not required promotion, first, to Candidate Member and were made full Politburo members at the same time as Andropov. The promotions of these three party hierarchs came at the height of détente—between Nixon's 1972 visit to Moscow and Brezhnev's visit in the summer of 1973 to the U.S.

These three were among the toughest in the Politburo about relations with the U.S. Shortly after his election, Grechko said:

> At the present stage the historic function of the Soviet Armed Forces is not restricted merely to their function in defending our Motherland and the other socialist countries.... The Soviet state supports the national liberation struggle and resolutely resists imperial aggression in whatever distant area of the planet it may appear.[3]

In a speech referred to earlier, Andropov redefined peaceful coexistence in such a fashion as to make the very concept impossible without surrender by non-communist countries to the USSR:

> Life demonstrates that as long as imperialism exists and still maintains its economic and military power, the real danger remains for the people of our country, and for other socialist countries, for all progressive forces and for world peace. . . . Our party and the Soviet government firmly uphold the cause of peaceful coexistence between the States with different social systems. But the Soviet people remember: The more we provide for the security of our motherland, the more we close the borders of the Soviet Union against the agents of imperialism, the more energetically and the firmer will be our counterforce against the enemy, the better results this course [peaceful coexistence] will produce.[4]

This speech was delivered in December 1967, a few months after Andropov became KGB head. Upon his becoming a full Politburo member, it was quite clear that his attitude towards peaceful coexistence hadn't changed at all:

> Recently the countries of the socialist commonwealth have increasingly encountered actions by imperialist forces that can be termed ideological sabotage. . . . Today the opponents of easing tension place special emphasis on sabotage in the field of ideology. As is known, an acute struggle between socialism and capitalism is unfolding in this area now. It could not be otherwise . . .
> In the sphere of ideology, imperialism is trying to use ways and means of sabotage aimed at, through deception and falsification, distorting the Soviet Union's peace-loving foreign policy. . . . Their [imperialists] goal comes down to undermining Soviet power from within and liquidating the gains of socialism.[5]

Andropov's promotion to full Politburo membership was a striking symbol of his importance in the Soviet hierarchy. Except for Beria, no previous secret police chief had ever enjoyed full Politburo membership while heading the secret police. And no other KGB head had ever achieved what Andropov was to achieve in 1982—election as General Secretary of the Communist Party.

However, *Chekists* (the generic Soviet term for people who have served in the secret police) have often reached high Soviet posts, though not the very top like Andropov. The first head of the secret police, Feliks Dzherzhinskiy, was extraordinarily close to Lenin, and while he ran the secret police organization, then known as the *Cheka* and OGPU, he also supervised the national economy. Chernenko, Andropov's rival for the Party leadership and Brezhnev's "favorite son," was in the NKVD in 1938. Arvid Pelshe, the octogenarian member of the Politburo, began as a Chekist and was in the NKVD right through World War II. Geidar Aliyev spent 28 years in the KGB, became the party First Secretary of Azerbaijan, a Politburo member, and presently is First Deputy Premier of the Council of Ministers. Eduard Shevardnadze spent seven years as MVD head in the Georgia republic, and became first party secretary of the republic and a Politburo candidate member. Aleksandr N. Aksenov, deputy KGB chief in Byelorussia went from MVD minister to chairman of the Byelorussian Council of Ministers. Valter Klauson was an NKVD official under Beria from 1937 to 1953 and is at this writing chairman of the Estonian Council of Ministers and candidate member of the Communist Party Central Committee.[6] Bulganin, Soviet Premier from 1955 to 1958, was also in the Cheka.

Andropov's success can be contrasted with the aborted success of Aleksandr Shelepin, KGB chief from 1958 to 1961, and with the story of Andropov's predecessor, Vladimir Ye. Semichastny, KGB chairman from 1961 to 1967. During the early 1960s, Shelepin looked the rising star in Khrushchev's firmament. At one time Shelepin held simultaneous membership in the Secretariat of the Central Committee, deputy premier of the Chairman of the Council of Ministers, and chairman of a new

Party-State Control Committee. Khrushchev permitted Shelepin to put in Semichastny, a Shelepin client, as KGB chairman. And after Khrushchev's ouster, Shelepin became a
member of the Presidium (later the Politburo) of the Central
Committee. This was an extraordinary array of overlapping
institutions in the Soviet hierarchy.[7]

Semichastny's contribution to the KGB and to Soviet internal
propaganda was his article in *Pravda,* May 4, 1965, which
praised the traditions and the activities of the Soviet secret
police agencies while glossing over the crimes of the Stalin era.
The article praised Soviet intelligence agents for their "honor-
able work in the struggle with the enemy." A series of Soviet
press articles followed Semichastny's contribution in the form
of a publicity campaign that included the glorification of the
Soviet spy, Col. Rudolf Abel.

When Shelepin's power base eroded, it was the end for
Semichastny. However, the KGB chief had had his own troubles. One of them, reportedly, was the fact that Svetlana Alliluyeva, Stalin's estranged daughter, had been allowed to leave
the USSR for India, carrying the ashes of her late Indian hus-
band, and had then sought political asylum at the U.S. Embassy
in New Delhi. This embarrassment was blamed on Semichastny. Khrushchev discusses the Alliluyeva affair with some
candor in his memoirs.[8] The Alliluyeva flight occurred in March
1967, and Semichastny was dismissed shortly thereafter by the
Politburo.

Another more serious contretemps might have threatened
Semichastny's career even earlier. On October 30, 1963, the FBI
in New York captured three KGB officers and an American
engineer at a New York rendezvous. Two of the KGB officers
were untouchable because they worked for the U.N. and, therefore, had diplomatic immunity. The third officer was an Amtorg
trading corporation chauffeur, a position that afforded no com-
parable immunity. The evidence against him was sufficient to
ensure his conviction in an American court.

Khrushchev being out of town, Semichastny got approval from Brezhnev, the number two, to frame as a U.S. spy Professor Frederick C. Barghoorn, the Yale University political scientist and a leading U.S. academic expert on Soviet affairs, who was visiting Moscow. Thereby one could arrange an exchange of "prisoners"—one American Sovietologist for one KGB agent. The KGB arrested Barghoorn as he was entering his hotel. His arrest on espionage charges was kept secret for several days. On November 14, 1963 at a press conference, President John F. Kennedy denounced the arrest and demanded Barghoorn's release. Khrushchev was furious at the embarrassment, not because of the arrest but because the KGB hadn't known that Barghoorn was a friend of the President or that Kennedy would make it a personal issue. Barghoorn was released on November 16.[9]

In any case, it was not Khrushchev who got rid of Semichastny because Semichastny became part of the conspiracy (along with his patron, Shelepin) that ousted Khrushchev in a coup d'état in October 1964. In fact, Semichastny even met Khrushchev at the Moscow Airport after Khrushchev's return from a holiday on October 13, 1964, and drove him to the Politburo meeting where they were waiting to give Khrushchev the bad news, that he was through.

For his timely decision and cooperation, Semichastny was promoted from candidate member of the Central Committee to full member and got three more years as KGB chairman. It is ironic to speculate that had Khrushchev kept in place his original appointee, Ivan A. Serov, as KGB chairman, he might have survived—as he had, with Serov's support, the earlier ouster move in 1957, unsuccessfully engineered by Molotov, Malenkov, Kaganovich, and others.[10]

Andropov's appointment to replace Semichastny in May 1967 was another triumph for the Brotherhood and Suslov. The man selected for the position had now had several years of high-level party work that took him all over Eastern Europe, Cuba, and the People's Republic of China. He had made the acquaintance of the leaders of ruling parties in the Communist world. Chairmanship of the KGB was a logical promotion for him, especially so since he had had a relationship with the secret police for more than 30 years.[11]

The Semichastny-Andropov succession showed once more the significance of patron-client relationships in Soviet politics. Had Andropov been guilty of similar accidents—Alliluyeva or Barghoorn—it would not have mattered very much because Andropov's patron, Suslov in particular and the Brotherhood in general, would have protected him. Since Shelepin wasn't totally disgraced until 1974–1975, Semichastny was sent as Deputy Premier to the Ukrainian Republic.[12]

How does an outsider measure the achievements of a KGB chairman? Since there is not much "inside information" except for what is available from former KGB officers who defect, and since there is no political sub-science, "comparative defection," to determine whose information is more reliable and useful than any other, we are left with "outside information" as the basis for our analysis.

While Andropov has gotten extraordinarily good press in the West as a wily secret police operator, one could make a strong case for Lavrentii Beria as far abler than Andropov. Beria, at one point, was regarded as an intellectual sort of chap, just as Andropov was at his appointment. A number of Western newspapers referred to Andropov's "intellectual" look due to the rimless glasses he used to wear. The same used to be said of Beria, Robert Conquest writes, "who (like Himmler, too) wore pince-nez and whose much-noted 'scrutinizing gaze' gave the impression of an incisive mind working behind them."[13]

It should be remembered that under Beria's chairmanship Stalin was able to penetrate America's atomic weapons research center during World War II and after. It was probably one of the most successful penetrations in the history of espionage since it helped the Soviet Union obtain the kind of weaponry that it might have been unable to develop with its own scientific resources, either in quality of manpower or materials, for years to come. Such a cosmic intelligence coup was all the more striking because U.S. counterespionage—the FBI and later, the CIA—were at the height of their powers and, therefore, afforded the KGB genuine trouble. From 1967 on, when exposes about the FBI and CIA began to be published in the U.S., the FBI and CIA were progressively weakened, in part because of their own self-inflicted wounds. In other words, Beria had a stronger intelligence agency opposing him during his 15 years than Andropov had during his similar time span.

In addition, large sectors of American and Western public opinion regarded the Soviet Union as a beneficent power, whose ethics were probably equal to if not superior to those of the U.S. In 1946, for example, the former U.S. Ambassador to the Soviet Union, Joseph E. Davies, said that "Russia in self-defense has every moral right to seek atomic-bomb secrets through military espionage if excluded from such information by her former fighting allies."[14] One cannot downplay a Soviet achievement of such magnitude, a onetime high-ranking American diplomat's justification of Soviet espionage against his own country.

Such an achievement could well have been the result of Beria's extraordinary ability and signal successes, under Stalin's direction, in penetrating the foreign service corps, intelligence agencies, and parliaments of Britain, the U.S., France, and Canada during the Cold War. Ambassador Davies had, during his wartime service in Moscow, demonstrated that he probably was a member of Lenin's category of "useful idiots."

However, other diplomats, parliamentarians, and intelligence agents were more consciously dedicated, and the Soviets used great skill in exploiting such willing and witting converts to the cause of Soviet foreign policy.

One cannot ignore the tremendous success of the Stockholm Peace Appeal, a purely KGB-inspired international movement in the late 1940-s and early 1950s which obtained half-a-billion signatures for "peace." This "peace" campaign melted away like a summer snow (as had the Communist campaign against Fascism upon the signing of the Nazi-Soviet non-aggression pact in August 1939) with North Korea's invasion of South Korea in June 1950. Yet it was not long before the U.S. found itself facing charges of germ warfare on the Asian mainland.

As to whether or not Beria should be credited with successes like the Stockholm Peace Appeal, the British intelligence penetration, the U.S. Department of State and other government agency penetrations, the Canadian Parliament and External Affairs department penetrations among many other examples, there is this to be said:

Whenever a decision was taken by the Politburo or by Stalin (and it will be true today with Andropov) to pursue a given foreign policy initiative, all kinds of covert action and clandestine collection operations were then and are now orchestrated in support of that initiative.

In fairness to Andropov, life was a lot simpler for a KGB chairman under Stalin than it was under Khrushchev and Brezhnev. As Leonard Schapiro has noted, under Stalin there was "an all-embracing tyranny, with its terror and its ubiquitous spies, with its cowed population which knew the danger of even thinking—let alone uttering—any kind of idea that had not been clearly and specifically approved by the regime. It is all very much more complicated now." For one thing, naked terror has to a large extent been replaced by more subtle methods of intimidation, such as the control over employment and over privileges.[15]

The most common methods of punitive control by the KGB over dissidence and resistance include threats of expulsion from the Party; deprivation of professional status including the right to work in one's area of training; loss of job or sometimes an entire family's means of livelihood; denial of higher education to family members; revoking residence permits for larger cities, especially Moscow; denial of medical treatment; cutting off telephone service, either temporarily or permanently; greater than normal restrictions on travel; psychiatric institutions; exile, prison and prison camps, and forced labor.[16]

Perhaps the unique achievement of the secret police during the Andropov era was the expertise the KGB and their scientific staff developed in the fields of psychiatry and pharmaceutics based on studies of pharmaco-dynamics, a branch of pharmacology dealing with the reactions between drugs and living structures. Such expertise was used in dealing with dissident workers, intellectuals, and other deviates defined in Soviet law as antisocial or parasitical.[17] It was the substitution of zombiism for terrorism, drugging or committing to institutions the rebellious instead of using Stalin's untidy methods of mass physical destruction of Soviet citizens by shooting, starvation, inanition, and overwork in slave labor camps.

The misuse of psychiatry in the Soviet Union has been the subject of criticism by innumerable psychiatrists in Western countries. So serious has been this criticism that the Soviet Union withdrew from the World Psychiatric Association in February 1983 rather than face the possibility of an investigation and suspension from the association at its July 1983 world congress.[18]

Under Andropov's administration, the misuse of psychiatry became widespread and systematic. It became the expression of deliberate government policy, about which even the United

Nations General Assembly passed a resolution in 1981 which declared that "the detention of persons in mental institutions on account of their political views or on other non-medical grounds is a violation of their human rights."[19]

There is some debate as to the number of political psychiatric institutions in the USSR. Whatever the disagreement, there is agreement that the number of such institutions increased with Andropov's arrival on the scene as KGB chief. General Petro Grigorenko, a victim of one of these hospitals and later exiled from the USSR, says that when Andropov came on the scene, there were three. Between 1967 and 1974, eight more were added, and as of 1982, there were thirty. The U.S. Mission to the U.N., however, claims that there are twelve.[20]

One drug administered to dissidents is sulfazine, a mixture of sulfuric acid in peach oil, which "was discovered and used in the West in the 1930s but has no respected position in present-day Western pharmacology." Other drugs used are insulin to bring on shock on non-diabetic individuals, aminazin, which produces extreme depression, and reserpine.[21]

In recent years and especially since Andropov's rise to power, there has been a tendency in the Western media and among Western statesman like Vice-President Bush to downplay the importance of the KGB in Soviet affairs.[22] Yet those who know how the Soviet Union functions have come to quite different conclusions about the importance of the KGB. For example, Marshal Tito in an authorized biography was quoted about the NKVD, the KBG's predessor organization:

> During the past fifteen years [from 1953], an important role has been acquired by the intelligence service, the NKVD. Instead of a weapon to fight counterrevolution, it has grown into a force in itself; instead of being an instrument of the revolution, it has become a power above Soviet society. The entire activity of the

country, the Party, the whole foreign policy—all rests upon the intelligence service; its reports are given priority, it really rules the country.[23]

Has there been much change in the relationship between the secret police and the Party itself? The KGB is and it always has been an *imperium in imperio,* a state within a state, which is why it was feared not only by the Soviet peoples but by Party leaders as well. It is much more than just an espionage agency and secret police army. As Walter Laqueur has pointed out, the Soviet system "needs the KGB to survive and yet it is always a potential threat to the ruling bureaucracy. . . . While the Soviet Union has always been a police state, the police have never run it." Harry Rozitske, a former CIA executive, has written that "the singular power of the KGB derives from its combining both the functions of internal security and secret foreign operations, as if the FBI and CIA in the U.S. were operating under a single chief."[24]

One of the most effective methods of ensuring internal security long used by the secret police is forced labor. As noted earlier, Andropov is no stranger to the use of forced labor on the massive scale that characterized the Stalin era. Even though forced labor practices have undergone some change since Stalin's death, the USSR still exploits forced labor on a large scale to such a degree that it is no exaggeration to say that the Soviet forced labor system is the largest in the world, with an estimated total Soviet penal population of four million persons: 2 million incarcerated in a network of 1,100 forced labor camps; 2 million living as unconfined forced laborers, as probationers or parolees or other categories. Probationers are forced laborers sentenced directly to construction sites instead of incarceration. They live in mobile trailers or fenced areas. Parolees are forced laborers released from camps to serve the remainder of their sentences at construction sites.[25]

While administration of these camps is not under the direct control of the KGB, it is the KGB that supplies manpower for them, since the police agency is concerned with putting down dissidents, religious leaders, deviants, and so-called anti-Soviet elements. Large numbers of the forced laborers are categorized as common criminals guilty of infractions of the criminal code. Others are borderline cases, between common criminals and political prisoners. Some 10,000—perhaps more—can be described as political and religious prisoners.[26]

Charges of forced labor have been under investigation by the International Labor Organization for thirty years following a U.N. report submitted May 1953 by a U.N. Committee on Forced Labor.[27] The question has developed great urgency in recent years because of charges that forced labor is being used in the construction of the export pipeline to Western Europe. The investigations by the ILO and other organizations will go on, and so will Soviet forced labor.

The most serious episode in Andropov's KGB career—serious at least in the West—occurred at the moment of his triumph in November 1982. He was suspect—he, the KGB, and the Bulgarian secret police—as having arranged the attempt on the life of Pope John Paul II in St. Peter's Square in Vatican City on May 13, 1981.

Several mysteries present themselves when one begins to try to separate fact from rumor, evidence from allegation. But on one question, there is no mystery to be solved:

No matter what stories, rumors, gossip, "smoking gun" testimony may or may not confirm the KGB-Bulgarian connection, no one, except of course Soviet spokesmen, has suggested that any country but the Soviet Union and its secret police and satellite branches might have been the culprit. There are some

164 countries in the world, but it is an ironic tribute to Andropov's formidable reputation as the master plotter, ruthless and ingenious, that no other country has been singled out as the possible instigator of the shooting. And it is a well-deserved reputation. After all no other country in the twentieth century has been accused of so many successful assassinations ("wet affairs" in KGB slang) and abductions as has the USSR.[28]

Of course the *cui bono* motive is easily fixed on Andropov and the USSR—Poland, Lech Walesa, Solidarity—motives enough to plot the assassination of this turbulent priest. But probability is not evidence, and all there may be is suspicion on suspicion fed by tiny, tantalizing facts. What evidence has been uncovered so far about the KGB connection with the attempted assassination of the pope is circumstantial. There is no question, however, that if the Bulgarian involvement is authenticated then the Andropov connection becomes certain.[29]

One of the few defenses of Andropov and the innocence of the KGB is another ironic tribute to the KGB's reputation: Had the KGB really planned the affair, the pope would be dead and there would be no Mehmet Ali Agca, the would-be assassin, in the hands of the Italian police and courts to start blabbing. An unnamed diplomat was quoted early in 1983 as saying that: "The trouble with the Bulgarian theory is that the plot was so . . . so *unprofessional.*"[30]

There is one mystery that has not been easy to crack and that is the silence, the reticence, the unwillingness of the U.S. government and its intelligence agencies to get involved in the investigation, which was presumably proceeding in spring 1983. The same reticence was to be noticed among the Western powers. The possible reason?

"If Moscow is behind Agca and the Bulgarians," wrote *Newsweek,* "most Western governments would rather not know about it; the effects on arms control, trade and other East-West relations could be devastating."[31]

A similar point was made by Claire Sterling before a Joint Committee of Congress, the Commission on Security and Cooperation in Europe. The author of a best-selling exposé on international terrorism, Mrs. Sterling told the Commission on September 23, 1982:

> I can say from personal knowledge that none of the governments concerned really wanted to press this investigation to a conclusion, that all of them to some degree went to considerable length to avoid following the most promising indications, any indications that pointed eastward, to avoid looking the reality in the face, although I think all of them were reasonably sure, in a general way without specific or precise knowledge of details, who was behind this monstrous act.[32]

It may be that President Reagan, Prime Minister Thatcher, President Mitterand, Chancellor Kohl, and whoever is now the Italian Premier, all hope that their prudent behavior toward a fellow-statesman in trouble will be repaid by Andropov in some appropriate manner at some appropriate time. If that, indeed, is the motive for the tight-lipped, eyes-heavenward demeanor of Western statesmen, then it is equally prudent to anticipate Western disappointment at Kremlin ingratitude before so noble and charitable an act of sovereign indulgence.

There is a huge and burgeoning literature about the KGB that deals extensively with its manifold activities, at home and abroad, with its capacity for subversion and terrorism, its organization of subventioned fronts—labor, peace, women, students, journalists, doctors—wherever and whenever necessary as occasioned by the zigs and zags of Soviet foreign policy and imperial aims. Few who have studied the operations of the KGB and its predecessor agencies have sought to minimize its effectiveness.

And the KGB is effective because it is geared to a single

objective—ideological supremacy on behalf of the Soviet Union
—and it is as prepared for ideologico-political warfare as the
Soviet regime is for nuclear and non-nuclear warfare. Its effectiveness also arises from the fact that no matter who is the head
of the secret police agency, its institutional memory and its
institutional objective is always there. No matter the shakeup,
no matter the purges and executions of KGB executives and
rank-and-file, characteristic of the Stalin era, the KGB has first
call on the resources and on the population of the USSR, particularly the latter from among whom the KGB recruits its vast
network of informers.

The KGB has had its share of defeats but its triumphs have
been many, especially since the weakening of the CIA to such a
degree that some informed people "believe that the CIA has been
'turned around' and that revitalizing the agency, instead of
starting a new one, would merely strengthen the possible KGB
penetrators in the CIA right now . . ."[33]

Under Andropov, the KGB has become a *corps d'élite* in Soviet
politics. Add to the KGB the manpower of the satellite police
agencies, and there is a formidable force against the weakened
and probably well-penetrated non-Communist intelligence
agencies.

The KGB has also kept pace, as have Soviet scientists, with
new scientific discoveries and their applications. As Richard
Helms, former CIA director, said: "Under Andropov, the Soviet
Union has refined and expanded its intelligence targets. The
new focus in on technology."[34]

To put it less delicately, the new focus means a tremendous
concentration in America's Silicon Valleys of KGB manpower.

Having strengthened the home front by crushing the dissident movements into voicelessness, Andropov now sits in a
position of power where the KGB directorates will be far more in
evidence than ever before in the history of the Soviet secret

police. The increase in KGB activity in the West has resulted in expulsion of Soviet "diplomats" and "journalists" by Western governments. In April of 1983, the French government expelled 47 Soviet "diplomats." However, the all-time record for such reprisals by a Western government is held by Britain, which, in 1971, expelled 105 Soviet "diplomats" and "journalists."

Andropov's greatest achievement—and it antedates his accession to the post of General Secretary—has been to create a passionate demand in the United States and Western Europe for disarmament of one side only. The demonstrations, the sit-ins, the lie-downs, the propaganda are almost completely against American arms while Soviet military power grows without eliciting similar protests from those who reprobate the U.S. defense budget. This is not to suggest that the "peace movement" is KGB-controlled. It is merely to call attention to a great feat in public relations and opinion manipulation by Andropov's talented specialists, who know the West's weaknesses.

17

The Challenges Within: Can Andropov Survive?

YURI Andropov reached the pinnacle of personal power on November 12, 1982. He may not be able to savor his achievement long. At the age of 68, when he took office as General Secretary of the Soviet Communist Party, he was the oldest to attain that exalted position. Brezhnev was 58 years old when he reached the top, Khrushchev 59, Malenkov 51, Stalin 50, and Lenin 47.

But there is this great difference between Andropov's arrival on the scene and those of his predecessors. The Soviet Union today, *militarily*, has never in its history been as powerful as it confronts the *glavnyi vrag*, the Soviet phrase for the main enemy—the United States. No matter how one counts the tanks, the manpower, the missiles, the battleships, the submarines, the planes, at the very minimum the USSR today is the equal of the U.S. in military power. Some military experts say that the USSR is ahead, far ahead of the U.S. in military power, whether nuclear or non-nuclear.[1]

There is also a vast difference between Andropov and his peers, the younger ones as well as his own contemporaries. That difference relates to his utter lack of preparation for the job of administering a virtual subcontinent afflicted by enormous social and economic problems that cry for some solution.

Andropov never studied engineering or agronomy; he never managed a factory, nor did he ever direct a city or industrial region. Nor can it be assumed that a man who spent 15 years as head of the KGB and before that in strictly Party ideological and staff work as a sub-Politburo apparatchik, that such a man will have any more than an autodidactic appreciation of economics. Such deficiencies in knowledge or experience could not be attributed to Party leaders like Brezhnev, Viktor Grishin, Vladimir Dolgikh, and Andropov's possible successor, Mikhail Gorbachev, who is concerned with agriculture.

One can attribute Andropov's selection over Chernenko as General Secretary to his acute political cunning, his control of police dossiers on everybody right up to Brezhnev's family.[2] It is also possible that he was selected because of apprehension among the Party chieftains that matters at home needed a firm repressive hand and who better than a man experienced in successfully putting down unrest and dissidence.[3]

According to *The Economist,* Andropov won over Chernenko because, judging from their Party careers, Andropov "had more solid political experience to offer and because over the years he had been able carefully to build up the kind of independent constituency within the party that Mr. Chernenko lacked."[4]

Since the Khrushchev years have demonstrated that it is possible to oppose the General Secretary and sometimes get away with it, Politburo members like the disaffected Chernenko, might have exacted an agreement from Andropov that he would be no more than a *primus inter pares,* a first among equals. Chernenko, Andropov's rival for the top spot, in proposing Andropov's election, stressed the need for collective leadership. In mourning Brezhnev's passing ("it will be extremely difficult to make good the loss we have suffered with the death of Leonid Ilyich") he said: "It is now doubly—triply—important to conduct affairs in the Party collectively. Harmonious joint work in all Party organs will ensure further success both in building communism and in our activities in the international arena."[5]

However the new Andropov regime works out, its economic difficulties will be enormous and more difficult to solve than ever. Soviet industrial performance has been steadily declining, and this decline will accelerate as manpower shortages spread throughout the economy. There is already and will continue to be insufficient increments in domestic capital investment during the 1980s.[6] U.S. banks will be unable to lend the Soviets as much money as they did during the Brezhnev era because the euphoric days of petrodollar windfalls seem to be over. With the coming end of the U.S. recession and lowering of domestic interest rates, borrowing demands will increase within the United States. Plus the unhappy realization by the U.S. banking industry that the Soviet bloc COMECON countries owe the West an estimated $90 billion that these Communist countries cannot service.[7] Thus far, East-West "trade" during the years of détente has, in the final analysis, been no trade at all. The USSR sold some oil, gold, and diamonds to the West, but mostly the USSR bought goods from the West with funds borrowed from Western banks, which eventually will have to be repaid probably by Western taxpayers. East-West trade is really in the nature of a Western welfare program for the COMECON countries.

In the 1980s, the Soviet Union will badly need a leader who is a successful economic manager and an expert in agriculture.

Andropov, the party functionary, the secret police chief, the ideologue-in-chief since Suslov's passing, lacks adequate experience to fill such a role. The Soviet leaders who ran the economy (one might say, ran it into the ground) under Brezhnev may be unwilling to serve Andropov in the same capacity since, like Gorbachev, they are his natural competitors for eventual power. In the foreseeable future, therefore, the logic of events and the logic of the internal struggle for power will force the Politburo to replace Andropov, the political transitionalist, by an economic manager. Or by a Red Army general who understands the relationship between arms, agriculture, and economics.

It is not widely known in the West that food rationing in peacetime is no longer unusual in the Soviet Union. So much has been officially admitted by Eduard Shevardnadze, an alternate member of the Politburo.[8] And this was not the first occasion that rationing had been introduced in peacetime. We have the official admission in a Soviet publication in 1965 that during the Khrushchev years there were, literally, breadlines.[9]

The Soviet Union, in 1982, suffered its fourth disastrous harvest in a row. There is no reason to expect that future harvests will be much better than the preceding ones. The Soviet target for grain production during the 1981–1985 Five Year Plan was to average at least 238 million metric tons (mmt) per year. In actual fact, the annual yields were:

> 1979—179 mmt
> 1980—189 mmt
> 1981—165 mmt (estimate of the O.E.C.D.)
> 1982—170 mmt (estimate of U.S. Agriculture Dept.)[10]

The old alibi, weather, is no longer acceptable, although Brezhnev used it as his explanation for poor grain production. The major responsibility for the agricultural and food crisis is the utter inadequacy of economic investment in Soviet agriculture, especially (a) the neglect of fallow fields, (b) the lack of crop rotation, (c) the shortage of fertilizer, and (d) the constant breakdown of agricultural machinery. Together, these factors have produced a tremendous amount of soil erosion, a condition that cannot be corrected in a short period of time nor can it correct itself as, say, the weather can. At this writing, the Soviet government has no program to halt soil erosion.[11]

Under Andropov, even more than was the case under Brezhnev, the USSR will continue to depend upon the West for grain, farm machinery, technology, and credits. What might, however, appear to be a bleak picture is lightened somewhat by the fact that the U.S. is committed to sell grain to the USSR. In 1983, another disastrous harvest is expected, the fifth in as many years, a record unprecedented since the Biblical days of Joseph and Pharaoh in Egypt. The USSR will have to purchase at least 46 million metric tons annually on the world market to supply feed for livestock and to replace stock changes in the USSR's strategic grain reserve.

All other grain-exporting countries combined—Argentina, Canada, Australia, and the European Community—cannot provide this amount of grain. Therefore, despite its expressed reluctance to buy on the American market, the USSR must come to the U.S. Fortunately for the USSR the present Administration is committed to selling the USSR as much as half of the grain requirements, 23 mmt. Thanks to American business generosity, the Soviets were in the recent decade able not only to keep their livestock at a level of subsistence and to prevent human starvation, but, more importantly, they were able to accumulate an impressive amount of strategic grain reserves, more than 90 mmt. This amount is enough to compensate for the domestic harvest shortages for the next 8-to-12 years, at least at subsistence levels for the population.[12]

West European and Japanese bank consortia appear eager to finance by Western government guaranteed loans at low rates of interest (less than eight percent), the USSR's major project for the 1980s—the six Siberian pipelines, only one of which is intended for gas export to Western Europe.

The Soviets recently revealed that the entire six-pipeline project cost is 25 billion rubles. At the same time, it is known and the Soviets themselves admit it, that the West is providing, in a form of bartered commodities valued at $15 billion, a sum that presumably would in time be repaid in Soviet natural gas.[13]

At the official rate of exchange, the Western supply of $15 billion worth of pipes and other technology is worth more than the 11 billion rubles, the nominal proceeds of the rate of exchange. Thus about one-half of the entire project—or about three pipelines—will be built on the basis of the Western commodity supply while only one pipeline is intended to serve Western energy needs. However, since certain of the commodities being supplied by the West—56-inch pipe or 25 megaton rotors and compressors and other items that the USSR is incapable of producing—the entire volume of Western technology items, worth $15 billion, is far more than is needed for one or for three pipelines.

In fact, the entire Soviet project of six pipelines, five of which will serve Soviet domestic and military needs, will have been built on the basis of Western technological and financial aid. Therefore, one can conclude that under the disguise of one export pipeline, the Soviets are solving their energy needs for the present decade and, perhaps, beyond, by the generosity of Western banks, Western industrial firms—in short, Western governments.[14]

At a time of declining petroleum prices, the entire natural gas deal will yield none of the expected benefits for Western Europe. Soviet repayments for the $15 billion worth of barter become even more questionable when Soviet energy needs, domestic and especially military, have been satisfied.

But whatever happens on the industrial front, the crisis that appears insoluble is in agriculture, and, given the dedication of the Politburo leadership to the status quo—centralization—in agriculture, it is unlikely that there will be the kind of positive change that would alleviate the crisis, let alone solve it.

We have referred earlier to Gorbachev as a coming man in the Politburo. We have no intention of predicting the course of Soviet leadership struggles; such prophecies have a short life. Gorbachev, however, is an example of why the USSR cannot solve its agricultural crisis. Gorbachev was appointed in November 1978 as CPSU secretary in charge of agriculture at a special Plenum devoted to the agricultural question. Usually several years pass before a Party secretary becomes, first, an alternate or candidate member and then a full member of the Politburo. Gorbachev beat the record. In October 1980, only two years after joining the secretariat, he was appointed a full Politburo member.[15] And only three months after he joined the supreme Party body, he had formulated the most radical reforms in the history of the Soviet economy since the 1920s.

On January 18, 1981, the CPSU Central Committee violated the usual procedure of discussing major decisions at the Party Plenum. The Central Committee issued a decree on the subject of private subsistence plots.[16] The decree was forced upon the Party because of the U.S. grain embargo, which the Carter Administration had imposed on the USSR because of the Soviet invasion of Afghanistan. The grain embargo was a severe blow to the Soviet economy.

According to the decree, private enterprise was to be encouraged to produce more milk, meat, beef, poultry, eggs, and vegetables. Then current limits on the use of private land for farming and animal husbandry were abolished, although the land itself remained State property. The peasants could farm the land and sell the produce, but they could not buy or sell the land. The State imposed one condition, that additional livestock output derived from the private plots could be sold to the socialized sector with—*mirabile dictu*—a negotiable price. This proviso was significant since it seemed to hint at a market approach.

Sales of socialized livestock to private households were encouraged with no requirement that the meat and milk they produce be sold to the socialized sector. In addition, plot growers were granted other concessions that enabled them to sell food produce and livestock for profit.

The USSR State Bank was instructed to provide credits to private plot holders. Livestock could be sold to the private sector on liberal credit terms. Peasants were to be allowed to buy truck farm machinery with 50 percent cash advances from State banks for use on the expanded plots. These reforms were far-reaching and can be described as a second NEP [New Economic Policy] in the animal husbandry branch of agriculture. Some Soviet economists went a step further and suggested extending this reform to Soviet agriculture as a whole.

Six months later, in the summer of 1981, two leading Soviet economists openly proposed in an academic journal a radical restructuring of the links between the industrial and agricultural sectors. The proposal meant that the leading sectors of agriculture would be practically excluded from the central planning system.[17]

There is little question that such changes would have been popular with the Soviet public, a popularity that might even have spilled over onto Brezhnev and his associates. But the reforms never got a chance to be put into practice. Brezhnev, Prime Minister Tikhonov, and other officials went out of their way to criticize a scheme that entailed, according to their perceptions, a departure from a centrally planned and therefore controlled economy either in agriculture or the economy as a whole.

The reform decree, it is now known, was promulgated January 18, 1981 with great reluctance by the Central Committee.

Neither *Pravda* nor *Kommunist,* the main party organs, carried the news of the decree. In fact, the text was published in only one academic agricultural journal and in a specialized agricultural paper.[18] Indeed, the Central Committee imposed upon itself a strange self-censorship in failing to issue the decree.

Ten weeks after passage of the Central Committee decree, April 1, 1981, President Reagan lifted the U.S. grain embargo and American grain exports began to move to the USSR. Thereby the USSR was enabled to solve what had been previously an unmanageable problem, namely, providing sufficient feed for livestock. The cautious, first step toward reform came to an abrupt stop. The decree wasn't mentioned in the Soviet press again. There was no point in recounting how central planning had almost ceased to be, at least, in food production.

While the majority of Politburo members were delighted with the course of events, Gorbachev's adherents, most of them trained experts, began to publish articles in economic and agricultural journals, articles that implied criticism of Brezhnev's agricultural policies. Three such articles actually appeared in the leading Central Committee journal, *Kommunist* (No. 13 [1981], Nos. 2 and 12 [1982].[19] Publication of such articles was a rather extraordinary departure from Party discipline and one that seemed to indicate the existence of a Gorbachev lobby even among Central Committee ideologists.

This episode is important in understanding the future course of Soviet domestic policies. There is a split at the top, one that Andropov will have to deal with. Recently two long-time supporters and appointees of Brezhnev and Chernenko, the Soviet Minister of Agriculture, Valentin Mesiats, and the Soviet Minister of Procurement, Gregory Zolotukhin, published articles on future prospects for the Soviet food economy. Both officials implied that to solve the food problem, policy-makers would have to go beyond the routine bureaucratic measures adopted by the Party Plenum in May 1982.[20]

What can be reported about the course of this inner Party split is that Andropov is siding with the conservatives, not with Gorbachev and the would-be "reformers." This can be seen by Andropov's action, upon taking power, in dismissing Petr Alekseev, editor-in-chief of *Izvestiya* and by Soviet standards, a "liberal," a "reformer." Alekseev was for agricultural reform and was Gorbachev's spokesman.[21] Alekseev's predecessor on *Izvestiya* had been L. N. Tolkunov, appointed after Khrushchev's ouster. Tolkunov had been Andropov's first deputy at the time Andropov had been in charge of the Central Committee department of liaison with ruling Communist parties.[22]

Western analysts have ignored the meaning of Andropov's action at the end of 1982 in appointing Tolkunov as editor-in-chief of *Izvestiya,* the position he had held during the first years of Brezhnev's tenure.

Alekseev's article in *Kommunist* (No. 2, 1982) criticized seventeen years of Brezhnev's agricultural policies. In other words, in the Party's main ideological journal, *Kommunist,* the then editor-in-chief of *Izvestiya* and other writers like Academician V. Mozhin (*Kommunist,* No. 13, 1981) and two economists like E. Krylatykh and A. Lifanchikov in the academic journal, *Voprosii Ekononiki* (No. 7, 1981) were attacking certain principles of the planned economy. These articles were written while Brezhnev was still alive.

Alekseev's dismissal early in Andropov's rule and Alekseev's replacement by a hard-line, ultra-conservative, anti-agricultural reformer like Tolkunov tells us a great deal more about the course of the economy, specifically, and reform, generally, under Andropov than all the fairy tales about Andropov's love of Scotch, jazz, and Jaqueline Susann's novels.

The long and short of it is that Andropov has come to power determined to change nothing, to ease no burdens. There will be no "thaw," the metaphor once used after Stalin's demise to express hope in the future. Changes in the economy? Why bother when the West is there to help with grain shipments, technology, and manufactured goods on easy credit terms?

There are more important matters to work on—future relations with China, the crisis in Poland for which there can be no end so long as Poles are Poles and there is a Polish Pope, the Afghanistan quagmire, the "star war" scenarios of President Reagan, the refusal of German voters in 1983 to pay any attention to Soviet suggestions on how to vote in the Bundestag elections, U.S. dominance—for the moment—in the Middle East, what happens after Khomeini goes.

Trying to change things leads to disaster, as Khrushchev learned to his sorrow when he tried "to shake up the ossified state and party bureaucracy."[23] But every new Soviet leader wants to change things, if only to show the Soviet peoples and the outside world that what went before was inferior and that we must not think of the ugly, decadent past but of the radiant present and the even more radiant future. If he could, the new Soviet leader, like Robespierre and Danton, would remake Time and 1983 would become the Year One, just as the French revolutionaries wiped out the year 1792.

So we see Yuri Andropov now in his Year One announcing a campaign against corruption, slackness at the work place, back to law-and-order, down with violators of the law, down with crooks, chiselers, and layabouts. The Western press was full of such nonsense for a few weeks after Andropov emerged as the Kremlin winner. One of the few Sovietologists to understand the ineradicable interpenetration of corruption in the structure of Soviet society is Alain Besançon who, describing corruption as "a sickness of communism," has written:

> As a result, in the confrontation between "them" [the Party] and "us," between the Party and civil society, corruption is for civil society a symbol of health. It is a manifestation of life, of a pathological existence but also of something which is worth more than death. Corruption translates itself by a rebirth of personal

life, for the very figure who is trafficking in corruption thereby becomes an individual, a person who has won something. The relations among men, instead of being molded in the melting pot ideology, returns to the terra firma of reality: personal interest, the argument over what is mine and what is yours, a negotiated partnership between citizens which allows them a certain autonomy.[24]

Andropov is just the man to try and rid himself of "corruption" because, like his mentor, Suslov, he is a Marxist-Leninist ideologue and Marxist-Leninist socialism cannot permit "corruption" to exist because it is against the ideology.

However, the truth is that Andropov won't wipe out corruption for three reasons. First, if he should by any chance try to enforce his edicts, the Soviet economy and Soviet productivity will grow even worse. The "second economy," or the "gray-black" economy, is what makes the Soviet state function. The "second economy" is what makes life bearable for everybody. The consumer can obtain various kinds of food, goods, and services otherwise unobtainable in official shops. The people who provide these foods, goods, and services profit and can in turn better their lives through the "second economy."

The "second economy" system is what provides the incentives for people to produce. To weaken these incentives by a drive against "corruption" will decrease what productivity exists now. Brezhnev was more flexible, and those under him tolerated the "corruption" because they were afraid of what might happen if it were stopped. The only way to stop the "gray-black" economy is to execute people for "economic crimes" or to jail them or to exile them to the virgin lands of Siberia.

Second, the main target of Andropov's anti-corruption drive will be the factory workers, because that's where the problem of productivity exists. He has already made it clear by publicity campaigns that there will have to be discipline at the work-place.

And the campaign will be based on the policy, initiated by Stalin, of fear and punishment. But the Soviet worker works no more than he has to for all the rewards he gets either in money or goods or services. The tremendous absenteeism is the natural adjustment by workers to the low state of morale. Neither fear nor punishment will induce him to work harder.

The third reason why the Andropov fight against corruption will not work is that it is not directed against the biggest reason for low productivity in the Soviet Union—alcoholism at the work-place. It is no reflection on Soviet workers, but many of them, men and women, are drunk, half-drunk, glazed when they work. That is why machinery is broken and products are of low quality. Alcoholism was an issue in the USSR—for a short while—during the Brezhnev era. Declining productivity is caus- ally related to alcoholism and absenteeism—but Andropov has not at this writing raised the question.

The reason has to do with Soviet tax policy, Cuban sugar, and the Soviet budget. The Soviets in 1979 bought Cuban sugar at 44¢ a pound when the world price was about 10¢. The Soviets also sell petroleum to Cuba at half the world market price.[25] To compensate for the negative economic impact of subsidizing Cuba, the Soviets have been using imported Cuban sugar at home.

From 1963 onward, a year after the Soviet-American missile crisis over Cuba, the Soviet Union began to import Cuban sugar at an almost frenzied rate. Soviet distillers began to process sugar into alcohol, a highly inefficient and wasteful method of alcohol production. As calculated by Dr. Vladimir G. Treml, the leading U.S. expert on Soviet alcohol manufacture, in terms of Soviet prices, sugar-produced alcohol is twice as expensive as alcohol produced from corn and about 57 percent more expen- sive than that produced from other grains or potatoes.[26]

The single most important article in Soviet industry and the most important sector of the Soviet budget is—alcohol. Dr. Treml estimated that during the last 15 to 20 years, Soviet turnover taxes collected on the sale of alcoholic beverages, vodka mostly, in retail trade comprised some 11 to 12 percent of all State revenues and *more than one-third of all taxes paid by the Soviet population.* Taxes on alcohol in the 1960s and the 1970s actually exceeded reported Soviet defense spending.[27]

Given the importance of liquor to Soviet finance, the Kremlin dreads above all the prospect that the Soviet consumer, no longer able to purchase state-produced vodka because of the price, will turn to moonshine, home brew (*samogon*).[28] The government has continued to raise the price of alcohol significantly over the past twelve years. Recently prices went up three times in succession by some 12 to 14 percent on each occasion. These price increases have, according to Soviet sources, had a two-fold purpose: to diminish the USSR's devastating alcoholism and to cope with hidden inflation, by withdrawing more cash from the population at a time of increasing wages. But there is a hidden third reason: the steep increase in the proportion of subsidized Cuban cane sugar used in the production of Soviet alcohol.

Despite the putative Soviet attempt to fight alcoholism, the Soviet leadership has been forced to encourage it. The Kremlin's number one priority is to subsidize Cuba and her destabilizing activities in the Western hemisphere even if it means declining productivity of the Soviet economy and deterioration in the health of the Soviet population.

The primitive Andropov approach to management of industry is about the worst possible approach to improving or raising worker productivity. As far as working conditions are concerned there are a number of important basic facts about the USSR and its food supply:

Soviet farmers do not have enough feed for their livestock, thus the animals are undernourished.

During the recent past, the already inadequate supply of milk and meat has decreased by at least three percent annually.[29]

Milk is available only to small children and by doctor's prescription for anyone else.

In many places meat is rationed at one kilogram per month per working person.

Average food consumption per capita in the USSR now stands at below the recommended, 3,000 calories per day. (This recommended average was reached but once in recent years, in 1979, after the exceptionally good harvest of 1978.[30])

There is one more crisis that will someday soon arrive on the Soviet scene. It is one that doesn't seem to concern the Politburo and Andropov, himself, or other Marxist-Leninist "conservatives." It is the demographic crisis.[31]

During the last 65 years, the USSR has suffered a succession of demographic disasters on a super-scale: populations have been wiped out because of civil war, liquidation of workers and peasants opposed to the regime, the effects of enforced industrialization, the collectivization of agriculture, the purges, the Gulag archipelago, the successive man-made famines, and, of course, World War II.

As if all these disasters were not enough, the Soviet Union is now experiencing a striking rise in its general mortality rate. Fertility is declining. In most of the Soviet Union, the fertility rate no longer suffices for the mere replacement of generations. Russians, Latvians, Ukrainians, Estonians all face declining birth rates. The ethnic Russians will begin to diminish in absolute numbers of the population from 1995 onward.

There are many reasons for this crisis, which mounts with each passing year. The average duration of life declined in the USSR from 69.5 years in 1960/70 to 68.0 in 1978/79. The respective figures for ethnic Russians are 68.6 years in 1969/70 to 66.9 in 1978/79. Duration of life of an average male in the USSR is now below 62 years and that of ethnic Russian males does not exceed 60.5 years.

As far as the declining fertility of Soviet European nationalities is concerned, fertility is limited not only by voluntary birth control but also by government policy. Since the USSR produces few contraceptives and those produced are of low quality, most women of non-Muslim origin, therefore, resort to induced abortions. Given the inadequate state of Soviet health services, abortions are performed by surgical methods—dilation and curettage—which are apt to be harmful to the woman. There are more than 2.5 induced abortions per one live birth in the USSR as a whole. On an average, six abortions occur during the fertile period of each ethnic Russian woman, a rather sad world record.

With each additional surgical abortion the risk of sterility increases. At least 75 percent of those women who have reached the age of 33 or 34 no longer are capable of giving birth. Most women in their early thirties do not want any more children, with the result that about 95 percent of Russian women no longer reproduce after the age of 33. Unless the Soviet Union embarks on a series of striking policy changes that would improve the quality of life, the ethnic Russians are on the road to ethnic extinction.

On the other hand, the Muslim peoples in the Soviet Union continue to multiply. Owing to the rapid rate of natural Muslim increase, greater than three percent a year, and to the declining natural increase of the ethnic Russians, an important demographic change has occurred: the ethnic Russians are today no longer a majority, but rather a plurality, in the Soviet Union.

By the year 2050, the ethnic Russians will constitute less than one-third of the population. Their position in the twenty-first century might, demographically, increasingly resemble that of the South African whites, with all the portentous consequences.

There are many forces working at cross purposes in the USSR. One of the most important in the country's power balance at the top is the military. They know, as the beneficiaries of the system, that the Soviet infrastructure is a shaky one, even though their armed might and their share of the national budget is as great, if not greater, than it ever has been. Both Brezhnev and Andropov have pledged to maintain Soviet military power above all other domestic considerations. But the military know the problems of the country probably better than the Politburo because they know the recruits that are drafted into the services. One can get more than a glimpse of what it is like inside the Soviet armed forces from recent interviews with Soviet deserters in Afghanistan, who have spoken on television or in newspaper interviews. The lack of enthusiasm for service in Afghanistan and the absence of loyalty to those in command and to the Soviet government is striking, according to Anatoly Zakharov, a Russian private and originally a farm worker, who deserted the Red Army in Afghanistan. Resentment among conscripts is now so widespread that NCOs and officers have been shot by their own men. Severe beatings of conscripts by the NCOs is routine, living conditions are poor: 30 conscripts are crowded into one tent. Poor sanitation—food kitchens stand alongside open latrines—and cramped living conditions have resulted in outbreaks of hepatitis, intestinal diseases, and even cholera. Food rations are meager: There is a lack of meat, salt pork is the common substitute. The soldier-witness, Zakharov, said that the Soviet soldiers were always hungry.[32]

It is difficult to believe that these conditions, which will only grow worse under Andropov or anybody else in the Politburo so long as they adhere to a passé ideology, can continue. Yet it will continue because Andropov and his Brotherhood have learned the right mixture to keep down public resentment without resorting to mass terror, starvation, or executions.

But for how long can this continue? Ruthlessness and repression alone cannot solve the Soviet Union's economic, demographic, and political problems. There are indications that the Soviet peoples are not so easily intimidated as they were in the 1930s and the postwar 1950s. Even though industrial strikes are much more difficult to launch than in Poland, a number of strikes have recently broken out in the USSR, e.g., in the Russian industrial areas of the Volga and the Urals and other regions. There have been spontaneous food riots, most recently in the city of Kalinin, an important industrial center in central Russia with a population of 500,000 and just 100 miles from Moscow.

If the KGB is not enough, then the military will have to step in. Just as it was a Polish general, Jaruzelski, who saved the Communist Party in his country, so could it be a Soviet marshal with a baton already in his knapsack who could present the "Bonapartist" solution to the Soviet crisis.

For Lenin, imperialism represented the highest stage of capitalism. We can perhaps paraphrase Lenin and say that military governance may one day both be the highest stage of communism—and its last.

Chapter Notes

1. Image Making

1. Edward J. Epstein, "The Andropov Hoax: The Americanization of Yuri," *The New Republic* (February 7, 1983), pp. 18-21.

2. Biographical Fiction, Biographical Facts

1. Speech by Konstantin Chernenko in *Pravda*, November 13, 1982, p. 1.
2. "Yuri Vladimirovich Andropov," *Pravda*, same day, same page.
3. All the "truths" of the latest official biography are derived from the article referred to in *Pravda*, the official Soviet daily. The counterpoints

listed hereafter will be noted and discussed separately, in detail in later chapters.

3. The Beginning: 1914–1930

1. *Otchetnye Svedeniia o deiatel'nosti Zemleustroitel'nykh Komissii Na 1 ianvaria 1916 g* (Data report on the activities of Commissions of Land Reallocation by January 1, 1916) (Petrograd, 1916), pp. 2-3, 11-13, 89-91.

   Izvestiia Zemskogo Otdela MVD (Reports of Land Department of the Ministry of Interior), no. 7 (Petrograd, 1915), pp. 242-43; no. 8 (Petrograd, 1916), pp. 218-19.

   P. N. Pershin. *Uchastkovoe Zemlepol'zovanie v Rossii. Khutora i otroba, ikh rasprostranenie za desiatiletie 1907-1916 gg* (Individual Allotment Land Usage in Russia. Farms and Their Proliferation for the Ten years 1907-1916) (Moscow, 1922), passim.

2. *Great Soviet Encyclopedia,* A translation of the Third Edition, vol. 2. (New York-London: Macmillan Publishers, 1973), p. 96.

   Ezhegodnik Bol'shoi Sovetskoi Entsiklopediia 1981 (Great Soviet Encyclopedia's Yearbook, 1981) (Moscow, 1981), p. 565.

   Deputaty Verkhovnogo Soveta SSSR. Vos'moi Sozyv (Deputies of the Supreme Soviet of the USSR. 8th Convocation) (Moscow, 1970), p. 23.

3. It is known that Andropov has two children—Igor Yur'yevich Andropov, 37, who in 1974-1975 was a senior researcher at the Soviet Institute of the U.S.A. and Canada. In "Soviet Active Measures," Hearings before *Permanent Select Committee on Intelligence,* House of Representatives, 97th Congress, 2d session, July 13-14, 1982, p. 73. It is also reported that he has a daughter, Irina, married to an actor, Alexander Filipov. The son is now reported to be with the Soviet Foreign Office. "Letter from Moscow," *New Yorker,* (January 31, 1983), pp. 108, 113 and 117. Andropov is said to be a widower. *Time,* November 22, 1982, p. 19.

4. *Rech'* (Speech) (St. Petersburg, June 14, 15, and 16, 1914).

5. *Russkie Vedomosti* (Russian Herald) (Moscow, June 14, 15, and 16, 1914).

6. *Pravda* (The Truth), November 13, 1982, p. 1.

7. N. Movchin, "Enlistment of the Red Army in 1918-1921," *Grazhdanskaia Voina 1918-1921* (Civil War of 1918-1921), vol. 2 (Moscow, 1928), pp. 17, 89.

8. A. G. Naporko, *Ocherki Razvitiia Zheleznodorozhnogo Transporta SSSR*

(Outlines of the Development of the Railway Transport in the USSR) (Moscow, 1954), pp. 84–85.

P. F. Metel'kov, "The Labor Achievement of Railroad Workers," *Iz Istorii Grazhdanskoi Voiny i Interventsii 1917-1922* (On the History of Civil War and Intervention 1917-1922) (Moscow, 1974), p. 317.

9. V. T. Sukhorukov, *XI Armia V Boiakh na Severnom Kavkaze i Nizhnei Volge. 1918-1920 gg* (The Eleventh Army in the Battles in the Northern Caucasus and Volga Valley) (Moscow, 1961), pp. 44–47, 52–56, 74–80, 86–91, 102-7, 123-43, 161-83, 196–97, 253.

A. I. Denikin, *Ocherki Russkoi Smuty* (Outlines of Russian Turmoil), vol. 3 (Berlin: Slovo Publishers, 1924), pp. 148–52, 177–89, 212–37.

William Henry Chamberlain, *The Russian Revolution,* vol. 2 (New York: Macmillan and Co., 1935) passim.

Peter Kenez, *Civil War in South Russia, 1918* (Berkeley: University of California Press, 1971), pp. 184–90 and passim.

Peter Kenez, *Civil War in South Russia, 1919-1920* (Berkeley: University of California Press, 1977), passim.

10. V. Krasnov, "Memoirs on the Years 1917-1920," *Arkhiv Russkoi Revoliutsii* (Archives of the Russian Revolution), vol. 8 (Berlin, 1923), pp. 142-65.

M. S. Bernstam, "Demographic Implications of Communist Extermination of Populations," *Novyi Zhurnal* (The New Review), vol. 143 (New York, 1981), pp. 162–215.

4. Great Leap Forward: 1930-1937

1. For a detailed discussion of Stalin's terror of the 1930's, see Robert Conquest, *The Great Terror: Stalin's Purge of the Thirties* (New York: The Macmillan Co., 1968); Aleksandr I. Solzhenitsyn, *The Gulag Archipelago, 1918-1956,* vols. 1-3, (New York: Harper & Row, Publishers, 1973- 1978); Moshe Lewin, *Russian Peasants and Soviet Power: A Study of Collectivization* (London: Allen & Unwin, 1968).

2. *Istoria Ukrains'koi RSR,* vol. 2 (Kiiv, 1958), p. 336.

"The Triumph of the Leninist Principles," *Molodoi Kommunist* (The Young Communist), no. 12 (1962), p. 8.

3. *Great Soviet Encyclopedia,* A Translation of the Third Edition, vol. 2 (New York-London: Macmillan Publishers, 1973), p. 96.

   Ezhegodnik Bol'shoi Sovetskoi Entsiklopediia 1981 (Great Soviet Encyclopedia's Yearbook, 1981) (Moscow, 1981), p. 565.

   Deputaty Verkhovnogo Soveta SSSR. Vos'moi Sozyv (Deputies of the Supreme Soviet of the USSR. 8th Session) (Moscow, 1970), p. 23.

   Pravda (The Truth), November 13, 1982, p. 1.
4. Mikhail Karavai, *Politotdel* (Political Department) (Moscow, 1934), pp. 32–48, 60–64, 88–97.

   Pravda (The Truth), January 24, 1933, p. 1.

   E. N. Oskolkov, *Pobeda Kolkhoznogo Stroia V Zernovykh Raionakh Severnogo Kavkaza* (The Victory of the Collective Farm System in the Grain Producing Areas in the Northern Caucasus) (Rostov, 1973), pp. 179–211, 253–292.

   B. Sheboldaev, "Break the Sabotage of Seeding and Procurements Which Was Organized by Farmers in the Kuban Regions," *Sotsialisticheskoe Pereustroistvo* (Socialist Reconstruction), no. 6 (Rostov, 1932), pp. 2–11.

   A. I. Osmanov, *Likvidatsiia Kulachestva Kak Klassa V Dagestane* (Liquidation of Farmers as a Social Class in the Daghestane) (Makhachkala, 1972), pp. 84-174.

   Mikhail Soloviev, *My Nine Lives in the Red Army* (New York: David McKay Co., 1955), pp. 50–68.
5. Frank Lorimer, *The Population of the Soviet Union: History and Prospects* (Geneva: League of Nations, 1946), pp. 162–63.
6. *Great Soviet Encyclopedia,* A Translation of the Third Edition, vol. 2 (New York-London: Macmillan Publishers, 1973), p. 96.

   Ezhegodnik Bol'shoi Sovetskoi Entsiklopediia 1981 (Great Soviet Encyclopedia's Yearbook, 1981) (Moscow, 1981), p. 565.

   Deputaty Verkhovnogo Soveta SSSR. Vos'moi Sozyv (Deputies of the Supreme Soviet of the USSR. 8th Convention) (Moscow, 1970), p. 23.

   Pravda (The Truth), November 13, 1982, p. 1.
7. *Deputaty,* p. 23.
8. *Pravda,* November 13, 1982, p. 1.
9. A. A. Zhdanov, "Lessons of Political Mistakes of Saratov Provincial Party committee," *Spravochnik Derevenskogo Kommunista* (Handbook of a Rural Communist) (Moscow, 1936), pp. 451–54.
10. N. S. Patolichev, *Ispytanie Na Zrelost'* (Maturity Test) (Moscow, 1977), pp. 102–8.

E. Kasimovskii, *Velikie Stroiki Kommunizma* (Great Construction Works of Communism) (Moscow, 1951), p. 53.

Rybinskii i Uglichskii Gidrouzly. (Rybinsk and Uglich Gydro-electric Scheme), Ed. A. B. Vinter (Moscow, 1949), pp. 26-31.

11. Ibid.
12. U. G. Saushkin, *Velikoe Preobrazovanie Prirody Sovetskogo Soiuza* (The Great Remaking of Nature in the Soviet Union) (Moscow, 1952), passim.
13. Solzhenitsyn, *op. cit.,* vol. 2, pp. 77-120.
14. A. Lebed and B. Iakovlev, *Transportnoe Znachenie Gidrotekhnicheskikh Sooruzhenii SSSR* (The Significance of the Hydrotechnical Construction of the USSR for Transportation) (Munich, 1954), p. 98.

N. S. Patolichev, *Ispytanie Na Zrelost'* (Maturity Test) (Moscow, 1977), pp. 102-8.
15. *Great Soviet Encyclopedia,* A Translation of the Third Edition, vol. 2 (New York-London: Macmillan Publishers, 1973), p. 96.

Ezhegodnik Bol'shoi Sovetskoi Entsiklopediia 1981 (Great Soviet Encyclopedia's Yearbook, 1981) (Moscow, 1981), p. 565.

Deputaty Verkhovnogo Soveta SSSR. Vos'moi Sozyv (Deputies of the Supreme Soviet of the USSR, 8th Convention) (Moscow, 1970), p. 23.

Pravda (The Truth), November 23, 1982, p. 1.
16. V. V. Pokshishevskii, ed., *Volga* (Moscow, 1954), p. 94.
17. Lebed' and Iakovlev, *op. cit.,* pp. 92-99.

Patolichev, *op. cit.,* pp. 102-8.

Bol'shaia Sovetskaia Entsiklopediia (Great Soviet Encyclopedia) First Edition, vol. 50 (Moscow, 1944), p. 23.
18. Patolichev, *op. cit.,* pp. 102-8.

5. Patrons and Clients: 1937-1940

1. Yuri V. Andropov, "Fifty Years Guarding the Security of the Soviet Motherland," *Izbrannye Rechi i Stat'i* (Selected Speeches and Articles) (Moscow, 1979), p. 112. However, for Andropov's reservations about the KGB in the early 1950s, see ibid, p. 113.
2. I. V. Stalin, "On the Shortcomings of Party Work and on the Measures for Liquidating the Trotskyites and other Double-Dealers," *I. V. Stalin,*

Works, vol. 1 (XIV) (Stanford: The Hoover Institution Press, 1967), pp. 196–97.

3. Ibid., p. 379.
4. Robert Conquest, *The Great Terror: Stalin's Purge of the Thirties* (New York: The Macmillan Co., 1968), pp. 279, 457–59.
5. N. S. Patolichev, *Ispytanie Na Zrelost'* (Maturity Test) (Moscow, 1977), p. 160.
6. *Belomorsko-Baltiiskii Kanal imeni Stalina. Istoriia Stroitel'stva* (The White Sea-Baltic Canal Named in Honor of Stalin. History of Construction) (Moscow, 1934), pp. 101–8.

   The White Sea Canal. Being an Account of the Construction of the New Canal Between the White Sea and the Baltic Sea (London: Marx House, The National Centre for Marxist and Left Literature, 1935), pp. 30, 87–103.

   Patolichev, *op. cit.,* p. 160.
7. Aleksandr I. Solzhenitsyn, *The Gulag Archipelago, 1918–1956,* vol. 2 (New York: Harper & Row, 1975), pp. 98–99, 102.

   Patolichev, *op. cit.,* p. 105.
8. Patolichev, *op. cit.,* pp. 102–8, 126–35.

   Belormorsko-Baltiiskii, pp. 101–8.

   Elena Kerber, *Kak Sovetskaia Rossiia Boretsia S Prestupnost'u* (How Soviet Russia Fights Crime) (Moscow, 1933), pp. 150, 154–55.
9. Patolichev, *op. cit.,* pp. 105, 126–28, 135, 160.

   G. N. Kupriyanov, *Za Liniei Karel'skogo Fronta* (Behind the Line of the Karelian Front) (Petrozavodsk, 1975), p. 15. For further details see chapter 6.
10. Patolichev, *op. cit.,* pp. 79–82.

    A. I. Shakhurin, "Aviation Industry on the Eve of the Great Patriotic War. From the Memoirs of a Minister," *Voprosy Istorii* (Problems of History) no. 2 (Moscow, 1974), pp. 81–82.

    Khrushchev Remembers (Boston: Little, Brown and Co., 1970), pp. 252–56.
11. Patolichev, *op. cit.,* pp. 74–77.

    Leonard Schapiro, *The Communist Party of the Soviet Union* (London: Eyre & Spottiswoode, 1960), pp. 440–51.

    R. Conquest, *Power and Policy in the USSR. The Study of Soviet Dynastics* (London: Macmillan & Co., 1961), pp. 71, 80.

    Pravda, April 6, 1940, p. 4; April 18, 1940, p. 1.

Jonathan Harris, "The Origins of the Conflict Between Malenkov and Zhdanov: 1939-1941," *Slavic Review*, June 1976, pp. 287-303.

12. Patolichev, *op. cit.*, pp. 68-82.

Bol'shaia Sovetskaia Entsiklopediia (Great Soviet Encyclopedia), 3d ed., vol. 19 (Moscow, 1975), p. 277.

Ibid. 2d ed., vol. 32 (Moscow, 1955), p. 229.

Ukrain'ska Radians'ka Entsiklopediia (Ukrainian Soviet Encyclopedia), vol. 10 (Kiev, 1962), p. 567.

13. Patolichev, *op. cit.*, pp. 79-82.

Bol'shaia, 3d ed., vol. 29 (Moscow, 1978), p. 310.

Shakhurin, *op. cit.*, pp. 81-82.

14. Patolichev, *op. cit.*, p. 160.

15. Ibid.

Iaroslavskii Krai V Dokumentakh i Materialakh, 19171977 (Yaroslavl Province in Documents and Materials, 1917-1977) (Yaroslavl, 1980), pp. 111-12.

16. Patolichev, *op. cit.*, pp. 92-95.

6. Between Two Wars: 1940-1941

1. Merle Fainsod, *Smolensk Under Soviet Rule* (New York: Random House, 1958), p. 423.

2. Ibid.

Robert Conquest, *The Great Terror: Stalin's Purge of the Thirties* (New York: The Macmillan Co., 1968), pp. 457-59.

3. *Pravda,* April 1, 1940, p. 1; April 6, 1940, p. 1.

4. *Khrushchev Remembers* (Boston: Little, Brown and Co., 1970), p. 156.

5. P. Ia. Egorov, *Marshal Meretskov* (Moscow, 1974), pp. 53-54.

6. K. A. Meretskov, *Na sluzhbe Narodu* (At the Service of the People) (Moscow, 1968), pp. 177-78.

7. V. M. Molotov, "Report About Foreign Policy of the Soviet Government," *Pravda,* March 30, 1940, p. 1.

Meretskov, *op. cit.*, pp. 180-81.

8. Molotov, *op. cit.*, p. 1.

9. *Khrushchev Remembers,* p. 155.

10. Ibid., p. 154.

11. *Pravda,* April 18, 1940, p. 1.

12. *Pravda,* April 4, 1940, p. 2.

 Kommunisticheskaia Partiia Sovetskogo Soiuza V Rezoliutsiiakh i Resheniiakh S'ezdov, Konferentsii i Plenumov TsK (Communist Party of the Soviet Union, Resolutions and Decisions of Congresses, Conferences and Plenums of the Central Committee), 8th ed., vol. 5 (Moscow, 1971), p. 426.

13. N. S. Patolichev, *Ispytanie Na Zrelost'* (Maturity Test) (Moscow, 1977), pp. 3–6, 84–85, 96–99.

14. Ibid., p. 98.

15. *Pravda,* April 1, 1940, p. 1; April 27, 1940, p. 5; April 29, 1940, p. 2.

 Ocherki Istorii Karel'skoi Organizatsii KPSS (Outlines of the History of the Karelian Organization of CPSU) (Petrozavodsk, 1974), pp. 291, 309–12.

 G. N. Kupriyanov, *Za Liniei Karel'skogo Fronta* (Behind the Line of the Karelian Front) (Petrozavodsk, 1975), pp. 14–15.

16. Kupriyanov, *op. cit.,* p. 15.

17. *Nezabyvaemoe* (Unforgettable) (Petrozavodsk, 1967), p. 340.

18. *Pravda,* April 29, 1940, p. 2.

 Kupriyanov, *op. cit.,* pp. 65, 72.

 P. S. Prokkonen, "Rear—For the Front," *Nezabyvaemoe,* p. 262.

 Kareliia V Gody Velikoi Otechestvennoi Voiny. Dokumenty. Materialy (Karelia During the Years of the Great Patriotic War. Documents and Materials) (Petrozavodsk, 1975), pp. 52, 55, 120, 335–37.

19. *Karelia V Gody,* pp. 53, 86–87.

20. Ibid., pp. 86–87, 97–98.

 Kupriyanov, *op. cit.,* pp. 36–37.

 A. A. Shpak, *Podvig Iunosti* (Heroic Deeds of the Youth) (Petrozavodsk, 1969), p. 87.

21. *Nezabyvaemoe,* p. 345.

 Pravda, April 29, 1940, p. 2.

 Kupriyanov, *op. cit.,* p. 7.

 Ocherki, pp. 295, 575.

 Kareliia V Gody, pp. 45, 55.

22. *Ocherki,* p. 310.

 Ocherki Islorii Karelii (Outlines of Karelian History), vol. 2 (Petrozavodsk, 1964), p. 325.

23. Branko Lazitch and Milorad M. Drachkovitch, *Biographical Dictionary of the Comintern* (Stanford: The Hoover Institution Press, 1973), pp. 209–10.

24. Kupriyanov, *op. cit.*, pp. 79, 228.
25. Patolichev, *op. cit.*, pp. 96-99.
26. Ibid., pp. 83-85, 96-99.
    Khrushchev Remembers, pp. 119-25.
27. Robert Conquest, *Power and Policy in the USSR. The Study of Soviet Dynastics* (London: Macmillan & Co., 1961), pp. 31-32, 80.
    Werner G. Hahn, *Postwar Soviet Politics. The Fall of Zhdanov and the Defeat of Moderation, 1946-53* (Ithaca: Cornell University Press, 1982), pp. 26-27, 141, 147.
    Patolichev, *op. cit.*, pp. 83-85, 91, 113-14.
    Jonathan Harris, "The Origins of the Conflict Between Malenkov and Zhdanov: 1939-1941," *Slavic Review*, June 1976, pp. 287-303.
28. Kupriyanov, *op. cit.*, pp. 36-37.
    Prokkonen, *op. cit.*, pp. 262-63, 268-70.
    Ocherki, pp. 295, 309, 535.
    Kareliia V Gody, pp. 54, 97-98, 409.
    Pravda, April 27, 1940, p. 5.
29. *Ocherki*, p. 311.
30. Aleksandr I. Solzhenitsyn, *The Gulag Archipelago, 1918-1956*, vol. 3 (New York: Harper & Row, 1978), pp. 387-88.
31. R. A. Medvedev, *K Sudu Istorii* (Let History Judge) (New York: Alfred A. Knopf, 1974), pp. 992-93.
32. *Ocherki*, p. 311.
33. The Karelo-Finnish Republic population in 1941 can be estimated as 550,000 persons. It was 470,000 in 1939 and 650,000 in 1959. (*Naselenie SSSR. 1973. Statisticheskii Sbornik*. Moscow, 1975, pp. 14-15.) If at least 200,000 people were settled in 1940-41 in the Republic (i.e., 48,000 families of at least four people per family), then about 120,000 people, conservatively estimated, were deported from the Republic to the northern territories. In fact, the total population of Karelian and Finnish ethnic identity declined in all of the USSR from 396,000 in 1939 to 260,000 in 1959. (*Pravda*, April 29, 1940, p. 2. *Sovremennye Etnicheskie Protsessy v SSSR*. Moscow, 1977, pp. 487-89. *Itogi Vsesoiuznoi Perepisi Naseleniia 1959 goda. Vol. SSSR*. Moscow, 1962, p. 186.) Part of the decline, which totaled 136,000 persons (and even greater if we take into account the natural increase, that is number of births minus the number of natural deaths), was due to assimilation and ethnic re-identification, meaning that Karelians and Finns in the 1959 census listed themselves as Russians. (See Robert A. Lewis, Richard H. Rowland, and Ralph S.

Clem, *Nationality and Population Change in Russia and the USSR. An Evaluation of Census Data, 1897-1970.* New York: Praeger, 1976, pp. 256-58.) Another part of this decline can be attributed to war losses, both military and civilian, which are known to be about 14,000. (A. A. Shpak. *Podvig Iunosti.* Petrozavodsk, 1969, p. 86.) The residual of these two factors—the re-identification and war losses—can be estimated as 60,000 persons, who actually perished as a result of Soviet actions.
34. *Ocherki*, p. 312.

7. The Mysterious Death of an Adversary

1. *Sovetskaia Voennaia Entsiklopediia* (Soviet Military Encyclopedia), vol. 4 (Moscow, 1977), pp. 83-86.

   K. A. Meretskov, *Na Sluzhbe Narodu* (At the Service of the People) (Moscow, 1968), pp. 220-28, 368-91.

   Nezabyvaemoe. Vospominaniia O Velikoi Otechestvennoi Voine (Unforgettable: Memoirs about the Great Patriotic War) (Petrozavodsk, 1967), pp. 15-164.
2. G. N. Kupriyanov, *Za Liniei Karel'skogo Fronta* (Behind the Line of the Karelian Front) (Petrozavodsk, 1975), p. 12.
3. *Ocherki Istortii Karel'skoi Organizatsii KPSS* (Outlines of the History of the Karelian Organization of CPSU) (Petrozavodsk, 1974), p. 338.

   Sovetskaia Voennaia, vol. 4, pp. 83-86.
4. *Nezabyvaemoe*, p. 24.

   Kupriyanov, *op. cit.*, pp. 17-26, 210.
5. Kupriyanov, *op. cit.*, passim.

   Kareliia v Gody Velikoi Oteshestvennoi Voiny. Dokumenty. Materialy (Karelia During the Years of the Great Patriotic War. Documents and Materials) (Petrozavodsk, 1975), pp. 33, 36, 42, 52, 54, 66, 70, 72, 120, 132, 138, 144, 174, 192, 314, 351. For the details see later in chapter 7.
6. Kupriyanov, *op. cit.*, p. 17.

   Sovetskaia Voennaia, vol. 4, pp. 83-86.

   Vnutrennie Voiska V Velikoi Otechestvennoi Voine. 1941-1945 gg. Dokumenty i Materialy (Internal Troops During the Great Patriotic War, 1941-1945. Documents and Materials) (Moscow, 1975), pp. 98-191, 693.
7. *Nezabyvaemoe*, p. 24.
8. Ibid., p. 25.

9. *Ocherki,* p. 326.
   Andropov, *op. cit.,* p. 22.
10. *Kareliia v Gody,* p. 36.
11. Andropov, *op. cit.,* p. 22.
12. *Kareliia v Gody,* pp. 53–56, 58–59.
    P. S. Prokkonen, "Rear—for the Front," *Nezabyvaemoe,* pp. 262–63.
    Vnutrennie Voiska, pp. 547–48, 693, 702.
13. Ibid.
14. *Vnutrennie Voiska,* pp. 126–29.
15. *Kareliia v Gody,* pp. 53–56, 58–59.
    Prokkonen, *op. cit.,* pp. 262–63.
16. *Kareliia v Gody,* pp. 43–44. 53 ff.
    Ocherki, pp. 327–28.
    Kupriyanov, *op. cit.,* pp. 36–37.
    Andropov, *op. cit.,* p. 112.
    Khrushchev Remembers (Boston: Little, Brown and Co., 1970), p. 329.
17. Kupriyanov, *op. cit.,* pp. 64–65, 228.
    Kareliia v Gody, pp. 43–44, 176.
    A. A. Shpak, *Podvig Iunosti* (Heroic Deeds of the Youth) (Petrozavodsk, 1969), p. 75.
18. Andropov, *op. cit.,* p. 112.
19. *Sovetskaia Voennaia,* vol. 4, p. 85.
    Kupriyanov, *op. cit.,* p. 66.
20. *Ocherki,* p. 328.
    Sovetskaia Voennaia, vol. 4, p. 85.
    Kupriyanov, *op. cit.,* p. 122.
21. Kupriyanov, *op. cit.,* p. 79.
22. For his detailed biography see Branco Lazitch and Milorad M. Drachkovitch, *Biographical Dictionary of the Comintern* (Stanford: the Hoover Institution Press, 1973), pp. 6–7.
    Ul'ias Vikstrem, *Toivo Antikainen* (Petrozavodsk, 1970).
23. V. M. Virolainen, "Along the Steel Main Railroad Lines," *Nezabyvaemoe,* pp. 303–4.
    Vikstrem, *op. cit.,* pp. 227–30.
24. Vikstrem, *op. cit.,* pp. 212–29.
    Virolainen, *op. cit.,* pp. 303–4.
25. Vikstrem, *op. cit.,* p. 210.
26. Ibid., pp. 217–19.
27. Ibid., pp. 224–30.
    Virolainen, *op. cit.,* pp. 303–4.

28. Virolainen, *op. cit.*, p. 303.
    Vikstrem, *op. cit.*, p. 230.
29. Vikstrem, *op. cit.*, p. 222.
30. Vikstrem, *op. cit.*, pp. 227-29.
    Virolainen, *op. cit.*, p. 304.
31. Vikstrem, *op. cit.*, p. 230.
32. Ibid., pp. 234-35.
33. *Kareliia v Gody,* p. 276.
34. *Ocherki,* p. 357.
    Kareliia v Gody, p. 276.
    Kupriyanov, *op. cit.*, p. 228.
35. Shpak, *op. cit.*, p. 129.
36. Kupriyanov, *op. cit.*, p. 211.
37. Ibid., p. 228.

8. Storming—Women and Children First

1. *Kareliia v Gody Velikoi Otechestvennoi Voiny. Dokumenty. Materialy* (Karelia During the Years of the Great Patriotic War. Documents and Materials) (Petrozavodsk, 1975), p. 43.
2. Ibid.
    Resheniia Partii i Pravitel'stva po Khoziaistvennym Voprosam (Decisions of the Party and the Government on the Economic Issues), vol. 3, 1941-1952 (Moscow, 1968), p. 35.
3. P. S. Prokkonen, "Rear—For the Front," *Nezabyvaemoe. Vospominaniia o Velikoi Otechestvennoi Voine* (Unforgettable: Memoirs about the Great Patriotic War) (Petrozavodsk, 1967), p. 266.
4. *Ocherki Istorii Karel'skoi Organizatsii KPSS* (Outlines of the History of the Karelian Organization of CPSU) (Petrozavodsk, 1974), p. 330.
5. *Kareliia v Gody,* p. 42.
6. Ibid., p. 43.
    Ocherki, p. 330.
7. Prokkonen, *op. cit.*, pp. 266–67.
    Ocherki, pp. 330–31.
8. *Kareliia v Gody,* p. 43.
9. *Ocherki,* pp. 330–31.
    Prokkonen, *op. cit.*, pp. 266–67.

10. G. K. Kozlov, *V Lesakh Karelii* (In the Forests of Karelia) (Moscow, 1963), pp. 58-66.

    Ocherki, pp. 330-31.
11. V. M. Virolainen, "Along the Steel Main Railroad Lines," *Nezabyvaemoe,* p. 299.
12. Aleksandr I. Solzhenitsyn, *The Gulag Archipelago, 1918-1956,* vol. 2, (New York: Harper and Row, 1975), pp. 139-40.
13. Prokkonen, *op. cit.,* p. 267.

    Virolainen, *op. cit.,* p. 299.
14. See chapter 5.
15. Prokkonen, *op. cit.,* pp. 267-69.

    Virolainen, *op. cit.,* pp. 301-2.
16. *Ocherki,* pp. 331-32.
17. Virolainen, *op. cit.,* pp. 299-300, 339.

    Prokkonen, *op. cit.,* pp. 268-69.
18. *Ocherki,* p. 332.

    Prokkonen, *op. cit.,* p. 269.
19. Virolainen, *op. cit.,* p. 300.
20. Prokkonen, *op. cit.,* pp. 268-69.
21. Ibid.
22. *Ocherki,* p. 339.

    Prokkonen, *op. cit.,* p. 271.
23. *Ocherki,* pp. 339, 345.
24. Ibid., p. 339.
25. *Strana Sotsialisma* (The Country of Socialism) (Moscow, 1941), p. 300.
26. Calculated from: *Godudarstvennyi Plan Razvitiia Narodnogo Khoziaistva SSSR Na 1941 god* (State Plan of the Development of the National Economy of the USSR for the Year 1941) (Moscow, 1941), American Council of Learned Societies Reprints, Russian Series No. 30. (Baltimore: Universal Press, n.d.), pp. 67-68, 141-42, 671, 673.
27. *Ocherki,* p. 338.
28. Prokkonen, *op. cit.,* p. 272.
29. *Ocherki,* pp. 338-39.

    Prokkonen, *op. cit.,* p. 272.
30. *Ocherki,* p. 339.
31. Ibid.

    Prokkonen, *op. cit.,* p. 272.
32. *Ocherki,* pp. 339-40, 346.

    Prokkonen, *op. cit.,* pp. 272-73.

33. *Ocherki,* pp. 339–40.
34. Ibid., p. 340.

9. Andropov's Career Falters: 1944–1945

1. For a detailed analysis see Robert Conquest, *Power and Policy in the USSR: The Study of Soviet Dynastics* (London: Macmillan, 1961), pp. 79–94.

   Werner G. Hahn, *Postwar Soviet Politics: The Fall of Zhdanov and the Defeat of Moderation, 1946-53* (Ithaca: Cornell University Press, 1982), passim.
2. G. N. Kupriyanov, *Za Liniei Karel'skogo Fronta* (Behind the Line of the Karelian Front) (Petrozavodsk, 1975), p. 72.
3. Hahn, *op. cit.,* pp. 25–44.
4. *Pravda,* July 6, 1938.
5. See chapter 6.
6. Yu. V. Andropov, "About the Love for a Native Domain," *Komsomol'skaia Pravda,* June 13, 1943, No. 138, p. 2.
7. *The New York Times,* February 22, 1983, p. 1.
8. Yu. V. Andropov, *Izbrannye Rechi i Stati* (Selected Speeches and Articles) (Moscow, 1979), pp. 28–33.
9. I. M. Petrov, "Heroic Deeds of Karelian Youth in Civilian Labor," *Nezabyvaemoe. Vospominaniia o Velikoi Otechestvennoi Voine* (Unforgettable: Memories About the Great Patriotic War) (Petrozavodsk. 1967), p. 266.
10. *Ocherki Istorii Karel'skoi Organizatsii KPSS* (Outlines of the History of the Karelian Organization of the CPSU) (Petrozavodsk, 1974), pp. 360–61.

    Sovetskaia Voennaia Entsiklopediia (Soviet Military Encyclopedia), vol. 4 (Moscow, 1977), pp. 85–86.
11. Hahn, *op. cit.,* pp. 26–27.
12. Ibid., pp. 26–28.
13. *Pravda,* April 29, 1940, p. 2.
    Ocherki, p. 577.
14. *Ocherki,* pp. 363–65.
15. Ibid., p. 364.

    Deputaty Verkhovnogo Soveta SSSR: Vos'moi Sozyv (Deputies of the Supreme Soviet of the USSR, Eighth Session) (Moscow, 1970), p. 23.

16. *Ocherki,* p. 365.
17. *Sovetskaia Voennaia,* vol. 1 (Moscow, 1976), p. 193.
    Deputaty, p. 23.
    Pravda, November 13, 1982, p. 1.
18. *Leninskoe Znamia* (Lenin's Banner) (Petrozavodsk) May 10, 1945, pp. 1-2.
    Karelia v Gody Velikoi Otechestvennoi Voiny. Dokumenty. Materialy (Karelia During the Years of the Great Patriotic War: Documents and Materials) (Petrozavodsk, 1975), p. 402.

10. The Brotherhood: 1945-1953—Part I

1. Leonard Schapiro, *The Communist Party of the Soviet Union* (London: Eyre & Spottiswoode, 1960), pp. 505-54.
   Robert Conquest, *Power and Policy in the USSR: The Study of Soviet Dynastics* (London: Macmillan & Co., 1961), pp. 154-227, 232-33.
   Werner G. Hahn, *Postwar Soviet Politics: The Fall of Zhdanov and the Defeat of Moderation, 1946-53* (Ithaca, N.Y.: Cornell University Press, 1982), pp. 136-60, 198-223.
2. A. S. Chuianov, *Na Stremnine Veka* (On the Chute of the Century) (Moscow, 1976), pp. 40-52.
   N. S. Patolichev, *Ispytanie na Zrelost'* (Test of Maturity) (Moscow, 1977), pp. 68-74, 96-99, 113-14, 160, 171, 279-85.
3. Schapiro, *op. cit.,* pp. 528-54.
   Conquest, *op. cit.,* pp. 154-227, 292-328, 346-47, 376-79.
   Khrushchev Remembers (Boston: Little, Brown & Co., 1970), p. 377.
4. Chuianov, *op. cit.,* pp. 40-52.
   Patolichev, *op. cit.,* pp. 68-74, 96-99, 113-14, 160, 171, 279-85.
5. For the detailed account, see I. P. Leiberov, *Na Shturm Samoderzhaviia. Petrogradskii Proletariat v Gody Pervoi Mirovoi Voiny i Fevral'skoi Revoliutsii Iul'. 1914-Mart 1917* (March Against the Autocracy. The Petrograd Proletariat during Years of WW I and the February Revolution. July 1914-March 1917) (Moscow, 1979).
6. Patolichev, *op. cit.,* pp. 96-99, 113-14, 279-85.
   Schapiro, *op. cit.,* pp. 505-21.
   Khrushchev Remembers, pp. 251-52.

Hahn, *op. cit.*, pp. 43–45, 53–57, 65–66, 77, 106–9.

Conquest, *op. cit.*, pp. 33, 40, 71–75, 87–88, 95.

Bol'shaia Sovetskaia Entsiklopediia (Great Soviet Encyclopedia), 2d ed., vol. 2 (Moscow, 1950), p. 434.

7. N. G. Kuznetsov, "On the Eve," *Neva*, no. 5, (Leningrad, 1965), p. 161.
   Khrushchev Remembers, pp. 306–7.

8. *Party and Government Officials of the Soviet Union, 1917–1967,* ed. by Edward L. Crowley et al. (Metuchen, N.J.: The Scarecrow Press, 1969), pp. 59–60, 97, 99.

   Sovetskaia Istoricheskaia Entsiklopediia, vol. 11 (Moscow, 1968), p. 274.
   Khrushchev Remembers, pp. 251–53.

   Patolichev, *op. cit.*, pp. 279–84.

   Conquest, *op. cit.*, pp. 82–88.

   Hahn, *op. cit.*, pp. 26–35, 41–45, 51–53.

9. V. V. Kolotov, *Nikolai Alekseevich Voznesenskiy* (Moscow, 1976), passim.
   R. A. Medvedev, *K Sudu Istorii* (Let History Judge) (New York: Knopf, 1979), pp. 965–70.

   Khrushchev Remembers, pp. 251–53, 598.

   Hahn, *op. cit.*, pp. 26–35, 41–45, 51–53.

   Patolichev, *op. cit.*, 279–84.

10. Chuianov, *op. cit.*, p. 61.

    A. I. Shakhurin, "Aviation History on the Eve of the Great Patriotic War," *Voprosy Istorii* (Questions of History), no. 2 (Moscow, 1974), pp. 81–82.

    Khrushchev Remembers, pp. 252–53.

    Hahn, *op. cit.*, pp. 51–52.

11. Patolichev, *op. cit.*, pp. 279–85.

    B. A. Abramov, "Organizational-Party Work of the CPSU During the Years of the Fourth Five-Year Plan," *Voprosy Istorii KPSS* (Questions of the History of the CPSU), no. 3 (1979), pp. 58–65.

    Istoriia Kommunisticheskoi Partii Sovetskogo Soiuza (History of the Communist Party of the Soviet Union), vol. 5, part 2 (Moscow, 1980), pp. 39–43, 216–20.

12. *Sovetskaia Istoricheskaia Entsiklopediia* (Soviet Historical Encyclopedia), vol. 11 (Moscow, 1968), p. 115.

13. *Ocherki Istorii Karelii,* pp. 404, 415.
    Ocherki Istorii Karel'skoi Organizatsii, p. 426.

14. *Pravda,* November 13, 1982, p. 1.

Chapter Notes

15. *Sovetskaia Voennaia Entsiklopediia* (Soviet Military Encyclopedia), vol. 1 (Moscow, 1976), p. 193.
16. *Ezhegodnik Bol'shoi Sovetskoi Entsiklopediia, 1981* (Yearbook of the Great Soviet Encyclopedia, 1981) (Moscow, 1981), p. 565.
17. *Deputaty Verkhovnogo Soveta SSSR Vos'moi Sozyv* (Deputies of the Supreme Soviet of the USSR, the Eighth Session) (Moscow, 1970), p. 23.
18. Conquest, *op. cit.,* p. 71.
19. *Ocherki Istorii Karel'skoi Organizatsii KPSS* (Outlines from the History of the Karelian Organization of the CPSU) (Petrozavodsk, 1974), p. 535.
    Belaruskaia Savetskaia Entsyklapedyia (Byelorussian Soviet Encyclopedia), vol. 2 (Minsk, 1970), p. 508.
    Conquest, *op. cit.,* pp. 179, 181–82, 187–88, 197–98, 203–8.
    Hahn, *op. cit.,* pp. 142–46, 196–97.
20. Patolichev, *op. cit.,* pp. 282–84.
21. Ibid.
22. See notes 8 and 9.
23. Patolichev, *op. cit.,* p. 284.
24. *Kommunisticheskaia Partiia Sovetskogo Soiuza v Rezoliutsiiakh i Respeniiakh S'ezdpv Konferentsii i. Plenumov TsK* (Communist Party of the Soviet Union in Resolutions and Decisions of the Congresses, Conferences and Plenums of the Central Committee), 7th ed., vol. 3 (Moscow, 1954), pp. 551–52.
    Khrushchev Remembers, pp. 279–81.
    Conquest, *op. cit.,* pp. 178–86.
25. Patolichev, *op. cit.,* pp. 282–83.
    Hahn, *op. cit.,* pp. 53–55, 209–23.
26. *Kommunisticheskaiia Partiia Sovetskogo Soiuza v resoliutsiiakh i Resheniiakh S'ezdov, Konferentsii i Plenumov TsK.* (Communist Party of the Soviet Union Resolutions and Decisions of the Congresses, Conferences and Plenums of the CC), 8th ed. vol. 6 (Moscow, 1971), pp. 195–209, 277–80.
27. *Sovetskaia Istoricheskaia,* vol. 10 (Moscow 1967), p. 593; vol. 11 (Moscow 1968), p. 527.
    Hahn, *op. cit.,* pp. 213–14.
28. *Belaruskaia,* p. 508.
    Abramov, *op. cit.,* pp. 58–65.
    Hahn, *op. cit.,* 38–43, 53–57, 65–77, 209–23.
29. Leonid I. Brezhnev, *Vozrozhdenie* (The Rebirth) (Moscow, 1978), p. 6.

V. N. Gusarov, *Moi Papa Ubil Mikhoelsa* (My Papa Killed Mikhoels) (Frankfurt-am-Main: Possev-Verlag, 1978), pp. 90-92.
30. Patolichev, *op. cit.*, pp. 282-83.
31. Estimates based on Patolichev, *op. cit.*, p. 283.
   Hahn, *op. cit.*, pp. 53-57, 213-23.

11. The Brotherhood: 1945-1953—Part II

1. Khrushchev secret speech to the Twentieth Party Congress. In *Khrushchev Remembers* (Boston: Little, Brown & Co., 1970), pp. 614-15.
   Ibid., pp. 276-77.
2. *Istoriia Kommunisticheskoi Partii Sovetskogo Soiuza* (History of the Communist Party of the Soviet Union), vol. 5, part 2 (Moscow, 1980), pp. 216-26.
   Werner G. Hahn, *Postwar Soviet Politics: The Fall of Zhdanov and the Defeat of Moderation, 1948-53* (Ithaca: Cornell University Press, 1982), pp. 38, 109.
3. *Istoriia Kommunisticheskoi,* pp. 39-40.
   Hahn, *op. cit.*, pp. 38, 109.
4. *Istoriia Kommunisticheskoi,* pp. 39-40, 43, 216-20, 225-26.
   B. A. Abramov, "Organizational-Party Work of the CPSU During the Years of the Fourth Five-Year Plan." *Voprosy Istorii KPSS* (Questions of the History of the CPSU), no. 3 (1979), pp. 58-61.
   Hahn, *op. cit.*, pp. 38, 109.
5. See Chapter 9.
   On the Zhdanovite tactics in the ideology issue, see Hahn, *op. cit.*, pp. 19-43.
6. *Sovetskaia Istoricheskaia Entsiklopediia* (Soviet Encyclopedia of History), vol. 10 (Moscow 1967), p. 593.
7. Ibid., vol. 13 (Moscow 1971), pp. 966-67.
   Bol'shaia Sovetskaia Entsiklopediia (Great Soviet Encyclopedia), 2d ed., vol. 2 (Moscow, 1950), p. 434; vol. 32 (Moscow, 1955), p. 229.
   Abramov, *op. cit.*, p. 61.
   Deputaty Verkhovnogo Soveta SSSR Vos'moi Sozyv (Deputies of the Supreme Soviet of the USSR. Eighth Session) (Moscow, 1970), p. 355.
   N. S. Patolichev, *Ispytanie Na Zrelost'* (Test of Maturity) (Moscow 1977), pp. 279-81.

Hahn, *op. cit.*, pp. 38–43, 53–55, 65–66, 77, 109, 201–5, 213–14.

8. *Sovetskaia Istoricheskaia,* vol. 7 (Moscow, 1965), p. 707.

   Robert Conquest, *Power and Policy in the USSR* (London: Macmillan 1961), p. 91.

   Branko Lazitch and Milorad Drachkovitch, *Biographical Dictionary of the Comintern* (Stanford, Calif.: Hoover Institution Press, 1973), pp. 209–10.

9. *Pravda,* December 14, 1946.

   Sovetskaia Istoricheskaia, vol. 12 (Moscow 1969), p. 700.

   Abramov, *op. cit.*, pp. 60–61.

   Patolichev, *op. cit.*, pp. 281–84.

   Hahn, *op. cit.*, pp. 53–55, 65–66, 213–14.

10. *Istoriia Kommunisticheskoi,* vol. 5, part 2, pp. 39–42.

    Abramov, *op. cit.*, pp. 58–61.

    Conquest, *op. cit.*, p. 84.

    Hahn, *op. cit.*, pp. 44–45, 51–53, 65–66, 213–14.

11. *Bol'shaia,* 2d ed., vol. 2, p. 434; vol. 32, p. 229.

    Bol'shaia, 3d ed., vol. 19 (Moscow, 1975), p. 277.

    Khrushchev Remembers, p. 236.

    Hahn, *op. cit.*, pp. 44–45, 51–53, 61–63.

12. *Kommunisticheskaia Partiia Sovetskogo Soiuza v Rezoliutsiiakhi Resheniiakh S'ezdov, Konferentsii i Plenumov TsK* (Communist Party of the Soviet Union in Resolutions and Decisions of the Congresses, Conferences and Plenums of the CC), 7th ed., vol. 3 (Moscow 1954), pp. 495–550.

    Ibid., 8th ed., vol. 6 (Moscow 1971), pp. 173–79, 194–260.

    Istoriia Kommunisticheskoi, vol. 5, part 2, pp. 205–26.

    Abramov, pp. 58–63.

13. *Kommunisticheskaia,* 8th ed., vol. 6, pp. 173–79, 210–60.

14. N. S. Khrushchev, *Stroitel'stvo Kommunizma v SSSR i Razvitie Sel'skogo Khoziaistva* (Construction of Communism in the USSR and Development of Agriculture), vol. 8 (Moscow 1964), p. 265.

15. *Khrushchev Remembers,* pp. 227–44.

16. Abramov, *op. cit.*, p. 63.

17. *Kommunisticheskaia,* 8th ed., vol. 6, p. 194.

    Bol'shaia, 2d ed., vol. 2, p. 434; vol. 32, p. 229.

    Bol'shaia, 3d ed., vol. 19, p. 277.

    Khrushchev Remembers, p. 236.

    Hahn, *op. cit.*, pp. 44–45, 51–53, 61–63.

18. Abramov, *op. cit.*, pp. 58–63.

    Istoriia Kommunisticheskoi, vol. 5, part 2, pp. 225–27.

Michael S. Voslensky, *Nomenklatura: Die Herrschende Klasse der Sowjetunion* (Nomenklatura: The Ruling Classes of the Soviet Union) (Vienna, Verlag Fritz Molden, 1980).

19. N. Yanevich, "Institute of World Literature in the 1930s-1970s," *Pamiat'.Istoricheskii Sbornik* (Memory: Historical Collection), vol. 5 (Paris: Editions La Presse Libre, 1982), p. 116.
20. Conquest, *op. cit.,* p. 74.
21. Abramov, *op. cit.,* pp. 61–63.
    Istoriia Kommunisticheskoi, vol. 5, part 2, pp. 41, 216–19.
    Ukrain'ska Radians'ka Entsiklopediia (Ukrainian Soviet Encyclopedia), vol. 10 (Kiev, 1962), p. 567.
    Belaruskaia Sovetskaia Entsyklapedyia (Byelorussian Soviet Encyclopedia), vol. 2 (Minsk, 1970), p. 508.
    Kommunisticheskaia, 8th ed., vol. 6, pp. 195–209.
    Khrushchev Remembers, pp. 228–44.
    Hahn, *op. cit.,* pp. 56, 64–66.
22. *Sovetskaia Istoricheskaia,* vol. 12 (Moscow 1969), p. 700.
    Ezhegodnik Bol'Shoi Sovetskoi Entsiklopediia 1981 (Yearbook of the Great Soviet Encyclopedia, 1981) (Moscow 1981), p. 594.
    Hahn, *op. cit.,* pp. 53–54, 109, 210–14.
23. *Ocherki Istorii Karel'skoi Organizatsii KPSS* (Outlines of the History of the Karelian Organization of the CPSU) (Petrozavodsk, 1974), pp. 384–85.
24. *Ocherki Istorii Karelii* (Outlines of the History of Karelia), vol. 2 (Petrozavodsk, 1964), p. 424.
25. *Ocherki Istorii Karel'skoi Organizatsii,* p. 371.
26. Ibid., pp. 372, 377.
27. Ibid., pp. 372, 377.
    Ocherki Istorii Karelii, p. 424.
28. *Ocherki Istorii Karelii,* p. 426.
29. Yu. V. Andropov, "Studies and Education of the Leading Soviet Cadres," *Pravda,* February 1, 1949, p. 3.
30. Ibid.
31. *Sovetskaia Istoricheskaia,* vol. 11 (Moscow, 1968), p. 274.
32. Hahn, *op. cit.,* pp. 12, 94–97, 102–5, 108–9.
33. *Khrushchev Remembers,* pp. 253, 313, 597–98.
34. *Sovetskaia Istoricheskaia,* vol. 12, p. 700.
    Hahn, *op. cit.,* pp. 77, 109, 210–11.
35. Conquest, *op. cit.,* pp. 92–93.
36. *Istoriia Kommunisticheskoi,* vol. 5, part 2, p. 220.

Abramov, *op. cit.*, p. 64.

Conquest, *op. cit.*, pp. 92–93.

Hahn, *op. cit.*, pp. 53, 94, 97, 102–5, 108–9, 204.

37. A. S. Chuianov, *Na Stremnine Veka* (On the Chute of the Century) (Moscow, 1976), pp. 40–41.

38. *Sovetskaia Istoricheskaia,* vol. 12, p. 700.

    V. V. Kolotov, *Nikolai Alekseevich Voznesenskii* (Moscow, 1976).

    R. A. Medvedev, *K Sudu Istorii* (Let History Judge) (New York: Knopf, 1974), pp. 965–70.

    Khrushchev Remembers, pp. 246–57, 597–98.

    Hahn, *op. cit., pp. 129–36.*

39. *Ocherki Istorii Karel'skoi Organizatsii,* p. 372.

40. Ibid., p. 387.

    Yu. V. Andropov, *Izbrannye Rechi i Stati* (Selected Speeches and Articles) (Moscow, 1979), pp. 42–45.

41. *Ocherki Istorii Karel'skoi Organizatsii,* pp. 388–89, 553.

42. *Ocherki Istorii Karelii,* p. 575.

43. Aleksandr I. Solzhenitsyn, *The Gulag Archipelago, 1918–1956,* vol. 2, (New York: Harper & Row, 1973), p. 116.

44. *Ocherki Istorii Karel'skoi Organizatsii,* pp. 388, 533.

45. Ibid., pp. 388–89.

46. Conquest, *op. cit.,* pp. 92–95.

    Hahn, *op. cit.,* pp. 51–53, 65, 136–37, 140, 213–14, 218–19.

47. *Pravda,* February 24, 1950.

    Ezhegodnik, 1981, p. 594.

    Bol'shaia, 2d ed., vol. 2, p. 434; vol. 32, pp. 229–230.

    Bol'shaia, 3d ed., vol. 19, pp. 296–97.

    Hahn, *op. cit.,* pp. 56–57, 102–4, 108–9, 140, 213–14.

48. *Belaruskaia,* vol. 2, p. 508.

    Bol'shaia, 2d ed., vol. 32, p. 230.

    Sovetskaia Istoricheskaia, vol. 10, p. 593; vol. 12, p. 700.

    Ezhegodnik, 1981, p. 594.

    Deputaty, p. 283.

    Hahn, *op. cit.,* pp. 112, 136–40, 215–19.

49. *Ocherki Istorii Karel'skoi Organizatsii,* p. 389.

50. Ibid., p. 553.

51. Ibid., p. 389.

    Patolichev, *op. cit.,* p. 160.

52. Patolichev, *op. cit.,* p. 160.

    Ocherki Istorii Karel'skoi Organizatsii, pp. 389, 411, 545.

53. Yu. V. Andropov, "On the Party Control Over Producing Enterprises," *Pravda*, April 12, 1951, p. 2.

12. The Brotherhood: 1945-1953—Part III

1. *Pravda Ukrainy*, September 4, 1951.
   Sovetskaia Voennaia Entsiklopediia (Soviet Military Encyclopedia), vol. 3 (Moscow, 1977), p. 312.
   Bol'shaia Sovetskaia Entsiklopediia (Great Soviet Encyclopedia), 3d ed., vol. 9 (Moscow, 1972), p. 88.
   Ezhegodnik Bol'shoi Sovetskoi Entsiklopediia (Yearbook of the Great Soviet Encyclopedia, 1981) (Moscow, 1981), p. 577.
   Robert Conquest, *Power and Policy in the USSR: The Study of Soviet Dynastics* (London: Macmillan, 1961), pp. 154, 178–83.
   Werner G. Hahn, *Postwar Soviet Politics: The Fall of Zhdanov and the Defeat of Moderation, 1946-1953* (Ithaca: Cornell University Press, 1981), pp. 106, 142–43.
2. *Sovetskaia Istoricheskaia Entsiklopediia* (Soviet Encyclopedia of History), vol. 12 (Moscow, 1969), p. 700.
   Kommunisticheskaia Partiia Sovetskogo Soiuza v Rezoliutsiiahkh i Resheniiakh S'ezdov, Conferentsii i Plenumov TsK (Communist Party of the Soviet Union in Resolutions and Decisions of the Congresses, Conferences and Plenums of the Central Committee), 7th ed., vol. 3 (Moscow, 1954), pp. 606, 608.
   Deputaty Verkhovnogo Soveta SSSR. Vos'moi sozyv (Deputies of the Supreme Soviet of the USSR. Eighth session) (Moscow, 1970), pp. 23, 145, 423.
   Khrushchev Remembers (Boston: Little, Brown, 1970), p. 377.
3. *Khrushchev Remembers*, pp. 242–43.
   Hahn, *op. cit.*, pp. 142–43.
4. *Khrushchev Remembers*, pp. 235, 329.
5. *Pravda*, February 24, 1950.
   Bol'shaia, 3d ed., vol. 19 (Moscow, 1975), pp. 296–97.
   Khrushchev, p. 253.
   Conquest, *op. cit.*, p. 154.
   Hahn, *op. cit.*, pp. 106, 142, 196–97, 218–19.

6. Aleksandr I. Solzhenitsyn, *The Gulag Archipelago 1918- 1956*, vol. 1 (New York: Harper & Row, 1973), pp. 112, 157–59.
7. *Pravda*, October 19 and 20, 1946.
    Khrushchev, pp. 104, 256, 312, 528.
    Party and Government Officials of the Soviet Union, 1917-1967, ed. by Edward L. Crowley et al. (Metuchen, N.J.: Scarecrow Press, 1969), p. 99.
    Hahn, *op. cit.*, pp. 105–6, 124, 142, 194–97.
8. *Zarya Vostoka* (Dawn of the East), April 16 and 21, 1953.
    John Ducoli, "The Georgian Purges, 1951-1953," *Caucasian Review*, no. 6 (1958), pp. 54–61.
    Khrushchev, pp. 598–99.
    Conquest, *op. cit.*, pp. 129–53.
9. *Pravda*, January 30, 1953.
    Khrushchev, p. 599.
10. Cited from Khrushchev's tapes in Hahn, *op. cit.*, p. 143.
11. *Bol'shaia*, 3d ed., vol. 19, pp. 296–97.
    Ezhegodnik, p. 594.
    CIA Directory of Soviet Officials: National Organizations, A Reference Aid, CR 82-14044 (Washington, D.C., August 1982), p. 12.
12. *Deputaty*, p. 283.
    Pravda, April 6 and 7, and July 27, 1953.
    Pravda Ukrainy, June 13, 1953.
    Khrushchev, pp. 263–66, 330.
    Hahn, *op. cit.*, pp. 191–92.
13. *Khrushchev*, pp. 263–64.
14. Roy A. Medvedev and Zhores A. Medvedev, *N. S. Khrushchev: Gody U Vlasti* (N. S. Khrushchev, Years of Power) (New York: Columbia University Press, 1975), p. 47.
    A. S. Chuianov, *Na Stremnine Veka* (On the Chute of the Century) (Moscow, 1976), pp. 43–45.
    N. S. Patolichev, *Ispytanie Na Zrelost'* (Test of Maturity) (Moscow 1977), pp. 171, 282–85.
15. Conquest, *op. cit.*, p. 33.
16. *Pravda*, August 20, 1952, p. 1.
17. *Khrushchev*, pp. 276–80.
18. Ibid., p. 277.
19. Solzhenitsyn, *op. cit.*, vol. 1, p. 92.
20. *Belaruskaia Savetskaia Entsyklapedyia* (Byelorussian Soviet Encyclopedia), vol. 2 (Minsk, 1970), p. 508.
    Conquest, *op. cit.*, pp. 217, 224.

21. *Belaruskaia,* p. 508.
22. Ibid.
23. Khrushchev's Secret Speech in *Khrushchev Remembers,* p. 615.
    Khrushchev, pp. 278, 280–81.
24. *Sovetskaia Istoricheskaia,* vol. 7 (Moscow, 1965), pp. 707–8.
25. Ibid., vol. 12 (Moscow, 1969), p. 700.
    Kommunisticheskaia, 7th ed., vol. 3, pp. 606–8.
26. *Sovetskaia Istoricheskaia,* vol. 11 (Moscow, 1968), p. 527.
27. Ibid., vol. 12, p. 700.
28. Josef V. Stalin, "Economic Problems of Socialism in the USSR," *Sochineniia* (Works), vol. 16 (Stanford, Calif.: Hoover Institution Press, 167), pp. 300–4.
29. Ibid., pp. 294–304.
30. Khrushchev's Secret Speech, p. 611.
31. Conquest, *op. cit.,* pp. 173–75.
32. Zdenek L. Suda, *Zealots and Rebels: A History of the Communist Party of Czechoslovakia* (Stanford, Calif.: Hoover Institution Press, 1980), p. 246.
33. Ibid., pp. 240–41, 245.
34. Ibid., p. 247.
35. Ibid., pp. 247–49.
36. Conquest, *op. cit.,* p. 175.
37. Ibid., p. 166.
38. *O Partiinoi i Sovetskoi Pechati. Sbornik Dokumentov* (About the Party and the Soviet Press, Collection of Documents) (Moscow, 1954), pp. 636–37.
39. *Pravda,* January 13, 1953, p. 1, Editorial.
    Mikailov's speech, *Pravda,* January 22, 1953, pp. 2–3.
40. *Sovetskaia Istoricheskaia,* vol. 7, p. 707.
41. Ibid., vol. 11, p. 527.
    Kommunisticheskaia, 7th ed., vol. 3, p. 595.
42. *Ocherski Istorii Karelii* (Outlines of the History of Karelia), vol. 2 (Petrozavodsk, 1964), p. 452.
43. *Sovetskaia Istoricheskaia,* vol. 11, p. 527; vol. 12, p. 700.
44. Khrushchev's Secret Speech, p. 601.
45. *Khrushchev Remembers,* pp. 286–87.
46. Aleksandr M. Nekrich, *Otreshis' Ot Strakha* (Abandon Fear) (London: Overseas Publications, 1979), pp. 105–8.
47. Ibid., p. 132.
    Khrushchev Remembers, pp. 259–61, 308–9.
48. *O Partiinoi,* pp. 645–47.

13. No Room at the Top?

1. *The Soviet Diplomatic Corps, 1917-1967,* ed. Edward L. Crowley (Metuchen, N.J.: Scarecrow Press, 1970), p. 16.
2. *Sovetskaia Voennaia Entsiklopediia* (Soviet Military Encyclopedia), vol. 1 (Moscow, 1976), p. 193.
   The Soviet Diplomatic, p. 76.
3. *Sovetskaia Voennaia,* vol. 1, p. 193.
   Deputaty Verkovnogo Soveta SSSR. Vos'moi Sozyv (Deputies of the Supreme Soviet of the USSR. Eighth session) (Moscow, 1970), p. 23.
4. *Sovetskia Voennaia,* vol. 1, p. 193.
   The Soviet Diplomatic, p. 40.
5. Ibid.
   U.S. Department of State, Division of Biographic Information: Soviet Political Leaders. (Washington, D.C., July, 1957), p. 3.
6. *Soviet Political,* p. 3.
7. *Deputaty,* p. 23.
   Ezhegodnik Bol'shoi Sovetskoi Entsiklopediia, 1981. (Yearbook of the Great Soviet Encyclopedia, 1981) (Moscow, 1981), p. 565.
   Spravochnik Patiinogo Rabotnika (Handbook of the Party Worker) (Moscow, 1959), p. 500.
   Department of State, Biographic Directory No. 272, *Directory of Soviet Officials,* vol. 1 (Washington, D.C., August 1960), p. 4.
   Ibid., vol. 1, BA 63-13 (November 1963), p. I-A6.
8. *Sovetskaia Istoricheskaia Entsiklopediia* (Soviet Encyclopedia of History), vol. 7 (Moscow, 1965), p. 709.
   Deputaty, p. 23.
   Ezhegodnik, p. 565.
   Sovetskaia Voennaia, vol. 1, p. 193.
9. Ibid.
   Sovetskaia Istoricheskaia, vol. 12 (Moscow, 1969), p. 700.
   U.S. Department of State, Intelligence Research Aid. *Directory of Soviet Officials,* vol. 1, A 66-5 (Washington, D.C., February 1966), p. I-A3.
10. A. V. Antonov-Ovseenko, *Portret Tirana* (A Portrait of the Tyrant) (New York: Khronika Press, 1980), p. 343.
11. *Pravda Ukrainy,* March 19, 1953.
    Kommunisticheskaia Partiia Sovetskogo Soiuza V Revoliutsiiahkh i Rosheniiakh S'ezdov, Konferentsii i Plenumov TsK (Communist Party of the Soviet Union in Resolutions and Decisions of Congresses, Confer-

ences and Plenums of the Central Committee), 7th ed., vol. 3 (Moscow, 1954), p. 606.

Werner G. Hahn, *Postwar Soviet Politics: The Fall of Zhdanov and the Defeat of Moderation, 1946-53.* (Ithaca, N.Y.: Cornell University Press, 1982), p. 142.

12. *Pravda,* March 7 and 21, 1953, April 7, 1953.

Sovetskaia Istoricheskaia, vol. 11 (Moscow, 1968), p. 527; vol. 12 (Moscow, 1969), p. 700.

Kommunisticheskaia, 7th ed., vol. 3, pp. 603-8.

13. *Pravda,* February 26, 1954.

14. *Pravda,* March 7, 1953.

Kommunisticheskaia, 7th ed., vol. 3, p. 604.

Bol'shaia Sovetskaia Entsiklopediia (Great Soviet Encyclopedia), 3d ed., vol. 2 (Moscow, 1970), p. 194.

15. *O Partiinoi i Sovetskoi Pechati. Sbornik Dokumentov* (About Party and Soviet Press: A Collection of Documents) (Moscow, 1954), pp. 598-672.

16. *Pravda Ukrainy,* June 13, 1953.

Pravda, July 27, 1953.

Deputaty, p. 283.

Bol'shaia, 2d ed., vol. 51 (Moscow, 1958), p. 152.

17. *O Partiinoi,* pp. 647-49.

18. *Pravda,* November 20, 1953.

Robert Conquest, *Power and Policy in the USSR: The Study of Soviet Dynastics* (London: Macmillan, 1961), pp. 231-33.

Roy A. Medvedev and Zhores A. Medvedev, *N. S. Khrushchev, Gody U Vlasti* (N. S. Khrushchev: Years of Power) (New York: Columbia University Press, 1975), p. 47.

19. *The Soviet Diplomatic,* pp. 6, 8, 16.

20. Ibid., pp. 16, 152.

21. *The Soviet Diplomatic,* p. 51.

22. Ibid., p. 41.

Ezhegodnik, p. 594.

Antonov-Ovseenko, *op. cit.,* p. 360.

23. *Sovietskaia Istoricheskaia,* vol. 13 (Moscow, 1971), pp. 966-67.

24. *Deputaty,* p. 355.

Soviet Political Leaders, July 1957, p. 3.

Hahn, *op. cit.,* pp. 204-5.

25. *Sovietskaia Istoricheskaia,* vol. 11 (Moscow, 1968), p. 403.

Deputaty, p. 355.

B. A. Abramov, "Organizational-Party Work of the CPSU During the

Years of the Fourth Five-Year Plan," *Voprosy Istorii KPSS* (Questions of the History of the CPSU), no. 3 (1979), p. 64.

Hahn, *op. cit.,* pp. 201, 204-5.

14. Hungary: Revolution and Counterrevolution

1. United Nations: Report of the Special Committee on the Problem of Hungary, General Assembly, Official Records: Eleventh Session Supplement No. 18 (A/3592), p. 6., par 55 and p. 81, para 467.
2. Ibid., p. 5, para 47.

   Bennett Kovrig, *Communism In Hungary: From Kun to Kadar* (Stanford: Hoover Institution Press, 1979), pp. 205ff.
3. United Nations Report, *op. cit.,* p. 6, para 56 and 57.
4. Janos Radvanyi, *Hungary and the Superpowers* (Stanford, Calif.: Hoover Institution Press, 1972), p. 7.
5. United Nations Report, *op. cit.,* para 84, 611, 642–43 and Chapter XV.
6. Veljico Mićunović, *Moscow Diary* (New York: Doubleday, 1980), p. 88.
7. Ibid.
8. Major General Bela Kiraly, "How Russian Trickery Throttled Revolt," *Life* magazine (February 18, 1957), pp. 119–29.

   Also Professor Kiraly's article, "The First War Between Socialist States: Military Aspects of the Hungarian Revolution," in *The Hungarian Revolution Twenty Years After* (Canadian-American Review of Hungarian Studies III: 2 Fall 1976), pp. 115–23.
9. Radvanyi, *op. cit.,* pp. 21–23. Radvanyi is a former Communist diplomat of Hungary who was both participant and observer in these historic events. The *Peking Review* article he refers to was entitled "The Origin and Development of Differences Between the Leadership of the CPSU and Ourselves," no. 37 (1963), pp. 9–10.

   See Radvanyi, p. 162, footnote 20.
10. Radvanyi, p. 23.
11. Kiraly, *Hungarian Revolution,* p. 120.
12. Arnold Beichman, "Hungarian General Bares Soviet Army Capabilities," *Christian Science Monitor,* February 6, 1957. This was the first of two articles dealing with General Kiraly's military analysis of Soviet strategy in Eastern Europe.

13. Arnold Beichman, "Hungarian Refugee Tells Details of Soviet Control," *Christian Science Monitor* (February 11, 1957).
    Also Kiraly, *The Hungarian Revolution,* p. 119.
14. Kovrig, *op. cit.,* p. 313.
    For Tito's ambivalent attitude toward the Hungarian revolution, see *Yugoslavia and the Soviet Union, 1939-1973: A Documentary Survey,* ed. by Stephen Clissold (Oxford University Press, Royal Institute of International Affairs, 1976).
15. Mićunović, *op. cit.,* passim. The diary is full of long, bullying anti-Yugoslav diatribes by Soviet leaders as a kind of rhetorical gang-bang that took place almost every time Mićunović went around to the Kremlin. Worst of the critics, whose language bordered on "plain insults" was Suslov, says the diarist. For a choice sample, see p. 364.
16. *Khrushchev Remembers, op. cit.,* p. 377.
17. United Nations, *op. cit.,* p. 66.
18. United Nations, *op. cit.,* p. 67.
19. Mićunović, *op. cit.,* p. 159.
20. Radvanyi, *op. cit.,* pp. 11-12.
21. Radvanyi, *op. cit.,* pp. 37-41.
22. See chapters 13 and 16.

15. A Decade of Promise: 1957-1967

1. *Sovetskaia Istoricheskaia Entsiklopediia* (Soviet Encyclopedia of History), vol. 7 (Moscow, 1965), p. 709; vol. 11 (Moscow, 1968), p. 274; vol. 12 (Moscow, 1969), p. 700.
    Yuri V. Andropov, *Izbrannye Rechi i Stati* (Selected Speeches and Articles) (Moscow, 1979), pp. 57-107.
    Pravda, November 13, 1982, p. 1.
2. Robert Conquest, *Power and Policy in the USSR: the Study of Soviet Dynastics* (London: Macmillan, 1961), pp. 263-394, passim.
    Michael Tatu, *Power in the Kremlin: From Khrushchev to Kosygin* (New York: Viking, 1970), passim.
3. *Khrushchev Remembers: The Last Testament* (Boston: Little Brown, 1974), p. 290.
4. Ibid., p. 450.

5. *Bol'shaia Sovetskaia Entsiklopediia* (Great Soviet Encyclopedia), 2d ed., vol. 51 (Moscow, 1958), p. 152.
   Sovetskaia Istoricheskaia, vol. 11, p. 527.
6. *Sovetskaia Istoricheskaia,* vol. 11, p. 527.
7. *Kommunisticheskaia Partiia Sovetskogo Soiuza v Rezoliutsiiakh i Resheniiakh S'ezdov, Conferentsii i Plenumov TsK* (Communist Party of the Soviet Union in Resolutions and Decisions of the Congress, Conferences and Plenums of the Central Committee), 7th ed., vol. 4 (Moscow, 1960), pp. 90, 110-11.
8. Ibid., p. 110.
9. Tatu, *op. cit.,* p. 31.
10. *XXII S'ezd Kommunisticheskoi Partii Sovetskogo Soiuza, 17-31 Oktiabria 1961 goda. Stenograficheskii Otchet* (The 22d Congress of the Communist Party of the Soviet Union, October 17-31, 1961. Stenographic Report) (Moscow 1962), vol. 1, p. 396; vol. 2, p. 149.
11. For Khrushchev's view of the anti-Stalin speech and how it originated, see *Khrushchev Remembers* (Boston: Little Brown, 1970), pp. 341-53. In this chapter, Khrushchev makes a statement, startling from a Communist: "Criminal acts had been committed by Stalin, acts which would be punishable in any state in the world except in fascist states like Hitler's and Mussolini's," p. 343.
12. Cited in Conquest, *op. cit.,* p. 317.
13. *Sovetskaia Istoricheskaia,* vol. 11, p. 527; vol. 12, p. 700.
14. *XXII S'ezd,* vol. 2, pp. 405-6.
15. *Sovetskaia Istoricheskaia,* vol. 12, p. 700.
   Pravda, November 24, 1962, p. 1.

16. "The KGB Has A Very Long Arm"

1. *Time,* November 22, 1982, p. 19, col. 2.
2. *The New York Times,* June 22, 1967, p. 2.
   Pravda, May 19 and June 22, 1967.
   On July 5, 1978, there was a KGB name change from "KGB under the Council of Ministers," meaning it was nominally under control of the Soviet Government, to "USSR KGB." This change was reportedly con-

tested by Alexei Kosygin, then chairman of the Council of Ministers. Peter Deriabin with T. H. Bagley, "Fedorchuk, the KGB and the Soviet Succession," *Orbis,* 26:3 (Fall 1982), p. 627.

3. A. A. Grechko, "Rukovodiashchaia rol' KPSS v stroitel'stve armii razvitogo sotsialisticheskogo obshchestva" (The Leading Role of the CPSU in the Construction of the Military of the Developed Socialist Society), *Voprosy istorii KPSS* (Questions of the History of the CPSU), no. 5 (1974), p. 39.

4. Yuri Andropov, "Fifty Years Guarding the Security of the Soviet Motherland," in *Izbrannye Rechi i Stati* (Selected Speeches and Articles) (Moscow, 1979), p. 114.

5. *Current Digest of the Soviet Press,* "Andropov Defends Civil Rights in the U.S.S.R.," XXVII:23 (1975), p. 8.

6. Deriabin and Bagley, *op. cit.,* p. 635.

7. Philip E. Mosely, ed., *New Trends in Kremlin Policy,* "The Stalin Issue in Perspective" (Washington: Georgetown University Center for Strategic and International Studies, 1970), pp. 63–64.
   Also Deriabin and Bagley, *op. cit.,* p. 628.

8. *Khrushchev Remembers* (Boston: Little Brown, 1970), pp. 290–96.
   The New York Times, "Shakeup of Soviet K.G.B. Preceded by 'Mishaps,'" (May 20, 1967), p. 8.

9. John Barron, *KGB* (New York: Reader's Digest Press, 1974), pp. 63–65.

10. Deriabin and Bagley, *op. cit.,* pp. 627–28.

11. See Chapter 5.

12. *Facts on File,* Vol. XXVII, No. 1396 (July 27-August 2, 1967). On the very day of Andropov's appointment as KGB chairman, *Red Star,* the Soviet Defense Ministry newspaper, reported "a tragic death in the course of his duties," that of Major-General Vasily A. Lukshin, 55, a senior KGB officer. No details of Lukshin's death or of his duties were revealed. Ibid.

13. Robert Conquest, "The Real Man from SMERSH," *The New York Times Magazine* (November 5, 1967), pp. 36–37. Optimists in the 1930s once thought that Hitler as a potentially destructive force couldn't be taken seriously because he was a vegetarian.

14. *The New York Times,* "Davies Says Soviet Has Right To Spy," February 19, 1946.

15. Leonard Schapiro, foreword, Gayle Durham Hannah, *Soviet Information Networks* (Washington, D.C.: Georgetown University Center for Strategic and International Studies, 1977), p. vii.

16. Hannah, *op. cit.,* p. 63.

17. The literature on Soviet abuse of psychiatry and pharmacology is large and growing larger. Some useful reading: Valery Tarsis, *Palata 7* (Frankfurt-am-Main: Possev, 1974).

    Vladimir Bukovsky, *To Build a Castle* (New York: Viking, 1978).

    Sidney Bloch and Peter Reddaway, *Psychiatric Terror* (New York: Basic Books, 1977).

    Also, Walter Reich, "The World of Soviet Psychiatry," *The New York Times Magazine* (January 30, 1983), pp. 21ff.
18. "Soviet Psychiatrists Blackballed," *The Economist* (February 19, 1983), p. 38.

    Allan Brownfeld, "Why Moscow Withdrew from the International Psychiatric Community," *Washington Times* (March 4, 1983), p. 3C.
19. General Assembly Resolution 36/56B, cited in U.S. Mission to UN Press Release 148–(82), November 26, 1982, p. 1.
20. Petro Grigorenko, "Looking Beyond Brezhnev," *Freedom-At-Issue* (New York: Freedom House, No. 69), November-December 1982, p. 10.

    USUN Press Release, *op. cit.*, p. 2.
21. Ibid., p. 3.

    Barron, *op. cit.*, pp. 111–13.
22. Vice-President George Bush, who served briefly as CIA director from 1976 to 1977, greeted Andropov in Moscow after attending the Brezhnev funeral with the would-be humorous comment: "I feel I already know you, since we served in similar positions." *Time,* "Eyes of the Kremlin," February 14, 1983, p. 30. Nothing could be further from the truth than that the KGB chairman and the CIA Director are similar positions. The omnicompetence, omnipresence and utter ruthlessness of the KGB make the KGB chairman, qualitatively and quantitatively, different from that of the CIA director. See also the earlier reference in chapter 2 to Bush's interview with the *Christian Science Monitor,* also about the KGB and its putative frailties.
23. Vladimir Dedijer, *Tito* (New York: Simon & Schuster 1953), p. 255.
24. Walter Laqueur, "What We Know About the Soviet Union," *Commentary* (February 1983), p. 19.

    Harry Rozitske, *The KGB: The Eyes of Russia* (New York: Doubleday 1981), p. 62.
25. Report to the Congress on Forced Labor in the USSR, *U.S. Department of State,* February 9, 1983. An earlier interim report was submitted in November 1982 by the State Department. These reports are prepared in compliance with Senate Resolution 449 and Conference Report 97/891

which accompanied H.R. 6956, September 20, 1982.

26. *Op. cit.,* Tab 2. Report to the Senate Foreign Relations Committee and House Foreign Affairs Committee, "Country Reports on Human Rights Practices for 1982," *Department of State,* February 1983 (Washington, D.C.: Government Printing Office), p. 1025.

Also see David Satter, "The System of Forced Labor in Russia," *Wall Street Journal* (June 24, 1982), p. 28. Mr. Satter, former Moscow correspondent of the *Financial Times* (London), estimates that of a total work force of about 115 million persons, as many as 5 million are forced laborers.

27. Report Ad Hoc Committee on Forced Labor, UN Document E/2431, Economic and Social Council, 16th Session, Supplement No. 13 (May 1953).

28. Between 1926 and 1960, the Soviet secret police probably murdered or abducted from outside its own borders at least 55 opponents. For a list of names, dates, and places see *Famous Soviet Spies: The Kremlin's Secret Weapon* (Washington, D.C.: *U.S. News and World Report,* 1973), Appendix V, pp. 203–9.

29. *The New York Times,* "The Attack on the Pope: New Link to Bulgarians," Nicholas Gage, March 23, 1983, p. 1.

30. *Newsweek,* January 3, 1983, p. 26.

31. Ibid., p. 23.

32. Hearing before the Commission on Security and Cooperation in Europe, 97th Congress, 2d Session, "The Assassination Attempt on Pope John Paul II," (September 23, 1982), p. 4. Mrs. Sterling is the author of *The Terror Network.* Her article on the attempted assassination in the *Reader's Digest* for September 1982 formed the basis of the Congressional hearing.

33. Arnold Beichman, "Can Counterintelligence Come In From the Cold?" *Policy Review* (Winter 1981) No. 15, p. 95.

34. *Time* Magazine, (February 14, 1983), p. 42, col. 1.

17. The Challenge Within: Can Andropov Survive?

1. U.S. Department of Defense, *Soviet Military Power* (Washington: Superintendent of Documents, 1983), passim.

Also see Robert Jastrow, "Why Strategic Superiority Matters," *Commentary,* 75:3 (March 1983), pp. 27–32, especially p. 30.

2. For a discussion of KGB intrusions into the Brezhnev family, see Andrew Nagorski, "The Making of Andropov, 1982: Dirty campaign tricks, Soviet-style," *Harper's* (February 1983), p. 24.
3. "Moscow Pressing Harder on Dissent," *Wall Street Journal* (January 19, 1983), p. 27.
4. "The Andropov Era has begun," *The Economist* (November 20, 1982), p. 15.
5. Speech of K. U. Chernenko, *Pravda,* November 13, 1982, pp. 1–2.
6. L. I. Brezhnev, "Otchetnyi doklad TsK KPSS XXVI s'ezdy KPSS: Ocherednye zadachi partii v oblasti vnutrennei i Vneshnei Politiki, 23 February 1981." (General Report of the CC CPSU to the 26th Congress of the CPSU: Working Tasks of the Party in the areas of domestic and foreign policy. February 23, 1981).

   Ekonomicheskaia Gazeta, No. 9, (Moscow, February 1981), pp. 8–9.

   Thane Gustafson, "Soviet Energy Policy: From Big Coal to Big Gas," *Russia at the Crossroads: The 26th Congress of the CPSU* (London: Allen & Unwin, 1981), pp. 121–39.
7. Paige Bryan, Scott Sullivan, and Steve Pastore, "Capitalists and Commissars," *Policy Review,* 22 (Fall 1982), pp. 19–54.
8. E. Shevardnadze in *Zaria Vostoka* (Dawn of the East) Tbilsi, November 26, 1981.

   Also Marshall I. Goldman, "The Simple Truth About Moscow's Agricultural Policies," *The New York Times,* Letters, (December 21, 1982), p. 26.
9. P. Ye. Shelest, a Presidium member elected in November 1964, said: "We heard the slogan [that we must] catch up and overcome in the near future the United States in per capita production of meat and milk. We heard slogans about fulfilling the Seven-Year Plan in three or four years, [slogans] that we live well now and tomorrow we shall live better. But what did we have in fact? Breadlines!" *Plenum of the Central Committee of the CPSU,* March 24–26, 1965 (Moscow: 1965), p. 36.
10. *Narodnoe Khoziaistvo SSSR v 1979 godu. Statisticheskii Ezhegodnik* (National Economy of the USSR in 1979 Statistical Yearbook) (Moscow 1980), p. 247.

    Narodnoe Khoziaistvo SSSR v 1980 godu (Moscow 1981), p. 229.

    U.S. Department of Agriculture, Foreign Agricultural Circular, *Grains* FG-21-82 (July 13, 1982), pp. 1, 3.

Karl-Eugen Wadekin, "Soviet Agriculture's Dependence on the West," *Foreign Affairs,* 60(4) (Spring 1982), p. 888.

11. *Planovoe Khoziaistvo* (The Planned Economy), No. 3, (Moscow 1979), pp. 35–36.

Economika Sel'skogo Khoziaistva (Economics of Agriculture), No. 11 (Moscow 1979), pp. 35–36.

Wadekin, *op. cit.,* pp. 882–903.

12. Mikhail S. Bernstam, "Behind U.S. Grain Sales to the USSR, Re-Examining Soviet Grain Balances and Strategic Grain Reserves, 1971/72 to 1981/82," *Defense and Foreign Affairs,* No. 9 (September 1982), pp. 22–24.

13. Sergei Klepikov, "The Gas and Pipe Deal: Despite the Sanctions," *New Times,* No. 29 (Moscow: July 1982), p. 6.

14. *Ekonomicheskaia Gazeta,* No. 48 (Moscow, 1981).

15. *Ezhegodnik Bol'shoi Sovetskoi Entsiklopediia 1981* (Yearbook of the Great Soviet Encyclopedia, 1981) (Moscow 1981), p. 573.

16. "O Dopolnitelnykh Merakh Po Uvelicheniiu Proizvodstva Selskokhoziaistvennoi Produktsii v Lichnykh Podsobnykh Khoziaistvakh Grazhdan" (Resolution of the CC CPSU and the USSR Council of Ministers "On Additional Measures to Increase the Production of Agricultural Products by Citizens' Personal Auxiliary Farming Operations") *Selskaia Zhizn* (Rural Life), Moscow, January 18, 1981, p. 1. Also published in *Ekonomika Selskogo Khoziaistva,* No. 2 (1981), pp. 3–7. English translation published in the *Current Digest of the Soviet Press,* 33(5) (1981), pp. 15–17.

17. E. Krylatykh, A. Lifanchikov in *Voprosy Ekonomiki,* No. 7 (1981).

See M. Bernstam, "Agriculture Debate: Brezhnev at Fault," *Soviet Analyst,* 11(12), (June 1982), pp. 5–6.

18. See footnote 16.

19. V. Mozhin in *Kommunist,* No. 13 (1981).

Petr Alekseev in *Kommunist,* No. 2 (1982), pp. 27–35.

C. Bobylev in *Kommunist,* No. 12 (1982), pp. 38–45.

20. V. K. Mesiats, "Selskokhoziaistvennye Organy v Novykh Usloviiakh" (Agricultural Organs Under New Conditions). *Ekonomicheskaia Gazeta* No. 39 (September 1982), p. 2.

G. S. Zolotukhin, "Razvitie Materialnoi Bazy Zagotovok" (Development of the Material Basis of Procurements) *Ekonomicheskaia Gazeta,* No. 36 (September 1982), p. 2.

21. See M. S. Bernstam, "Agricultural Debate," pp. 5–6.

22. U.S. Department of State, Biographic Reference Aid, *Directory of Soviet Officials,* vol. 1. (Washington, D.C., November 1963), P. I-A6.
23. Adam Ulam, *Dangerous Relations* (New York: Oxford University Press, 1983), p. 313.
24. Alain Besançon, "Éloge de la corruption en Union soviétique" (In Praise of Corruption in the Soviet Union) *Présent soviétique, et passé russe* (Paris: Livre de Poche, 1980), p. 302.
25. U.S. Department of State, *Cuban-Soviet Impact on the Western Hemisphere,* No. 167 (April 17, 1980), p. 2.
26. Vladimir G. Treml, "Production and Consumption of Alcoholic Beverages in the USSR: A Statistical Study," *Journal of Studies on Alcohol* 36(3) (New Brunswick: State University of New Jersey 1975), p. 287.
    Also, Treml, "Alcoholism and State Policy in the Soviet Union," *Economic Development in the Soviet Union and Eastern Europe,* vol. 2, "Sectoral Analysis," ed. Zbigniew M. Fallenbuchl (New York: Praeger, 1976), p. 389.
27. Treml, *op. cit.,* 1975, p. 287; Treml, 1976, pp. 380, 382, 394.
28. Treml, *op. cit.,* 1976, p. 384.
29. *Narodnoe Khoziaistvo SSSR, 1922-1982* (National Economy of the USSR 1922-1982) (Moscow, 1982), p. 53.
    Pravda, (January 23, 1983), pp. 1-2.
30. *Effektivnost Narodnogo Khoziaistva* (Efficiency of the National Economy) (Moscow, 1981), p. 230.
    Voprosy Ekonomiki (Problems of Economics) No. 12 (1981), p. 105.
    Ekonomika Selskogo Khoziaistva, no. 10 (1982), p. 72.
31. For the detailed analysis on the demography of the Soviet population, see Mikhail S. Bernstam, "Demography of Soviet Ethnic Groups in World Perspective." Paper presented at the Conference on Soviet Nationalities at the Hoover Institution, Stanford University, April 1982. To be published in *The Last Empire: Nationalities in the Soviet Union,* ed. Robert Conquest (Stanford: Hoover Institution Press, forthcoming). See also Murray Feshbach, "The Soviet Union: Population Trends and Dilemmas," *Population Bulletin,* 37(3) (August 1982), pp. 3-43.
32. *Soviet Analyst,* vol. 12, no. 2, January 1983, pp. 4-5.

Index

on ideology, 15–16, 32–35, 78–79,
105–6, 162
as inspector, 14, 89, 91, 95–96,
98–99, 112, 117–18
and intellectuals, 156–57
in Karelo-Finnish Republic,
13–14, 23, 41–73, 75, 80–81,
88, 90–91, 99, 101, 104–9, 112
and KGB, 5–9, 13, 15, 30, 64, 92,
117, 122, 153, 162, 173–89
and Komsomol projects, 12–14,
24, 26–28, 34–35, 37–38, 45,
47, 49–50, 55, 60, 62–64, 70,
73, 81, 88, 112
and Kupriyanov, 48–49, 53–54,
62–64, 74–75, 90–91, 104,
106–9
and Kuusinen, 47, 100, 130–32
leader, election as, 3–6, 12,
15–16, 191–93
and Malenkov, 48, 74, 109–11
in *nomenklatura*, 103, 136
and Patolichev, 38, 41, 44–45,
47–48, 73, 83–84, 87, 92
on patriotism, 76–79
on peaceful coexistence, 174–75
in Petrozavodsk, 88–90
in Politburo, 7, 10, 15, 64, 117
Pope John Paul II assassination
attempt, 8, 185–87
postwar–1953 career, 88–96
power, 9–10
psychiatry, misuse of, 182–83
and purges, 12–15, 26, 35, 107–9,
116–20, 122, 128, 130, 132, 161
and Rappoport, 49, 68
Soviet media on, 12–16
and Stalin, 12–16, 34, 45, 95, 99,
116–20, 122, 134. *See also*
Brotherhood
and Suslov, 15–16, 131, 137, 143,
152–54, 160, 165, 167, 170,
172, 179, 202
Western reaction to, 6–8, 78,

179, 183, 200–201
and Western relations, 10, 12,
157–58, 174–75, 187–89, 195
and World War II, 14, 50–72, 74,
82
and Yegorov, 111–12
and Zhdanov, 26, 42, 44, 47–48,
74–77, 79–81, 90, 99, 106–9
Antikainen, Toivo, 58–61
Anti-Semitism. *See* Jews
Archangel Province, 69
Argentina, 195
Aristov, Averkii B., 84, 95, 124–25,
128, 138–39, 142
Arms control, 186, 189
Asia. *See* Central Asia; country
names
Atomic weapons, 7, 155, 180, 192
August 1914 (book), 18
Auschwitz, 29
Australia, 195
Austro-Hungarian Empire, 19. *See
also* Austria; Hungary
Azerbaijan, 18, 176

Baku, 18–19
Baltic Republics, 103
Barghoorn, Frederick C., 178–79
Bashir Province, 139
Baskakov, Mikhail I., 49, 56, 92,
121–23
Belomorsk, 53, 55, 67–68
Beria, Lavrentii P., 6, 15, 32, 46,
48, 84, 86, 106, 110, 114–17,
121–22, 124–25, 127–29, 134,
135, 138–40, 143, 175, 179–81
Besançon, Alain, 201–2
Black Hundreds, 20
Black Sea, 18–19
Bohlen, Charles, 157
Borkov, G. I., 87, 101
Brezhnev, Leonid, 3, 5, 15–16, 19,
33, 47, 82, 84, 117–18, 125–25,
138, 163, 165, 174, 176, 178,

246